AMERICAN CITY

THE FESLER-LAMPERT MINNESOTA HERITAGE BOOK SERIES

This series reprints significant books that enhance our understanding and appreciation of Minnesota and the Upper Midwest. It is supported by the generous assistance of the John K. and Elsie Lampert Fesler Fund and the interest and contribution of Elizabeth P. Fesler and the late David R. Fesler.

The series features works by the following authors:

Clifford and Isabel Ahlgren
J. Arnold Bolz
Wanda Gág
Walter Havighurst
Helen Hoover
Florence Page Jaques
Evan Jones
Frank A. King
David A. Lanegran
Meridel Le Sueur
George Byron Merrick
Grace Lee Nute
Sigurd F. Olson
Charles Edward Russell
Calvin Rutstrum
Ernest R. Sandeen
Timothy Severin
Robert Treuer
Charles Rumford Walker

AMERICAN CITY

A Rank and File History
of Minneapolis

CHARLES RUMFORD WALKER

Foreword by
Mary Lethert Wingerd

University of Minnesota Press
Minneapolis • London

TO THE RANK AND FILE EMPIRE BUILDERS

Originally published in hardcover by Farrar & Rinehart, Inc., 1937. Republished by arrangement with Henry Holt and Company, LLC.

First University of Minnesota Press edition, 2005

Published by the University of Minnesota Press
111 Third Avenue South, Suite 290
Minneapolis, MN 55401-2520
http://www.upress.umn.edu

Library of Congress Cataloging-in-Publication Data

Walker, Charles Rumford, 1893–
    American city : a rank and file history of Minneapolis / Charles Rumford Walker ; foreword by Mary Lethert Wingerd. — 1st University of Minnesota Press ed.
        p.   cm. — (The Fesler-Lampert Minnesota heritage book series)
    Originally published: New York : Farrar & Rinehart, 1937.
    Includes bibliographical references.
    ISBN 0-8166-4607-4 (pb : alk. paper)
    1. Minneapolis (Minn.) — History.   I. Title.   II. Series.
    F614.M557W35   2005
    977.6'579—dc22

                                                        2005004844

Printed in the United States of America on acid-free paper

The University of Minnesota is an equal-opportunity educator and employer.

14 13 12 11 10 09 08 07 06 05   10 9 8 7 6 5 4 3 2 1

CONTENTS

LIST OF ILLUSTRATIONS vii

FOREWORD ix
Radical Politics and the Minneapolis Labor Movement:
Legacies of an American City   *Mary Lethert Wingerd*

ACKNOWLEDGMENTS xxxv

INTRODUCTION xxxvii

    I. AMERICAN CITY 1

    II. THE GOLDEN AGE OF ECONOMIC EMPIRE . . . 9

    III. FATE OF THE RANK-AND-FILE EMPIRE BUILDERS 25

    IV. POLITICAL REVOLT AND THE WAR 45

    V. THE FARMER-LABOR PARTY IN POWER 59

    VI. 1934: CITY OF TENSION 79

    VII. THE FIRST CHALLENGE 93

    VIII. BATTLE IN THE STREETS 113

    IX. PERSONAL LIVES 129

    X. CIVIL WAR IN JULY 155

    XI. THREE CITIZENS AND THE FATE OF A CITY . . . 185

    XII. TRUCE BETWEEN THE PAST AND THE PRESENT . . 207

    XIII. EVERYDAY LIFE 223

    XIV. THE DYNAMO OF CHANGE 245

    XV. CROSSROADS 267

SELECTED BIBLIOGRAPHY 275

PUBLISHER'S NOTE

———

THE Fesler-Lampert Minnesota Heritage Book Series is designed to renew interest in the state's past by bringing significant literary works to the attention of a new audience. Our knowledge and appreciation of the culture and history of the region have advanced considerably since these books were first published, and the attitudes and opinions expressed in them may strike the contemporary reader as inappropriate. These classics have been reprinted in their original form as contributions to the state's literary heritage.

LIST OF ILLUSTRATIONS

AMERICAN CITY . . . . *frontispiece*
JIM HILL 12
BRIDGE SQUARE, MINNEAPOLIS, 1869 13
ST. PAUL AND PACIFIC, 1873 13
BUNKHOUSE IN THE NINETIES 28
THE WHEAT FIELDS OF MINNESOTA 29
IGNATIUS DONNELLY 48
LINDBERGHS, FATHER AND SON 49
FARM-HOLIDAY 66
"I HOPE THE PRESENT SYSTEM OF GOVERNMENT GOES RIGHT
   DOWN TO HELL" 66
AT THE STATE CAPITOL 67
"MONDAY'S BATTLE WAS A MILITARY ENGAGEMENT" . . . 116
THE BATTLE WAS REPORTED OVER THE RADIO LIKE A FOOTBALL
   GAME 117
THE FARMERS SET UP THEIR OWN MARKET 168
FATHER HAAS AND E. H. DUNNIGAN 168
POLICE OPEN FIRE ON TRUCKLOAD OF UNARMED STRIKERS . 169
A. W. STRONG 188
V. R. DUNNE 189
GOVERNOR FLOYD B. OLSON 204
ENTER THE NATIONAL GUARD 205
A LESSON IN CLASS POLITICS 220
THE STRIKERS' NEWSPAPER ANSWERS THE RED SCARE . . 221
BASEBALL 236
SWEDISH "MIDSOMMARDAGEN" 236
107° ABOVE 237
40° BELOW 237
STRIKE AT FLOUR CITY ORNAMENTAL IRON CO. . . . 252
FLOUR CITY 252
LEGENDARY BOLSHEVIKS—THE DUNNE BROTHERS . . . 253
STEWARD'S MEETING, 544 253
ANNOUNCING THE FIRST STRIKE SETTLEMENT 268
WHAT NEXT? 269

RADICAL POLITICS AND THE MINNEAPOLIS LABOR MOVEMENT: LEGACIES OF AN AMERICAN CITY

Mary Lethert Wingerd

———

Charles Rumford Walker and the Writing of *American City*

In the spring of 1936, Charles and Adelaide Walker packed up their family and set out for a yearlong sojourn in Minneapolis. They settled into a modest urban neighborhood and prepared to take the pulse of a city that had been rocked by a momentous labor conflict two years earlier. A small group of militant union organizers had led Minneapolis truckers in a brilliant campaign that cracked the open-shop citadel Minneapolis had maintained for three decades. Contemporary observers on both the right and left identified the conflict as an event of historic import. For labor sympathizers, the victory of General Drivers Local 574 of the International Brotherhood of Teamsters (IBT) was a harbinger of positive change for the fortunes of the labor movement. *Fortune* magazine perceived a more ominous portent, declaring that this "revolt in the Northwest" had left Minneapolis with "the clearest Left-Right alignment of any city in the land."[1]

The future was uncertain. With the United States mired in the most devastating depression in its history, the survival of capitalism itself was in question. Franklin Roosevelt and his team of New Dealers experimented with an assortment of strategies to stem the downward spiral and put the nation back on an even keel. Meanwhile, various forms of radicalism had won unprecedented political legitimacy among significant numbers of the population. A survey conducted in 1938 concluded that "three-quarters of the public believed that industry had failed in its social and economic responsibilities." In Minnesota, Farmer-Labor candidate Floyd B. Olson had won the state-house in 1930; four years later, on a substantially more radical platform, he was handily reelected along with numerous other Farmer-Labor party office seekers. At the 1934 party convention, Governor Olson declared to thunderous approval, "I am not a liberal. I am what I want to be—a radical."[2]

In such a volatile political climate, even Communism was no longer the political pariah of decades past. When *American City* debuted in 1937, the nation was as politically divided as it had ever been in its history. Thus, Walker's relatively even-handed treatment of the battles that shook Minneapolis won praise from reviewers across the political spectrum.[3] Rather than craft an apologetic for radical change, Walker had taken pains to present multiple perspectives of the conflict—a quality that enhances its worth as a work of social history. Nonetheless, the narrative was politically informed, and today, nearly sixty years after its original publication, *American City* has added historical value as a window onto the spirit of the times as well as a compelling contemporary narrative of the events of 1934. Thus, an understanding of the politics and person-ality of Charles Rumford Walker becomes an essential context within which to situate his work.

Walker and the Anti-Stalinist Left

Despite the "balanced" tone of the narrative, Walker was a self-proclaimed radical whose sympathies lay squarely with the working class. Though not formally affiliated with either Communists or Socialists, he had long been drawn to the principles of labor activism and social change that suffused the American left of the 1920s and 1930s. By background, Charles Walker was an unlikely revolutionary. Born in 1893, a descendant of New Hampshire's last colonial governor, Walker enjoyed a sheltered upper-middle-class childhood. Educated at Exeter and then Yale, where he was editor of the *Yale Literary Magazine,* he graduated in 1916 with stellar social credentials and without radical aspirations. To the contrary, along with thousands of other Ivy League romantics captivated by visions of martial glory, Walker eagerly enlisted as an officer to serve in the World War. There his political awakening tentatively began. The harsh realities of war, coupled with a natural empathy for life circumstances different from his own, raised troubling questions for young Charles about the social and political presumptions that had nurtured him.[4]

Once mustered out of the army, Walker put off embarking on his intended business career to find out for himself what life was like across the class divide. He bought some secondhand clothes and hired on as a helper at the Jones and Laughlin steel mill outside Pittsburgh. While his agenda was far from radical—he reasoned that by understanding workers better as three-dimensional human beings, he would become a more effective manager—Walker discovered that sharing the comradeship and the dangerous, dirty, and exhausting world of the steelworkers had inexorably shifted his sympathies to the working class. As he later wrote, "the twelve-hour day, as I observed it, tended either to destroy, or to make unreasonably difficult that normal recreation and participation in the doings of the family group, the church, or the community, which we ordinarily suppose is reasonable and part of the American inheritance." After leaving the mill, he briefly took a position in the personnel department of a firm in the copper industry but found that company policies clashed with his emerging social conscience. Driven by principle, he shifted his allegiance to labor reform, moved to New York, and embarked on a new career in journalism.[5]

New York in the 1920s was home to a vibrant circle of left intellectuals, writers, and artists that included Theodore Dreiser, John Dos Passos, James T. Farrell, Floyd Dell, and Herbert Solow. Walker soon became drawn into their orbit, though his politics as yet exhibited only a general leaning to the left. In the foreword to *Steel: The Diary of a Furnace Worker* (1922), which recounted the onerous conditions he experienced as a steelworker, he maintained a cautious stance: "There are certain inferences, I think . . . that can be made from this record. But no thesis has been introduced and no argument developed. I have recorded the impressions of a complex environment, putting into words sight, sound, feeling, and thought."[6]

As a journalist and assistant editor at the *Atlantic Monthly*, Walker's political sympathies acted as an undercurrent rather than the driving force of his writing. In his fiction, however—a working-class novel, *Bread and Fire* (1927), and a collection of short stories, *Our Gods Are Not Born* (1931)—he was a more forthright champion of the humanity and trials of working people.

Still, it was only after his marriage in 1928 to Adelaide George, a member of the Boston Repertory Stock Company, that Walker fully dove into radical politics. It appears that Adelaide inspired her husband to refine his sympathies into an articulated political philosophy. Returning from a monthlong writing assignment for *Colliers* in 1931, he learned that Adelaide had begun to volunteer for the Communist-led Unemployed Council.

Within the year she had become a member of the executive board of the National Committee for the Defense of Political Prisoners. Charles followed her into political activism. Once committed, he was tireless, lending his name, his pen, and his presence to a multitude of demonstrations for change spawned in the depths of the Depression. In 1933 the Walkers journeyed to the Soviet Union, replete with letters of introduction to key Soviet cultural figures. According to Adelaide, the Communists welcomed Charles because of his reputation for moderation and open-mindedness, which challenged stereotypes of radicalism as beyond the pale of respectability.[7]

However, after seeing Stalin's Russia firsthand, both Walkers returned to the United States disillusioned with the Communist party and soon joined sympathies with a small group of disaffected radicals who became known as the New York Intellectuals. Critiquing Stalinist Communism from the left for its betrayal of the revolutionary and democratic ideals of Lenin, these leftists supported the political philosophy of Leon Trotsky. Formally constituted as the Communist League of America, they were commonly known simply as Trotskyists.[8] The Walkers found an intellectual home among this group, and at this juncture of their political evolution Charles and Adelaide Walker turned their attention to Minneapolis.

With their shared political ideals, the Walkers functioned as a team. Adelaide cheerfully uprooted the family to settle for the better part of a year in Minneapolis, conducted most of the documentary research, and collaborated with Charles on framing the ideas and structure of *American City*. While Charles turned his considerable investigative and literary talents to bringing the story of the Minneapolis truckers to life, Adelaide devoted her political energy to the Nonpartisan Labor Defense League, a Trotskyist organization dedicated to "the struggle against capitalist oppression." As is apparent, Adelaide was a committed political actor in her own right.[9]

Minneapolis-Style Radicalism

According to Walker, his prospectus for *American City* was a hard sell. "Why Minneapolis?" skeptics asked. "From any point of view . . . both city and region were neither typical nor strategic to modern industrialism or to American life." Defending his site of study, Walker claimed that the faltering economy of Minneapolis and Minnesota—bogged down by more than a decade of agricultural depression—was an ideal laboratory for exploring the possibly crucial connection between economic decline and economic radicalism.[10] But beyond this investigative hypothesis, Minneapolis held an allure for Walker that neither San Francisco nor Toledo (the sites of other historic strikes in 1934), nor any other industrial city, could match. For the anti-Stalinist left, Minneapolis offered a singular ray of hope for the future. Seemingly out of nowhere, a handful of obscure, working-class Trotskyists had crafted an internally democratic, militant union movement and taken the city by storm.

Schooled in the logging camps, harvest fields, and railroad gangs of the Northwest rather than in the halls of elite universities, Vincent Dunne and Carl Skoglund were the strategic architects who built Local 574.[11] They had honed their revolutionary socialism first in the ranks of the IWW, then as Communist left-wing Farmer-Laborites. Expelled from Farmer-Labor ranks in 1924 for their Communist affiliation, in 1928 the dissident Trotskyists were ousted from the Communist party for their opposition to Stalin. They then reformed as the Communist League of America.[12] Along with Vincent Dunne's younger brothers, Miles and Grant, and a handful of fellow working-class Trotskyists, Dunne and Skoglund created and carried out the plan to organize the "open shop capital of America." Ordinary workers, they were virtual unknowns to the New York Intellectuals vanguard. Nonetheless, these "organic intellectuals" had achieved a singular success in 1934.[13] Not only had they built a powerful, democratic union, they had also won the loyalty and trust of the majority of workers throughout the city. This was a model that clearly merited further study.

In Walker's estimation, understanding this phenomenon and its potential for broader social change required more than a simple investigation of the struggle from the workers' perspective. He did not shy away from framing the conflict as "class struggle"—a term as threatening to mainstream America in 1936 as it is today—nor did he hesitate to make clear that his sympathies were with the workers. Still, in the humane style that had characterized his earlier work, Walker painted no cardboard villains. Instead, he attempted, with remarkable success, to portray a dynamic social text fraught with multiple perspectives, priorities, and forces that, taken together, reflected the life of the city.

Making Radicalism "Respectable"

Charles Walker may have been uniquely qualified to take on this task. Nurtured in the world of the upper class, with some experiential knowledge as both a manager and an industrial worker and with a genuine curiosity to hear all sides of an issue, he conducted an impressive range of interviews during his months in Minneapolis. A skilled and thoughtful interviewer, Walker's radical credentials gave him easy access to strike leaders and rank-and-file workers; his journalistic bona fides opened the door to the governor's office and to officials of the Citizens Alliance, the open-shop guardians of Minneapolis. As a neighbor, he could discuss the issues of the day over the back fence with ordinary Minneapolitans. And finally, perhaps because of shared Ivy League connections, he was granted extraordinary entrée to scions of the Minneapolis elite.[14] All these personalities emerge in the narrative as complex and thoroughly human individuals.

Though overtly muted, Walker's political agenda still clearly influenced his narrative choices. Notably, while he acknowledged Trotskyism as a key element in the forces at play, Walker chose to deemphasize the revolutionary underpinnings of the strike leaders, focusing instead on the rank-and-file rebellion. Nor did he detail the factional ruptures among the left that battered the movement or increasingly virulent assaults by anti-Communist red-baiters on the right.

Both during the strike and in the ensuing years, the union was fiercely attacked from both the left and the right for its Trotskyist "taint." In the end, opponents of the union would use its radical reputation as a weapon to beat it into submission.[15] Yet, without other points of reference, Walker's account might suggest that revolutionary politics was merely a sidebar to the union struggle. Certainly, this was true in the minds of rank-and-file workers whose radicalism rarely extended beyond the Farmer-Labor party. Their loyalty to the leaders of 574 was based on personal respect and trust without regard for political affiliation. The Trotskyists themselves never used the union to proselytize; however, they were forthright about their politics, which infused the structure of the union and the rhetoric of the struggle. When the Communist *Daily Worker* attacked the union leadership for settling with the employers and thereby betraying their revolutionary principles, strike leaders scoffed in return that they were building a union, not a revolution. Yet, it was clear in their minds that the union was the "instrument of the fight," the institutional foundation that would educate workers for bigger battles to come. Vincent Dunne was unwavering in his belief that revolutionary change would come one step at a time.[16]

During their months in Minneapolis, Charles and Adelaide Walker became ardent admirers of the Dunne brothers and very likely shared Vincent Dunne's hopes for the future.[17] Thus, Walker's choice to relegate radical politics to the margin in *American City* may have been a conscious strategy to advance a more long-term vision for change. By emphasizing the heroics and humanity of the movement and minimizing the revolutionary nature of the leadership's guiding principles, he offered a version of class struggle rooted in American values. In his telling, militant class struggle in Minneapolis had been imaginatively adapted to the American scene, "a strategy as flexible as it was bold to achieve practical success"—a message intended to allay fears of radicalism by incorporating it into a progressive agenda of benefit to society as a whole.[18]

The Problem of St. Paul

Walker also hoped that *American City* would serve another purpose: as a handbook for crafting a democratic social movement. He believed that the "militancy, foresighted leadership, and class understanding" that characterized the labor struggle in Minneapolis offered an invaluable organizing model for the labor movement, a turn away from the fragmentation of traditional American Federation of Labor (AFL) craft unionism to the worker solidarity that girded the industrial unionism of the newly formed Committee for Industrial Organization (CIO).[19] However, the record revealed a problematic limitation to worker solidarity. Workers in St. Paul, just down the Mississippi River, displayed little interest in the plight of their fellows in Minneapolis. St. Paul unions, including Teamsters Local 122, offered minimal support to the truckers, a circumstance that was a jarring note of discord—which may explain why St. Paul is entirely missing from the narrative.

While the businessmen of Minneapolis had relentlessly battered organized labor in Minneapolis for more than thirty years through the antiunion Citizens Alliance, St. Paul was known as a union stronghold; closed-shop contracts were the norm; and its mayor, a founder of the Farmer-Labor party, proudly carried a union card. Union culture in St. Paul was quite distinct from that in Minneapolis. The two cities had a long history of political, cultural, and economic rivalry. *Fortune* magazine in 1936 described the relationship as "outright hatred."[20]

This antipathy had deep roots. By the end of the nineteenth century, the industrial might of Minneapolis had relegated St. Paul to the role of a poor relation, and St. Paulites acutely felt the sting. If Minneapolis was experiencing what would prove to be a temporary period of economic decline, St. Paul, without an industrial base, had felt the pinch for the past thirty years. Founded as a trade and transportation hub, the city had watched its strategic importance gradually shrink. While Minneapolis industry boomed, serving a national and international market, St. Paul's precarious economy had become dependent on regional and local consumers. Contrary to Walker's hypothesis that economic decline fosters economic radicalism, in St. Paul it fostered a culture of compromise between business and labor. Most city businesses were relatively small and unable to bear the disruption of costly work stoppages; employers interacted with employees on a face-to-face basis, which made for qualitatively different relationships than those in the factories of Minneapolis with their hundreds or thousands of employees. And in St. Paul workers were key consumers as well as laborers.

Higher wages literally meant more consumer dollars to bolster the struggling local economy. Workers used that leverage to win fair wages, decent working conditions, and closed-shop contracts. In return they were willing to concede on demands that proved more than the local market could bear. Strikes seldom broke the surface of labor peace and most often were settled relatively amicably in labor's favor. In sum, local circumstances encouraged business to deal with organized labor rather than try to defeat it.[21]

In the doldrums of the 1920s, city businessmen had briefly tried to break the unions and establish an open-shop regime, but the result had been a public relations and economic fiasco. By 1934 the unions had recouped their losses, and business and labor had resumed their negotiated peace. With a distinctly local perspective, people closed ranks across class, ethnic, and religious differences to defend their city from "outsiders," especially those right next door in Minneapolis.[22]

The case of St. Paul suggested that worker solidarity might face some daunting obstacles. St. Paul unions regarded those in Minneapolis more as competitors—for both jobs and members—than as allies. Furthermore, the intransigence of Minneapolis business had spawned a militant culture that seemed alien to St. Paul unionists. As one member of Local 122 explained, Minneapolis teamsters were "a rough crowd . . . They had to be rough because they were facing a rough adversary." Nonetheless, their "style" wasn't comfortable to St. Paul union members who "didn't want any part of the violence" going on in Minneapolis.[23] Not surprisingly, such discordant sentiments did not find their way into Walker's narrative. The union culture that inspired his work was of another sort altogether. However, from a historical vantage point, the contrasting circumstances of St. Paul help illuminate the locally grounded nature of social protest and the difficulty in bridging parochial boundaries to create broad coalitions for change.

The Alternative Unionism of the 1930s

Minneapolis in the 1930s seemed a fertile seedbed for creating such a coalition, and *American City,* like all historical narratives, carried a political message. It was crafted to demonstrate to a general audience that militant unionism was not a threat but rather a positive force to benefit society. For working people across the nation, it was intended as a message of hope that with solidarity and commitment they too could achieve the victories that the Minneapolis truckers had won. For Walker himself, it represented his optimism that the principles of revolutionary socialism had taken root in Minneapolis and would grow to bring about the "achievement of a civilized world," one community at a time.[24]

In 1936 Walker's optimism seemed well founded. He captured Local 574 at the height of its success. Workers flocked into the union by the thousands, transforming what had been an impotent organization of a few hundred members into a seemingly unstoppable powerhouse. Throwing off the limitations of craft unionism, the teamsters had won the right to represent warehouse and shipping workers and all those "whose jobs were by any plausible definition related to trucking." They also offered membership to the unemployed, a strategy that Vincent Dunne declared had been critical to their success. The rank and file were fiercely loyal to the union, partly because it proved its effectiveness, but more important because they were active participants in creating policy and working for change. They had stood shoulder to shoulder during the strikes and continued to have essential roles to play. When a labor dispute arose anywhere in the city, the truckers put their vehicles and their bodies on the line to support the cause. Policy decisions were put before the membership for a vote. As one of the union leaders explained, "All in all, rank-and-file control over Local 574's affairs, including democratic selection of the leadership, had become a living reality. This was the mainspring of its strength."[25]

The leadership of 574 had crafted a model of what Staughton Lynde has described as alternative unionism, characterized by local autonomy and community-level organization. In Lynde's words, "this alternative unionism was democratic, deeply rooted in mutual aid among workers in different crafts and work sites, and politically independent. The key to the value system of alternative unionism was its egalitarianism." In the early 1930s workers in many cities across the country constructed similar versions of grassroots unionism, grounded in local conditions, creating the most vibrant and hopeful period of labor activism in American history. Nowhere was this movement more successful than in Minneapolis.[26]

Beyond *American City*

If Charles Walker had been able to see into the future, *American City* undoubtedly would have concluded on a more somber note. Behind the scenes, even as he chronicled the union's success, an array of opponents, on the left as well as the right, were at work to destroy labor's grand achievement.

Factionalism within the Left

Ideological inflexibility within the left had resulted in a long history of factional infighting that ranged from various incarnations of Socialism to the split between the Stalinist and Trotskyist wings of the Communist party. The Stalinist Communist party roundly hated the Trotskyists and was bent on discrediting them even if it led to the defeat of the truckers' struggle. As testament to the intensity of the ideological differences, Bill Dunne, the eldest of the Dunne brothers and a luminary in the Communist party, led the charge against his brothers and the union. During and after the 1934 strikes, Bill penned numerous attack articles in the *Daily Worker* denouncing his brothers at various turns as undemocratic, agents of the bosses, labor racketeers, and traitors to the workers' cause. He even appeared at a rally in Minneapolis in an attempt to discredit his brothers. The vast majority of the rank and file reacted with hostility to Dunne's charges and wholeheartedly supported their Trotskyist leaders. Nonetheless, the very public battle over which version of Communism should prevail had a negative cumulative effect. During the period of the Popular Front, beginning in 1935, the Communist party changed tactics from opposing the Farmer-Labor party to working from within. By 1936 Communists and Communist sympathizers had become influential in the left wing of the Farmer-Labor party, which eroded crucial political support for the union. In addition, public wrangling between the radical factions regularly reminded the general public (who made little distinction between various versions of Communism) of the "revolutionary" character of the union's top echelon. All this played into the hands of a growing coalition of antiunion red-baiters as the decade wound toward its end.[27]

The Business Counteroffensive

The 1934 strikes had wrought a public relations disaster for the Citizens Alliance. The general public blamed the Citizens Alliance and the businesses it represented for much of the violence that occurred. Meanwhile, Local 574 increased its prestige among workers by coming to the aid of labor actions throughout the city. A second round of violent strikes in other Minneapolis industries in 1935 further damaged the Alliance's public image, causing member employers to question the organization's tactics. Despite appeals by the Citizens Alliance for employers to hold the line, defections escalated as one major industry after another agreed to accept union representation. The Citizens Alliance was finally forced to acknowledge that the days of a union-free Minneapolis were over.[28]

Recognizing that aggressive suppression of union activity was no longer possible, in 1937 the Citizens Alliance formally disbanded; however, a new organization (with the same officers, board, street address, and members) was immediately formed. Though it claimed its mission was to promote labor peace, the Associated Industries of Minneapolis, as it was called, immediately set to devising less transparent strategies to tie labor's hands. Using its influence with political allies, the Associated Industries lobbied for antiunion legislation that included restrictions on striking and boycotts along with legally binding contracts as a means to strip the unions of the tactics of direct action—the most powerful weapon in their arsenal.[29]

The first order on the agenda was to eliminate the leadership of Local 544 (formerly 574). The Trotskyists soon found themselves attacked by an unrelenting barrage of red-baiting propaganda and fabricated charges of labor racketeering and other illegal activities. The antilabor businessmen behind this smear campaign were enthusiastically aided by a most improbable ally—the International Brotherhood of Teamsters.[30]

Labor's Own Worst Enemy

Daniel Tobin, president of the International Brotherhood of Teamsters, was no supporter of the Minneapolis local. Conservative, committed to the principles of craft and business unionism, and most dedicated to maintaining his personal power and authority, Tobin was incensed that 574 had launched the first of its strikes without the sanction of the International. Despite the fact that over three thousand new members poured into the union, his grudge against the strike leaders escalated with each victory they won. Tobin was painfully aware that workers' allegiance was to the local leaders rather than to the International. Moreover, by incorporating inside workers and the unemployed, 574 had transgressed the jurisdictional boundaries of craft unionism. Tobin was not about to allow such an insurrection in the ranks.[31]

Over the next six years, Tobin plotted various strategies to take control of 574. In 1935 he revoked the local's charter but found that the rank and file refused to abandon the "outlaw" 574. Defeated for the moment, the IBT was forced to issue a new charter to the resolute truckers, now designated as Local 544—a change in name only. During the next three years 544 proved itself perhaps the most effective union in the country. National membership in the IBT rose from 80,000 in 1933 to nearly half a million members in 1939, in large part due to the adoption of strategies first tested in Minneapolis—which only increased Tobin's determination to oust the Trotskyists and regain control of "his" union.[32]

Bent on discrediting the leadership, Tobin orchestrated several unsuccessful attempts to force the Trotskyists out. He authorized spies to infiltrate the union, launched various legal challenges, and when all else failed sent strong-arm enforcers to intimidate 544 loyalists. Finally, fed up with years of attack from their own international union, the Minneapolis teamsters voted to secede from the AFL and join the fledgling CIO.[33] Tobin frantically tried to halt the defection with tactics of persuasion, propaganda, and legalistic maneuvering. As added inducement, a crew of armed thugs roamed the streets of Minneapolis to beat recalcitrant defectors back into the AFL. Remarkably, the members of 544 stood firm against all the forces brought to bear against them. In the end, only the federal government would prove to have the power to finally bring the union down.[34]

State and Federal Power

The power of the state was a key actor both in facilitating the rise of 574 and in destroying the militant unionism that was the source of its power. New Deal protections for organized labor and President Roosevelt's words of support for union membership encouraged workers across the country to organize. In Minnesota, the political clout of the Farmer-Labor party created a particularly optimistic climate. Vincent Dunne freely admitted that the truckers could not have defeated the Citizens Alliance in 1934 without a sympathetic Farmer-Labor governor in the statehouse. Though Floyd Olson failed to live up to his "radical" claims, his political career was built on working-class support. A defeat for the truckers would have fatally injured his credibility. Each day that the strike dragged on, his political capital diminished, yet he was unable to bring the employers to heel. Federal mediators dispatched from Washington had no better luck. But just when the strike seemed about to be lost, the employers suddenly caved in—due to what Walker called rumors of "mysterious pressure from Washington." Pressure indeed. In a secret meeting between Olson and President Roosevelt held in Rochester, Minnesota, they had come upon a strategy to end the strike.[35]

The two preeminent banking entities in Minneapolis (and Minnesota), First Bank Stock Corporation and Norwest Banco, were major financial backers of the Citizens Alliance and its member businesses. They were also heavily indebted to the federal government through bailout loans issued to carry them through the Depression. In fact, 70 percent of the net worth of Norwest was controlled by the government through the Reconstruction Finance Corporation (RFC). Immediately after the Roosevelt/Olson meeting, federal strike mediators met with the presidents of the two mammoth financial institutions to convey the RFC's "concern" over the declining value of the collateral that secured Norwest's loans. Regrettably, if the situation continued, the agency might have to call in the loans. The bank presidents immediately responded to that veiled threat and used the enormous financial leverage they held over the business community to force the Citizens Alliance to capitulate.[36]

Four years later government played an equally pivotal role. The political winds had drastically changed. Republican Harold Stassen won the governor's seat in 1938 with a call for "labor peace," promising to bring an end to the "extremism" of "reactionary industrialists" and "irresponsible, radical labor agitators" who fueled needless conflict between business and labor. Stassen's version of labor peace came to fruition with the passage of the Minnesota Labor Relations Act in 1939, reviled by organized labor as the Stassen Slave Labor Act. Prefiguring the provisions of the Taft-Hartley Act by nearly a decade, the Minnesota act outlawed sit-down strikes, mandated cooling-off periods before striking, and prohibited secondary strikes, boycotts, and a list of other so-called unfair labor practices. Much of the bill had been crafted by the Minnesota Employers' Association and the Associated Industries of Minneapolis. Essentially, it stripped organized labor of its most effective tactics of direct action.[37]

Worse was yet to come from Washington. As the country moved ever closer to entering World War II, the Roosevelt administration took another look at the Minneapolis teamster troublemakers. The Trotskyists—now politically reconstituted as the Socialist Workers party—vocally opposed American involvement in the European war. Nationally, the membership of the Socialist Workers party amounted to no more than a few hundred persons—an insignificant protest group. Only in Minneapolis had they achieved any kind of influence—not as political dissidents but as architects of a militant labor movement that had shifted the balance of power a bit more than was anticipated in 1934.

Growing federal antagonism toward Minneapolis-style labor activism was already apparent in 1939 when nationwide strikes broke out among WPA workers, protesting wage cuts and layoffs. Workers in the Twin Cities, with strong support from 544, shut down WPA projects in St. Paul and Minneapolis for two weeks. Similar strike actions occurred in thirty-six other states, but, curiously, the government, claiming violation of the 1939 relief appropriation law, chose to prosecute strikers only in Minneapolis and St. Paul, handing down indictments against 162 strikers for "intimidation and conspiracy." Federal prosecutor Victor Anderson declared in court that "Minneapolis is not going to become the Moscow of America as long as I am district attorney"—a theme that foreshadowed other events already in motion.[38]

In June 1940, with the war escalating in Europe, the political climate in Washington ensured easy passage of the Alien Registration Act, sponsored by the rabidly antilabor congressman Howard W. Smith. Though innocuously titled, the Smith Act was actually the first federal peacetime antisedition and conspiracy act passed by the federal government since 1798 and a powerful weapon to use against antiwar dissidents, particularly Communists. The Trotskyists, who made no secret of their opposition to the war, were vulnerable to be sure, but as a threat to American policy the Socialist Workers party constituted a very insignificant position. However, other considerations put them directly in the line of fire for prosecution. Consequently, the first indictments issued under the provisions of the Smith Act were brought in Minneapolis against members of the Socialist Workers party, who, not coincidentally, were the leadership of Local 544.[39]

Daniel Tobin had spearheaded labor support for Roosevelt in his two previous election campaigns and maintained a close relationship with the president. In the fight to wrest 544 away from the CIO, he had called in that political debt for assistance from the White House. Roosevelt's immediate response was to publicly admonish the CIO for chartering Local 544. Two weeks later the Department of Justice raided the Minneapolis office of the Socialist Workers party, carting away boxes of Marxist literature (all of which was published and easily purchased material), "two red flags, and several pictures of Leon Trotsky."[40]

While ostensibly the case was based on alleged political conspiracy by the Socialist Workers party to overthrow the government, of the twenty-four defendants named in the indictment all but a few were key leaders of 544. In anticipation of the case, the FBI had compiled fat dossiers on several of the union's leaders that went back a number of years. In 1941 it had stepped up surveillance by infiltrating agents into the union to "observe the leadership."[41]

If the object of the prosecutions had truly been the Socialist Workers party, the logical location to be raided would have been its New York headquarters rather than a Minneapolis branch with only a few dozen active members. Quite clearly, the militant Minneapolis labor movement—not a subversive "Communist" plot—was the intended target.

The first instance of what would come to be called McCarthyism played out against the labor leaders in Minneapolis. Despite a prosecutorial case that failed to demonstrate any conspiracy to overthrow the government, eighteen defendants, including Vincent and Miles Dunne (brother Grant, unable to bear the strain, committed suicide during the time of the trial), Carl Skoglund, and most of the rest of the leadership of 544, were found guilty and sentenced to eighteen months behind bars. In 1943, after unsuccessfully appealing the case, the Trotskyists entered federal prison. In the final analysis, they were prosecuted for their *ideas* rather than for illegal actions.

Losses and Legacies

By the time the convicted labor leaders emerged from prison in 1945, the world had changed. The moment of possibility that fueled radical politics and a militant, democratic labor movement in the 1930s had passed, subsumed by the patriotic fervor of the nation at war. In service to wartime demands, government prohibitions limiting most forms of direct action and regulatory restrictions imposed by the National Labor Relations Board and the War Labor Board became the accepted order of the day. As a result, the alternative, community-based unionism that had energized worker activism was no longer possible, replaced instead by a contractual, bureaucratic, top-down style of labor negotiation that removed much of the decision-making process from worker control. In Minneapolis, the teamsters had been forcibly domesticated, returning to the IBT to protect what gains they could. The Trotskyists who had built the Minneapolis labor movement had no place in this new union culture: they had been rendered irrelevant. Vincent Dunne remained stalwart in his political beliefs to the end of his life, but his activities elicited little further government interest, though he

ran for public office several times as a member of the Socialist Workers party. According to his son, the government left
Dunne alone because "he wasn't important anymore."[42]

With the onset of the Cold War, radicalism of any sort—and
with it any challenge to a celebration of capitalism—had no
place within the bounds of political discourse. Disillusioned
leftists either retreated into silence, were hounded from public
life, or refashioned their politics to make peace with the perceived limits of political change. Charles Walker chose the latter course. Increasingly disheartened by splits among the left as
well as by counterattacks from the right, Charles and Adelaide
Walker turned away from radical politics. The assassination of
Leon Trotsky in 1940 marked the end of their self-definition as
"revolutionaries," and they retreated to a position "somewhere
between Norman Thomas and Franklin Roosevelt." Their slide
to the right escalated rapidly. By 1941 Adelaide had become a
campaign worker for Republican industrialist Wendell Willkie
in his presidential challenge to Roosevelt's reelection. Charles
became the assistant secretary of his alma mater, Yale University, returned to the Episcopal faith of his youth, and divided
his time between penning industrial relations studies and
translating works of classical Greek drama. Perhaps ancient
tragedies were easier to bear than those taking place around
him. Most of the other so-called New York Intellectuals followed similar courses of retreat. Many, including key theorists
of the anti-Stalinist left, embraced a neoconservative version
of anti-Communism. Others, like Walker, simply disappeared
from the public stage.[43]

The Minneapolis Trotskyists, following the lead of Vincent
Dunne, kept faith with the principles that had inspired them
in the 1930s. But blacklisted by Minneapolis employers, they
struggled to keep food on the table, helpless to stem the ero-

sion of the movement they had built. They must have asked themselves if all the sacrifices and struggle had been worth it in the end.

There can be no doubt that the battles of the 1930s had a lasting beneficial impact on workers' lives in Minneapolis, winning the right to organize and defeating the city's intransigent anti-union forces. Even the domesticated unions that emerged in the 1940s offered important protections for workers' rights that the Citizens Alliance had denied them. However, the bureaucratic and legalistic structure that has characterized the AFL-CIO since that time (the two organizations merged in 1955) has been a pale shadow of the promise of democratic unionism that flourished in the 1930s. Still, many of those who participated in the events in Minneapolis were personally transformed by the experience and carried the ideals of solidarity, self-respect, and democratic possibility wherever life took them. Marvel Scholl, married to one of the union leaders, described her participation in the strikes as "where I was a person," an experience that led to a life dedicated to social activism. Jake Cooper embarked on a political journey that began as a teenage striker in 1934, took him to prison as a defendant in the Smith Act trials, and did not falter when he later became an independent businessman. His lifelong participation in social and political struggles testified that social justice and business success can be mutually reinforcing. Countless other veterans of 544 schooled the next generation in democratic alternatives to the status quo, both inside and outside the labor movement.[44]

While individuals such as these nurtured and passed on the ideals of democratic unionism, too few people today are familiar with the events that rocked Minneapolis in the 1930s. History, after all, is written by the winners, and it becomes difficult to conceive of possible outcomes different from those that shape our daily lives. The republication of *American City* provides an important opportunity to revisit the grassroots activism that once fueled the Minneapolis labor movement. But it is more than the tale of a road not taken. The rise and demise of Local 574 can both inform and inspire future struggles for change. If the lessons of its legacy are carried forward, then history will have served us well.

Notes

1. "Revolt in the Northwest," *Fortune,* April 1936, 113.

2. Survey of the National Association of Manufacturers, cited in William Millikan, *A Union against Unions: The Minneapolis Citizens Alliance and Its Fight against Organized Labor, 1903–1947* (St. Paul: Minnesota Historical Society Press, 2001), 330; Millard L. Giske, *Minnesota Farmer-Laborism: The Third Party Alternative* (Minneapolis: University of Minnesota Press, 1979), 140–41, 188, 199.

3. See, for example, *New York Times Book Review,* March 21, 1937; *New Republic,* March 31, 1937, 25; *The Nation,* March 20, 1937; *Saturday Review of Literature,* March 27, 1937.

4. Biographical sketch, Charles Rumford Walker Papers, Minnesota Historical Society (hereafter MHS), St. Paul, Minnesota; Alan M. Wald, *The New York Intellectuals: The Rise and Decline of the Anti-Stalinist Left from the 1930s to the 1960s* (Chapel Hill: University of North Carolina Press, 1987), 56.

5. Charles Rumford Walker, *Steel: The Diary of a Furnace Worker* (Boston: Atlantic Monthly Press, 1922), 156; Wald, *New York Intellectuals,* 56.

6. Walker, *Steel,* vii.

7. Wald, *New York Intellectuals,* 56–57, 151; Dorothy Day, "Hunger Marchers in Washington," *Commonweal* 48 (December 24, 1932): 277–79.

8. Wald, *New York Intellectuals,* 151, 3–24; Mary Jo Buhle, Paul Buhle, and Dan Georgakas, eds., *Encyclopedia of the American Left* (Urbana: University of Illinois Press, 1992), 782–83.

9. Walker, this volume, xxxvi, xli; Wald, *New York Intellectuals,* 55–56, 104.

10. Walker, this volume, xxxviii–xxxix.

11. For extensive biographical sketches of the Dunnes, see Dale Kramer, "The Dunne Boys of Minneapolis," *Harpers,* March 1942, 388–98.

12. Vincent Dunne's son remembered the emotion-filled meeting of the Farmer-Labor Ward Club, held in Dunne's own living room, when the members tearfully expelled his father, their "good friend of many years," from the association. V. R. Dunne Jr., interview by Mary Wingerd, August 19, 1994, Minneapolis, tape recording.

13. I am indebted to Lawrence Goodwyn for the term "organic intellectual," defined here as one whose understanding of theoretical concepts is interpreted through experiential knowledge of working-class life.

14. The Dunne brothers, Skoglund, and other workers appear in the text undisguised, as does A. W. Strong, president of the Citizens Alliance. Most other interviewees are portrayed with pseudonyms. Walker's appointment book and interview notes reveal that among his sources were manufacturing heir Totten Heffelfinger; John Crosby, son of one of the founders of General Mills; and prominent attorney Richard Tighe. See appointment book and interview notes, Walker Papers, MHS.

15. For an account of the strikes and ensuing struggles of the union in which politics plays a central role, see the series of books by strike leader and Trotskyist Farrell Dobbs: *Teamster Rebellion* (1972), *Teamster Power* (1973), *Teamster Politics* (1975), and *Teamster Bureaucracy* (1977), all published by Monad Press, New York.

16. Dobbs, *Teamster Rebellion,* 100–101; Grace Carlson, interview by Carl Ross, July 9 and 14, 1987, Minneapolis, tape recording, MHS.

17. Wald, *New York Intellectuals,* 151.

18. Walker, this volume, 271–73.

19. Ibid., 271.

20. "Revolt in the Northwest," *Fortune,* April 1936, 112.

21. Mary Lethert Wingerd, *Claiming the City: Politics, Faith, and the Power of Place in St. Paul* (Ithaca, NY: Cornell University Press, 2001).

22. Ibid.

23. Gordon Larson, interview by Mary Wingerd, July 27, 1996, St. Paul, tape recording and notes.

24. Walker, this volume, 272–73.

25. Dobbs, *Teamster Power,* 30–31; Vincent Dunne Sr., interview by Lila M. Johnson, April 27, 1969, Minneapolis, tape recording, MHS.

26. Staughton Lynde, ed., *We Are All Leaders: The Alternative Unionism of the Early 1930s* (Urbana: University of Illinois Press, 1996), 2–3.

27. The breach between Vincent and Bill Dunne remained unhealed

throughout their lives. They never spoke again. Near the end of his life Vince said that, despite political disagreements, he carried no personal grudges toward anyone except his brother, who had tried to break the strike: that he could never forgive. Dunne Sr., interview; Dobbs, *Teamster Rebellion*, 98–99; Gieske, *Minnesota Farmer-Laborism*, 211.

28. Millikan, *Union against Unions*, 289–314.

29. Ibid., 315–18.

30. Ibid., 316, 323–42.

31. See Dobbs, *Teamster Rebellion*.

32. See ibid.

33. Thomas L. Pahl, "The G-String Conspiracy, Political Reprisal or Armed Revolt? The Minneapolis Trotskyite Trial," *Labor History* 8, no. 1 (1967): 36–39; Dobbs, *Teamster Bureaucracy*, 129–36; George Dimitri Tselos, "The Minneapolis Labor Movement in the 1930s" (PhD diss., University of Minnesota, 1970), 534–37.

34. Pahl, "G-String Conspiracy," 38–39.

35. Vincent Dunne Sr., interview; Walker, this volume, 218; Millikan, *Union against Unions*, 285.

36. Millikan, *Union against Unions*, 240–42, 284–87.

37. Ibid., 343–50.

38. Herman Erickson, "WPA Strike and Trials of 1939," *Minnesota History*, Summer 1971, 203–14.

39. See Millikan, *Union against Unions*, 338–42; Pahl, "G-String Conspiracy," 30–51.

40. Millikan, *Union against Unions*, 338–42; Pahl, "G-String Conspiracy," 32.

41. Pahl, "G-String Conspiracy," 30–51.

42. Dunne Jr., interview.

43. Wald, *New York Intellectuals*, esp. 151–52.

44. Marvel Scholl, quoted in Marjorie Penn Lasky, "Where I Was a Person: The Ladies' Auxiliary in the 1934 Minneapolis Teamsters Strikes," in *Women, Work, and Protest*, ed. Ruth Milkman, 181–205 (London: Routledge, 1985); Mark Harris, ed., *My Brother, My Comrade: Remembering Jake Cooper* (San Francisco: Walnut Publishing, 1994).

ACKNOWLEDGMENTS

IN the writing of this book I have of necessity become indebted to hundreds of persons; to workers, farmers, business men, leaders of political parties, students, and professional persons who have filled out the historical narrative by facts and by their own personalities. I want to thank them all here, as I have thanked many in person for the help they have given.

The sources for most of the material on the early history of the "empire" I have listed in a brief bibliography, but I wish to acknowledge the special debt I owe to the archives of the Minnesota Historical Society. For the lives of the "rank-and-file empire builders" I am especially indebted to Lynn and Dora B. Haines' "The Lindberghs" (Vanguard Press, New York, 1931) and Paul de Kruif's lifelike study of the Merritts, entitled "Seven Iron Men" (Blue Ribbon Books, New York, 1934). The interpretation of these lives is, however, entirely the author's.

For invaluable documentary material on the truck drivers' strikes I am indebted to Mr. Herbert Solow, and for much original material on the modern city and other assistance to Mr. Gordon Roth.

I wish to acknowledge a personal debt to Mr. Richard L. Tighe for his aid in acquainting me with many phases of the city's business and political life and to absolve him of any responsibility for my interpretations of the material or for any of the opinions or conclusions expressed in this book.

I wish to thank my wife, Adelaide George Walker, for not having been an inspiration in the writing of this book. Her services were of a different character. Nearly the whole of the documentary research was done by her. She introduced many of the specific illustrations as well as the general ideas embodied in the book. The plan of the whole was made and brought to completion in collaboration with her.

INTRODUCTION

———

THIS is the "biography" of one American city which in less than seventy-five years sprang from the frontier, moved into a "Golden Age" of economic maturity, and entered its decline. The book stresses the adventures and personal lives of ordinary citizens rather than of their economic or political rulers.

I have chosen the Northwest and one of its economic capitals, Minneapolis, as the theme of this biography. Conflicts there between social groups have been sharper and more frequent than in other sections, and in the last half dozen years their explosive and *decisive* character provides, I believe, an extraordinary laboratory for the dynamics of social and economic struggle in America.

A large section of the biography has been devoted to the delineation of a single event of recent history, the general truck drivers' strikes of 1934 which paralyzed the city's life. I make no apology for this emphasis. Frequently more can be learned of the character of an individual, a class, or a community in a few hours of crisis than in a lifetime of routine living. I believe this singularly true of the dramatic episode in question. The strikes' unparalleled scope and violence—compared with any other labor war of recent years in the Northwest—suggest that their roots were neither shallow nor recent. Further study reveals them inseparably interwoven with the whole fabric of the city's economy and its history. It might be added that the emphasis given the strikes, if not my treatment of them, is shared in Minneapolis by both sides of the controversy.

Like the business men and the workers of Minneapolis in what was virtually civil war for the city in the summer of 1934, this book frankly recognizes the fact of class conflict. So far as possible the interests, motives, and passions of both combatants are explored, as well as the role of the indifferent if not disinterested bystander. As faithfully and objectively as possible I have treated the strategies of this warfare, the activity of its general staffs, its political and military armament, its diplomacy and its treaties. No clash of class forces is without these institutions and implements to embody it. Above all I have attempted to treat the episodes of the struggle not as fortuitous, and as interruptions of history, but as part of it. American cities have actually written the most consistently militant and explosive chapters in labor warfare of any country.

The effects of the "class struggle" on the personal lives of men and women—on whatever side they find themselves— is a neglected chapter of American history. And so far as I am able I have given the living connection of these events in the lives of individuals, in their ways of making a living, in their emotions and in their basic beliefs. After all, the whole bundle of individual lives adds up to the life of the city.

Critics of this book—before it was written—insisted that the author's choice of Minneapolis was unfortunate. From any point of view, they remarked, both city and region were neither typical nor strategic to modern industrialism or to American life. As to the exploit; of the Farmer-Labor party and an unusually militant labor movement, they were a "sport" in American life, dependent on an accident of decline in the city's and state's economy. My critics advised instead the story of Detroit or Pittsburgh or some other typical and strategic citadel of industrial America.

Few will dispute that Minneapolis shares a cultural common denominator with all America as surely as any other city. But in other ways I believe her history exemplifies more sharply than most the impact of forces that are typical and universal. All America reflects the depression of the farmers' economy. Minneapolis responds more violently—but not dissimilarly—to this chronic and world-wide condition. Most of the diseases of our economic system visit the city, in a more acute stage—but the maladies are universal ones. That her decline, however, is also particular and regional, and that her economy is not strategic to American capitalism, cannot be questioned. Will this destroy the significance of her biography—except, say, as an economic curiosity—to American life? I believe in some ways it sharpens the significance. *Fortune* magazine, in its study of Minneapolis—cordially detested by most Minneapolitans—after discussing the proposed St. Lawrence waterway as a check to commercial decline, remarks, "If that hope is ever fulfilled, Jim Hill's dream [of a railroad "empire" heading up in the Twin Cities] may yet come true. If not, Minneapolis may see the beginning of the Revolution—or it may go the way of St. Paul." The author of this book cannot join the editors of *Fortune* in guessing the birthplace of the future American Revolution, but the *Fortune* comment hints at a relation between economic decline and economic radicalism which is crucial.

History has a way of choosing apparently nonstrategic sectors of the economic front for revolutionary experiments. If the experiments are successful they themselves become strategic for the whole front. Who would have guessed that a clericalist reactionary revolt in Spain—the most backward economic sector on the continent—would have posed sharply for Europe the question of Communism or Fascism? Far less importantly and at a level where the forces and objectives are more elementary ones, the fifty-year story of farmers' and workers' revolt in the Northwest may quite possibly have a limited, but strategic, meaning for the whole of American economy.

Workers and farmers in Minnesota, through the Farmer-Labor party and through trade unions, have won a remarkable *measure* of control over their own destiny. Possibly such instruments of effective rank-and-file control could only be perfected in a weakened economic area as they unquestionably have been in the city of Minneapolis today. And only perhaps through the accident of unusually clear-sighted leadership. It is difficult to imagine achievements comparable to the Farmer-Labor party's in recent years, or exploits comparable to those of Minneapolis trade unions, in Pennsylvania or in Michigan. But "engineering" principles can be employed in other sectors. The social and economic organism transmits with remarkable speed impulses felt at periphery points. And spread of ideas and morale is not limited by state or industrial lines. For this reason, the experiences of the Northwest have more than a regional interest for Americans.

Contrariwise and by the same token, a "right swing" throughout the whole country, such as a new world war might release, and the whole leftward development in the Northwest—militant unionization, Farmer-Labor party and all— might be swept away. However, for the present all political weathervanes are pointing left and not right.

Such a biography as this might have confined itself to the recent battles, economic and political, in the city's life with their remarkable dénouement. That history is a dramatic and significant one. But this would have left the story incomplete and largely unintelligible. I have preferred at the risk of the reader's impatience to examine briefly the economic bones of these "rank-and-file revolts" which lie buried in the "imperial" history of the Northwest, and to review the rise of its four main satrapies—timber, railroads, wheat and iron—because their growth is an economic primer in the rise of American Capitalism. Chapter I, American City, is a preview, so to speak, of the book and city as a whole.

Chapters I, II, and III as a group will enable the reader, I believe, to tie in the explosive character of the modern city with the wider history and perhaps the destiny of America. The remaining chapters, the bulk of the book, are the more intimate biography of persons and a city in what for them has been a life and death struggle for cultural and economic survival.

Workers and farmers of Minnesota in the battles—political and economic—related in this history have never wasted any pity on themselves. Their conception of their individual lives is not as sociological phenomena or as victims of events but as active participants. And this history of their adventures with the American economic system is in full accord with that point of view.

Although the main events of this history had long been known to the author, the bulk of the book was actually written in Minneapolis, where I settled for the purpose, in the spring, summer, and fall of 1936. I lived with my family in a small house in a central section and participated, as far as possible, in the life of the city. The construction of the book became a continual process of revision and discovery.

AMERICAN CITY

Minneapolis is like a man in his late thirties who made a tremendous success at twenty-five . . . he is pugnacious and his friends wonder where he is going next

AMERICAN CITY

Chapter I

AMERICAN CITY

THE city of Minneapolis is a man in his late thirties who made a tremendous success at twenty-five. His parentage is mixed and racial differences quarrel in his veins. Ideas, too, and emotions thwart each other in his head. He is not quite sure of himself. And yet—he is pugnacious and still young with plenty of blood in him. His friends wonder where he is going next.

Minneapolis isn't like any other city. Not like New York. It's not cosmopolitan. Nor is it like, say Detroit. Detroit is like a big company town—held down to the belt and the sales talk. Minneapolis is far more varied and more headstrong. Nor is it like Pittsburgh, which is crowded and smoky and tough like the steel it makes. Nothing like Kansas City, which has tried to be like Boston. Nor like Boston—St. Paul is proverbially the Boston of the Middle West. Minneapolis is like none of them. And yet, it shares the American common denominator with each of them.

Minneapolis is an imperial city at the headwaters of the Mississippi—half way between east and west America—strategic to the plains of Minnesota, the Dakotas, parts of Montana and Wisconsin. Looking down from the Foshay tower one sees the gorge of the Mississippi, broad levees for river traffic, and an incredible web of railroad trackage, with

1

shining arteries disappearing into the East and West. Along
the river banks and elsewhere are tall tubular elevators like
watch towers fortifying the flour mills.

Every city is supposed to have a personality, evident and
appreciable to sentient persons—visitor or native alike.
Minneapolis is no exception.

Physically and financially the city is close to the soil.
She is a farmers' city. Her leading industry, milling, grinds
his grain. The bulk of her commerce is with the agricultural
empire surrounding—almost invading—her. Farmers come to
her from all over the Northwest to sell grain and vegetables,
to market butter fat, and to borrow money. You see them with
their produce in the market; you see them on the streets of
Minneapolis in their overalls. And in high boots, with sun-
burned faces, eating in her restaurants; or over in St. Paul in
the state office building, in the governor's chamber, dirt
farmers with *bona fide* Minnesota manure on their boots,
singly or in delegations telling the legislature, telling the governor what to do. Democrat, Republican, Farmer-Labor—the
farmer is one-half of economics and two-third of politics in
Minnesota. He contributes all he can to the personality of
Minneapolis. But he doesn't dominate it.

Minneapolis does not look at the farmer as he looks at
himself—or at Minneapolis. He looks warily at Minneapolis
as "the city," as the home of the grain exchange, as the Wall
Street of the Northwest. She looks at the farmer eagerly and
with calculation as her best customer. For despite substantial
manufactures, Minneapolis is at bottom a city of commerce
and transportation, in fact as well as in spirit. Not only does
the citadel of warehouses tell you that, but you breathe it in
the atmosphere of her streets and her market place: those rows
of semitrailers backed up to eight freight depots, the trucks
on meat row and fish row, and the *fleets* of trucks loading at

the city's 991 wholesalers, or moving out of the city with everything from safety pins to cultivators to the villages and farms of the Northwest.

As with most persons, blood is a basic component of personality with all the racial inheritances it carries. Along the streets of Minneapolis, in factories and offices, singing their own songs in cafés, are fair-haired, blue-eyed Scandinavians who have come from Copenhagen, Stockholm, Oslo, to Minneapolis, the Norse capital of America. Fifty-six per cent of Minnesota's population is foreign born. Plenty of the Norse languages and German are still spoken, especially in the market with farmers driving in from Chaska, or Mankato or Faribault or Cloquet. Or the Scandinavian guttural makes over Middle Western Americanese. *Skoal!* at Norse beer joints. Herring and Swedish bread at "A bit o' old Sweden," the café in north Minneapolis.

This is the Northland. Last winter the thermometer stayed under twenty below zero for two months. In the Minneapolis Club, where descendants of New Englanders foregather, they lean to whiskey as a fuel in winter, and gin fizzes to cool them off in the summer. In the rest of Minneapolis—mostly—the beverage for both purposes is beer. The drys never got a real foothold in the Northland. Statistics show that Minnesota drinks more beer in a year than Kansas does in a decade. Swing music has invaded Minneapolis, infecting the nimble-jointed, but Minneapolis still has a dozen public dance halls advertising "Old-Fashioned Dances." Anglo-Saxon, French-Canadian, and Scandinavian youth all like to dance the Swedish schottische.

Scandinavian influence bites deeper than the old customs. The governor of Minnesota for six years was Floyd Bjorsterne Olson. All over Minneapolis are co-operative oil stations, stores, and factories. Over in St. Paul the Farmers' Union Central

Exchange displays a row of shiny red tractors with a "co-op" label on each. Like beer and the schottische, the ubiquitous "co-op" and the Norse governor are part of the city's personality.

Today there are Olsons and Petersons and Andersons in Minnesota politics. But look over the names of the bankers, or railroad directors, or the owners of the flour mills or timber lands. They are Walker, Weyerhauser, Pillsbury, Crosby, Bennett, Washburn. The Pillsburys came from New Hampshire, the Washburns and Crosbys from Maine; most of the "first families" came from New England, direct or via Ohio or Iowa. The rosters of the Minneapolis and the Woodhill Country Club contains no Norse names. Didn't the melting pot work in Minnesota, or hasn't there been time yet for a vertical infiltration? The city is a split personality.

I lived in Minneapolis in a two-story six-room house with a neat lawn around it, a sprinkler, and a garage. There are maybe fifty thousand houses like mine in Minneapolis, besides, of course, the larger ones. I don't mean that everybody has one. There are a few apartments and there are tiny cottages on the outskirts and flop houses and dollar-a-week flats around Bridge Square. But architecturally they overflow the city. (It is said that fifty-six per cent of Minneapolitans own their own homes.)

Builders transmute a regional quality into sticks and stones in spite of themselves. And the thousands of blocks of residential Minneapolis share with most American cities the peculiar mediocrity of the "brown era." Six rooms to ten rooms, one-family or duplex, gambrel roof or plain, the line of the roof and the proportion of parts are unfailingly wrong. And the colors are ugly ones from the drab brown side of the palette. Of course Minneapolis is no different from other American cities in her predilection for the brown heterodox

house, except that—very fortunately having fewer tenements—
she has more houses. The streets of Minneapolis are beautiful
in the summer because they are broad, and the number of
trees, hedges, and sprinkled lawns are phenomenal. Only when
the leaves fall and the gardens and lawns freeze does the
drab era exhibit itself nakedly.

Minneapolis is close to the soil. And though some of her
citizens have forgotten it, she is close to her recent beginnings
in the pioneer west. Seventy-five years ago Minneapolis was a
village of a dozen shacks near the Falls of St. Anthony. Her
inhabitants busied themselves shooting elk and Indians. Men
and cities that mature slowly have different personalities from
those who grow up fast, or skip stages to an early success.

There is still plenty of room in the city—more than in
most—with its boulevards, its lakes, and its half wild parks;
room for the bank president and the garage mechanic to go
swimming or skating or fishing within the city limits. Though
the bank president goes to Lake Minnetonka or the pool at
Woodhill and the mechanic to Lake Harriet, which is closer
to the six-room houses. And outside the city, lots of room in
Minnesota with its "10,000 lakes" for picnics and week-end
fishing. So that space, perhaps, is one thing which gives an air
of freedom, real or imagined, to the personality of the city.
Something apart from the geography contributes, too: the faces
of men and women on the streets, farmers in overalls and
workers in shirt sleeves on Hennepin Avenue, or jostling
against business men in the legislative halls across the river,
and on the steps of the Capitol.

In Minneapolis, cultural bases are melting in spots and
freezing in others.

An evangelist copying Coughlin adopts the radio in an anti-
vice campaign. He adds, "What Minneapolis needs to be rid

of far more than the gangsters are the Dunne brothers." (The Dunne brothers are insurgent Minneapolis labor leaders.)

Two old people, she in her sixties, he at seventy-four, stop going to church. They join the Townsend movement and play cards and eat ice cream at Townsend sociables. Every night they pray that God will inspire Congress to vote them $200 a month.

Floyd Bjornsterne Olson, governor of Minnesota, addresses the unemployed from the steps of the State Capitol. He says if Capitalism cannot prevent a recurrence of depressions, he hopes "the present system of government goes right down to hell!" The unemployed citizens of Minnesota cheer.

The "Citizens' Alliance," representing eight hundred Minneapolis employers, meets in honor of the ideals which built the city. The speaker talks about the economic system under which the eight hundred employers live. "In the first place it is somewhere between 20,000 and 40,000 years old," he says; ". . . it cannot be hurried."

The Greek Orthodox Church holds its synod in Minneapolis, affirming belief in a sixteen-hundred-year-old ritual.

In the Unitarian Parish House, the Theatre Union of Minneapolis plays "Squaring the Circle," a Soviet comedy, to an applauding audience.

The day I settled into my comfortable six-room house on Harriet Avenue, a lady came to the door and said she was from the "Welcome Wagon." She welcomed me to the city, and offered me food samples from the grocer and the baker. I thanked her. Sitting in my parlor—and unofficially—she confided to me that conditions in the city were terrible. She hinted that radicals and racketeers had established a malign dictatorship.

A few days later I was in the office of a grain merchant, scion of one of the "empire builders" of the Northwest. "In

1934, the Communist leaders of the truck drivers' strike captured the streets of the city. They even put strikers in as traffic officers!" he told me. "After the next election we shall put all the Communists and criminals who are ruining the city in jail."

Floyd Bjornsterne Olson, first Farmer-Labor governor in the United States, died in August, 1936. A rabbi, a Lutheran minister and a Catholic priest preached a sermon over him. Governor La Follette of Wisconsin delivered the funeral oration. He had the largest funeral in the history of the Northwest.

A descendant of one of Minneapolis' pioneers sums it up: "My grandfather was a banker in a small town in Minnesota," he says. "In those days you could make a loan on a man's face. And it was good security. It isn't any more. *Something has slipped.*"

In 1849 Minneapolis was a sawmill town on the Falls of St. Anthony. In sixty years, a vast explosion of economic energy—remarkable in human history—had made the city what it is today, what 50,000 annual convention delegates see, what the Civic and Commerce Association describes . . .

But beneath the surface, sometimes puncturing it, the city is restless, and in ferment, defiant to the new, defiant to the old, puzzled, explosive, trying to hold on to itself, trying to break loose and go places. Where?

The Employment Stabilization Research Institute, staffed with economists from the University of Minnesota, predicts that: "Barring some unforeseen, fortuitous circumstance, Minnesota faces the prospect of a decline in industry, bringing in its trail a decline in the standard of living . . . an increasing tax burden . . . a growing unemployed population."

"If the rest of the country," says one native of Minneapolis, who is an officer of the strongest trade union in the Northwest, "had the workers as well organized as in Minneapolis, I'd like to see the Fascists start something. Today—if they wanted to—the workers of Minneapolis could seize power."

"A Republican administration," says a business man of energy and vision, "will restore our liberties, jail our agitators, and give us peace and prosperity. We have a fine city, intelligent leaders, and hidden in our soil and laboratories are the seeds of an industrial expansion we have hardly tapped. The future is bright."

CHAPTER II

THE GOLDEN AGE OF ECONOMIC EMPIRE

HISTORY has permitted the average city in Europe a thousand years in which to make the transition from barbarism to maturity. Minneapolis, through a skipping and compression of historic stages from backwoods to civic maturity, achieved "civilization" in a little more than forty. Twenty years later, economic decline had already begun. The Golden Age, maturing in the nineties, continued for roughly a generation, and the imprint of that age in her economy and way of thought are crucial to the understanding of the city.

"Somewhat unsightly are the suburbs," remarks a Minneapolis visitor in the nineties. "Huge, unpainted pine rookeries, from which the high smokestacks pierce the sky; countless piles of lumber, freshly sawed and now spread out for seasoning by wind and sunshine . . . the arrow-like streets of the business section. . . . Vehicles of every known description, all going full tilt. . . . They say you never see a dog stop to scratch himself in Minneapolis . . . he has not the time. . . . the West Hotel is the finest edifice of its kind . . . this side of New York . . . yet . . . overshadowed by the lofty Lumber Exchange across the street, the name of Edison and his electric light and motor plant can be read all over the northward county . . . and the Guaranty Loan Company's building claims, perhaps without danger of denial, to be the finest office structure in the world."

And it was impossible in the Golden Age—as it is now—

9

to fail to compare or contrast Minneapolis with her sister city
of St. Paul.

"If we were to imagine the Twin Cities personified, we
would liken Minneapolis to a vigorous rustic beauty in short
skirts; while St. Paul we would describe as a fashionable,
marriageable urban miss, a trifle stilted and lacking color and
plumpness, but with more style and worldly grace than her
sister."

"St. Paul is the home of merchant and professional man,"
writes another observer of the nineties, "Minneapolis of the
lumber king and the miller. Lawyers abound in the old town,
artisans in the new. The former is Republican in the sense of
culture and conservatism; the latter, Democratic, even fiercely
so, in popular vim and enterprise. St. Paul, from lofty bluffs,
looks down upon the valley in content. Minneapolis, from
its level of a prairie, peers aloft at its twelve story cornices and
ever strives to climb."

Native and visitor alike, however, were careful to stress that
on a massive base of material wealth the Twin Cities were
second to none in the "refinements of civilization." Julian
Ralph warns:

"It may be necessary to say to the untraveled Eastern reader
that the appointments—and the tenants—of these mansions
reflect the best modern attainments of civilization as it has been
studied in the capitals of the world. One, at least, among these
houses has not its superior in New York so far as its size, its
beauty, and the character of its surroundings are concerned.
In its appointments it will be found that the elegances and art
triumphs of far more than Christendom have been levied
upon to testify to a taste that at no point oversteps the limits
cultivation has established. On the walls a number of master-
pieces of the Barbizon school hang side by side with the best

efforts of Munkacsy, Diaz, Tadema, Detaille, Meissonier and many other masters. Barye bronzes have their places in various rooms and the literature of two continents, freshened by the constant arrival of the best periodicals, is ready at hand and well marked for use. . . . It is no secret that this is the home of James J. Hill."

In the decades preceding the Golden Nineties an unparalleled economic expansion, explosive energy, and an unconquerable optimism had laid the physical foundations for the "appointments of these mansions—and the tenants" who reflected the last attainments of civilization. That this miraculous expansion would ever cease, that actual decline would overtake the empire in the twentieth century, would have seemed to contemporaries a blasphemy. In the sixties a St. Paul editor wrote: "Enclose St. Paul, indeed! Fence in a prairie fire! Dam up Niagara! Bail out Lake Superior! Tame a wolf! Civilize Indians! Attempt any other practical thing; but not to set metes and bounds to the progress of St. Paul!"

Speed of development has been characteristic of most of the North American continent, but the economic area of the Northwest exemplifies with classic precision the conditions and laws, so to speak, of this swiftness. And considered at each stage in its lifting and declining curve, this swiftness is an invaluable key to our American city.

Speed was made possible—on the physical side—by an imperial domain, ready and ripe for conquest. But the potential wealth of the Northwest had been in existence since the close of the Ice Age. It remained untapped until almost the close of the American Civil War, 1865 A. D. By that time, technical, historical, and human correlations were for the first time entirely adequate for its speedy conquest.

"Swiftness" certainly does not explain the origins or the

operative principle of American Capitalism under whose
auspices the Northwest was conquered and "turned into a
habitable land." But it throws it into dramatic relief and in
some ways gives a classic and "pure" demonstration of its
principles. There was here no feudalism to overlap or adulter-
ate pure industrial—or agrarian—Capitalism, and no time for
cultural anachronisms to incrust or obscure the pure process.
In a later chapter we will remark again on this phenomenon.
Here it is enough to emphasize what the reader has guessed
from the quotations of contemporaries, that the simplicity and
the unparalleled speed of capitalist development in the Northwest implanted in the empire builders an unqualified devotion
to its principles and to the "laws of human progress."

The physical and sensual evidence of wealth that grew by
the hour, and of a tangible and total civilization that conquered
the wilderness in a few decades, instilled into the empire's
rulers far more than a "devotion to sound business principles."
The mechanics of Capitalism became identified with their
own manifest destiny—how could it be otherwise?—and indeed, at moments, with a crusade for the spread of civilization
itself. In particular what might be called "the law of indefinite
expansion" became a part of their mental and moral outlook.
That a million-dollar market this year becomes in a decade a
billion-dollar one, that farms and cities and fortunes grow
endlessly from year to year seemed not isolated as a historical
coincidence but a veritable law of the universe, eternal, and
eternally rewarding to their devotion. This philosophical fruit
of swiftness which still governs the descendants of the empire
builders is a key to an understanding of the city.

For many years after the American Revolution, Minnesota
remained under the control of the Hudson's Bay Company.
But in 1816 the American Fur Company turned an early

© *Keystone View Co.*

JIM HILL
"The most confident, indefatigable, realistic, and ruthless of them all . . ."

BRIDGE SQUARE, MINNEAPOLIS, 1869
The Northern Pacific Exploring Expedition
"We took a backwoods country . . . connected it with railroads,
planted cities . . ."

ST. PAUL AND PACIFIC, 1873
"To acquire his first railroad it was alleged that Hill conspired with the
receiver for a false statement . . ."

harvest of Minnesota's wealth into American pockets. A rich toll of mink, fox, and beaver from the virgin forests of Minnesota flowed east each year to be traded into the hard cash of early American fortunes and especially into that of John Jacob Astor. But scarcely had the principal wealth of the fur trade been harvested than the first lumbermen from New York and Canada—but especially from Maine—displaced the hunter's rifle with the axe.

"We took a backwoods country," boast the timber kings, "dotted with a few squatters, Indians, and trappers. We cleared the land and it became the greatest granary in the world. We connected it with railroads, planted cities, and built a government. In less than fifty years our efforts transformed the wild timber lands of the Northwest into a modern economic state. Does human history offer any parallel in the building of an empire?"

The above is a composite of at least a score of official biographies of the "empire builders." And it cannot be said that the boast is an idle one.

It was not, however, until the great tide of immigration swept into the Middle West from Europe and the eastern states that the lumber interests rose to imperial heights. The entire Middle, North, and Far West began demanding houses, barns, stores, furniture, fences, wagons, and all the equipment of a civilization based on wood. The timber kings and their allies met the challenge.

The ease of acquisition of the timber lands by the lumber companies increased the swiftness of development and whetted the lumbermen's appetite for astronomical profits. Land grants to the railroads in Minnesota alone equaled in acreage two states the size of Massachusetts. However, when unable to obtain the land as a gift, the empire builders stole or bought it from the Indians for a trifle of its worth. Ninety per cent of the Chippewa's White Earth Reservation was "bought" by land and lumber companies after the Indians had been thoroughly "persuaded" by bad whiskey, and was paid for in large measure by due bills or tin money (redeemable at stores and saloons). When these sources disappeared, the timber kings turned to bribing the government land agents, or that failing, cut the timber anyway. Estes, timber agent for Iowa, Minnesota, and part of Wisconsin, reported in 1854 that in the Black River district 200,000,000 feet of pine had been cut from the public lands. On the Black River, sixteen lumber mills operated for a dozen years *entirely* on logs taken from public lands. The population of the empire was calling for houses, barns, and furniture, public sentiment favored "clearing the West," the profits of a manifest destiny were great. And the empire builders did not hesitate to fulfill that destiny.

First settlers in Minnesota brought with them, with surprisingly little adulteration, the culture and piety of New England. "The first legislature passed a law placing a Sunday ban on work and such diversions 'to the disturbance of the community as hunting, shooting and sport,' with a fine of three dollars for violation of the law. . . . Later, Minnesotans were forbidden by law to be present 'at any dancing' or at public shows on Sunday." These earlier moralities languished and died—as they did in New England—as the country grew in prosperity, in the addition of new blood mixtures, and in sophistication. But the dominance of New England names among the empire builders as well as of New England mental processes, remains. The empire builders today send their sons not to the University of Minnesota but to Harvard and Yale. Significantly, the greatest of the empire builders and the recipients of the empire's most substantial gifts were not—with a few exceptions—in the first wave of immigrant pioneers. They were in the second: lawyers, business men, and traders who came out in the seventies and eighties a few decades before the Golden Age.

In the *bona fide* pioneer days of the forties and fifties, men turned their hands to everything and anything in communities where professional grooves had not yet hardened. There was everywhere "the genial St. Anthony jack-of-all-trades who combined dentistry with his work as a jeweler and as a repairer of guns, locks, and umbrellas. The photographer would take your picture or pull your teeth as you preferred."

The same versatility applied as well to the upper ranks of the empire builders. Farm boys or young professional men arriving from the East in their twenties frequently found at sixty that they had made three or four fortunes instead of one. Starting, say with lumber, it was normal after the removal of the forests to turn sawmills and water power to the grinding of wheat, which became increasingly profitable in the eighties. A seat on the grain exchange followed and possibly a railroad dictatorship or two, if railroad building had not flowed earlier from an ownership of timber lands. In the nineties, another fortune—by way of competence for old age—might turn up in the Mesabi Range where to the surprise of geologists iron ore had been discovered. With this "start," the empire builder frequently spent his declining years as a bank president or United States Senator.

No wonder that the empire builders felt God was with them and the multiplication of mills, railroads, and fortunes identifiable with the eternal will.

The most confident, indefatigable, realistic, and ruthless of them all was Jim Hill. He also became the richest and most powerful. At forty, "Jim Hill was a short, thick-set man . . . with a massive head, large wrinkled features, long black hair and a blind eye. His unique exterior—like a 'grim old lion'— reinforced by a naturally stern manner gave him a formidable reputation in his territory. He was known always to be 'a very hard man in business,' among railroad men 'the hardest man to work for.' He carried everything in his head, worried, systematized, labored himself or drove on the others around him with unflagging energy. He had no small scruples; rough-hewn throughout; 'intolerant of opposition, despotic, largely ruling by fear'; his contemporaries said, 'he was also given to personal violence in the department offices of the road.'"

His railroads had the most powerful locomotives, the longest trains. His own headquarters in St. Paul were "solid and bare as a prison," his house "grimly strong as a feudal fortress," burglarproof and cycloneproof through the use of huge beams of steel. From that headquarters he governed the single most strategic factor in the economy of the growing empire—the railroads.

Jim Hill was born in Guelph, Canada, of Scotch-Irish parentage. He lived in a log house built by his father, who tilled the soil for a living, and he was the third of four children.

Coming to St. Paul he started in as a warehouse and commission man, and married Mary Theresa Mehegan, whom he met as a waitress. Before their marriage he sent her "to be educated" in a convent school in Milwaukee. She bore him ten children and made him a lifelong friend of the Catholic Church.

Jim Hill had imaginative foresight which resembled genius. More than any of his contemporaries, he plotted the empire in advance, envisioning flourishing cities and a million homesteads while the Northwest was still forest and prairie.

For a generation American railroad magnates had been milking railroads dry, and leaving them bankrupt. Jim Hill despised the practice, not because the stockholders and public were robbed, but because it was stupid—and in the long run, unprofitable.

Vigorously, he set out to populate the Northwest, along the routes of the Hill syndicate. In search of an enduring freight load his agents scoured Europe for immigrants and brought them back to the Northwest where they could ship their wheat over "Jim Hill's main line."

Hill, as his biographers record, "had no small scruples." To acquire his first railroad, it was alleged he conspired with the receiver for a false statement of its operating profits in order to drive down the purchase price. He ruined competing roads by discriminatory rates, and on one occasion hauled freight for nothing to drive the enemy into bankruptcy. His practices were no different from those of other contemporary captains of industry, except that they were more intelligent, ruthless, and successful.

To prevent government regulation, he bought and corrupted legislators, and controlled the press of the Northwest with the thoroughness characteristic of him. As a corollary to his system of railroads—through whose arteries flowed the economic life blood of the empire—he set up a political dictatorship. As the farmers remarked, it was impossible to get so much as a dog catcher's job without first obtaining an O.K. from the "throne room" in St. Paul.

Jim Hill's genius was that he overlooked nothing. He knew the Northwest needed coal. By the flood tide of empire, it was found that Hill, when he had been a commission agent, had quietly bought up most of the deposits in Montana. By the time the United States Steel Corporation came to operate the iron mines in the Mesabi, they found Jim Hill owned vast tracts of it. His syndicate reaped new revenues by leasing these tracts.

James J. Hill's life dream was to tie the markets of the

Orient to the American manufacturer, and the wheat fields of the Northwest to the Orient, via the Twin Cities and the Hill railroads. He sent agents into India, Japan, and China. Japanese business men were persuaded to mix American cotton with the short staple from India, which they had been using. And he lowered his rates so that Minneapolis flour could be sold profitably in Hong Kong.

Jim Hill worried ceaselessly about problems of locomotive construction; of railroad beds; of tillage and farm fertilizers; of markets, prices, and financial control; and he solved most of them in his own way. He worried about his competitors and smashed them or bought them out. He worried about political opposition, and broke it by persuasion or force. He also became increasingly worried over the rank and file of the empire which his agents had induced to come to America. Their strikes, their politics, and their morals worried him; he gave $50,000 for the endowment of a Roman Catholic Cathedral in St. Paul in order to strengthen "the only authority they fear or respect." "Look at the millions of foreigners," he said, "pouring into this country. What will be their social view, their political action, their moral status, if that single controlling force should be removed?" This is as much a matter of good business, he declared, as is the improvement of farm stock or the construction of a faultless railroad bed.

In thirty years, Hill and his partners took $407,000,000 *exclusive of dividends and other emoluments* out of the Great Northern. The total profits of the Hill syndicate up to 1910 were said to be $1,526,016,621.

More basic to the empire, however, than the wealth of the timber lands (which built the scaffolding of the empire out of wood, and financed most of it), and more basic than Jim Hill's railroads, were the vast agricultural prairies of the Northwest. At the heart of the area and serving as its market capital stood Minneapolis.

The meaning of this economic empire, in terms of our American city, was an influx of wealth and population and the setting up of an economy geared on an imperial scale. As the industrial corner stones of this prosperity were removed or corroded in later years, a load of economic and social problems fell on the shoulders of her citizens. This fact is all important to an understanding of the modern city. In addition, the psychology of an expanding economy remained with many of her economic rulers in an era of decline.

Charles Beadle, an Englishman who visited Minneapolis in 1887, wrote in his diary: "We went to one large flour mill, Pillsbury's . . . the whole concern works like a piece of clockwork and turns out some 7,000 barrels of flour in twenty-four hours. They have other mills making their output altogether 10,500 barrels daily, or sufficient to feed two cities the size of New York. They have two immense elevators in Minneapolis for storing wheat and have small ones at almost all the railroad stations in the surrounding wheat districts, all in communication with the chief office by wire. . . . The water power used in these mills as well as the mills belong to the Pillsburys, on whom I called, and found to be nice people."

Not only did the millers of Minneapolis own grain elevators "at almost all the railroad stations" throughout the Northwest "in communication with the chief office by wire," but through the Minneapolis Chamber of Commerce—the official grain exchange—they established a "buying monopoly," passed on the grading of wheat, and speculated in its sale. The small farmer and the farmers' co-operatives, however, were infallibly barred from membership and the millers even denied the jurisdiction of the courts over the rules and acts of the Chamber. The efficiency of this control in the interests of the millers' profits roused deep resentment among tne farmers, and together with freight-rate discriminations lay at the core of the farm revolts of the nineteenth century.

Throughout the Golden Age the wheat fields of Minnesota built the empire; but more significantly, they were strategic in a transformation of the whole economy of American industrialism. The sale of wheat to foreign countries was essential to this transformation, for wheat sold abroad paid for the import of machinery, which ultimately emancipated the whole country from economic dependence on Europe. Equally crucial if American industrialism was to succeed was an unlimited supply of food for the new manufacturing centers of the East. The Northwest set herself the task of supplying this basic food-fuel not only for her own expanding empire but for the country as a whole.

Decisively, the part played by the Northwest and its Twin City economic capital in nineteenth-century American Capitalism was not accessory—as it has since become—but strategic. The positive contributions of the Golden Age are a part of American life today and of the life of our American city. Inevitably they were achieved through methods of economic autocracy which roused resentment among the rank and file of the empire. And as a characteristic corollary of the system on which they were based they involved a huge waste of resources, human and material, that has taken revenge on the economy of the modern city. Both inheritances of the Golden Age are essential to an understanding of the class conflicts of a later day.

As if to round out her vital contributions of lumber, wheat, flour, and transportation, iron ore was discovered in Northern Minnesota in 1890. The reddish dirt of the Mesabi tested sixty-five per cent pure iron, the purest deposit in the world. "But for the acquirement of the Mesabi mines the colossal

United States Steel Corporation could not have been organized," writes Frick's biographer. The iron ore of the Mesabi, second only to wheat, was strategic to the forward march of American industrialism.

So far as I know no gold has ever been discovered within the confines of the empire. And the crown of the Golden Age was to be made of iron, not gold. However, Lewis Merritt, father of the discoverers, had told his sons that "the iron ore up under the Mesabi will be worth all the gold in California." And it was.

It would be a mistake to believe that only the governors of the four main satrapies of the empire—lumber, wheat, railroads, and iron—contributed to erecting a modern economic state in the Northwest or were its only beneficiaries. Their colleagues and lieutenants who manufactured boots and shoes for the multiplying millions of the Northwest, or who made furniture, or who supplied life insurance, reaped the rewards and swore undying fealty to the economic laws of imperial expansion. The whole process illustrated, even for the blind, the progressive role—as well as the wasteful chaos—of American Capitalism in the nineteenth century.

Even more important than the Golden Age to this history is the fact and the story of the empire's decline. The beginnings of retreat were manifest as early as 1910 but became undeniable even for optimists after the World War.

In certain spheres—not all—the decline of the empire was as meteoric as its rise. The lumber industry dwindled rapidly after 1910. And what amounted to a surgical removal of this one large industry—a major source of dividends, wages, and tax revenue—dumped a whole sheaf of social problems on the modern Minnesotan. The extinction of lumber meant a sucking of the economic life blood of the countryside; villages dependent on lumbering and on sawmills shrank or disappeared. And today, most of Minnesota's sixteen "cut-over counties" are bankrupt. The people have moved away if they could—or have remained to rot.

The first crack in the imperial plans of Jim Hill, to include not only the whole Northwest but the Orient as well in an empire based on freight, came with the opening of the Panama Canal and the establishment of the Interstate Commerce Commission. It proved cheaper to ship a load of freight from Seattle via the Canal to New York and thence by rail west than to send the same load by rail from Seattle to Ohio! Later freight-rate changes have further contracted the empire from its imperial scope to Minnesota itself, the Dakotas, and part of Wisconsin.

The opening of the Panama Canal, four thousand miles away, seemed like a fortuitous slap of fate against the railroad dictator. But after a half century other processes, more molecular and less dramatic, were to corrode the economy of the Northwest and with it the destiny of its Twin City capital. The great flour mills began a migration from Minneapolis to Buffalo and the South, though significantly, financial control lingered in Minneapolis.

Most basic to this history and most tragic of all for the city of Minneapolis has been the decline of agriculture. A generation before President Roosevelt called upon the farmer to slaughter his hogs and plough under his cotton, there were signs of "over production" in the Northwest. The War boom reversed for a time this disturbing trend, but during post-War "prosperity" the interrupted laws of political economy more than revenged themselves. Farm machinery and improved methods which had stepped up production during the War only added to the farmers' problems in a waning market when the War was over. Deflation of land values followed; and, more devastating, the slogan of "national self-sufficiency" swept over Europe and the export market for American farm products collapsed.

If the economic health of all America rests on the farm, the prosperity of our empire and of its market capital Minneapolis is far more directly based upon it. Mutual exchange of farm products for manufactures is the life blood of our American city, and the decline of agriculture—both regional and world-wide—becomes for her a problem of economic life and death.

Can agriculture revive, and enjoy a reasonably stable prosperity under Capitalism? No one in the empire has yet given a satisfactory answer. And yet this is the question that connects the local economic crisis of our American city with a far wider one—the ill health of Capitalism itself, not only in the empire but throughout the world.

A munificent nature, which endowed the Northwest with vast forests, wide prairies, and iron mountains, also in a measurable degree isolated her in the Northland and located her economic capital at magnificent but commercially unfavorable distances from the denser centers of the nation's population. In the post-War era just before the period in which the main body of our narrative begins, national manufacturing companies, chain-store syndicates and mail-order houses struck a blow—very difficult to parry—at the solid fabric of middle-sized businesses which supported the upper structure and had flourished not only in the Golden Age but long after. The "little business men" in the Twin Cities, small but "rugged individuals," found themselves in a life and death struggle not with the empire builders but with national monopoly.

The state of Minnesota and the city of Minneapolis are still central to the economy of a narrowed agrarian and industrial area. But the factors of decline from the Golden Age color her thinking today and perplex her citizens. And they furnish the economic setting for the city's explosive modern history, which is the theme of this book.

If the workers and farmers, the lumberjacks, shovel stiffs and factory operatives—rank-and-file builders of the empire— failed for the most part to share in the imperial spoil or to influence the confident policies of their masters in the period of the empire's expansion, they began to challenge both in the period of its decline.

CHAPTER III

FATE OF THE RANK-AND-FILE EMPIRE BUILDERS

THE swiftness of exploitation of the Northwest required not only captains and generals but an imperial army of buck privates and corporals. The first rank-and-file empire builders who extracted a fortune from the empire with their hands and lives were the Indians. They trapped the mink, beaver, otter, fox, and other living and primitive wealth and traded it for money, rifles, gewgaws, whiskey, and due bills. In the early days of the American republic fur was a major industry, and long before the empire builders arrived to take possession of their domain it had laid the foundation of the Astor fortune.

Astor's chief weapon in obtaining vast quantities of valuable furs from the Indians was the illegal sale or gift of whiskey, which debauched and ruined whole tribes. Indian Agent Sibley prophesied bloody revolts as a direct result of the methods of Astor's company.

But if the American Fur Company cheated and debauched the native tribes as an incident to a fortune in furs, the government swindled them on a far more grandiose scale. That portion of the Indians' land which the government paid for under the so-called treaties was purchased for two cents an acre. Much of the remnant in reservations which the United States thereupon guaranteed to the Indian and "his heirs forever," was maneuvered away by the land agents and lumber companies.

The Indians, like the rank and file of the white men who

followed them, did not view these conquests of the empire builders with indifference. But as savages they displayed even less appreciation than the white rank and file of the civilizing role of Capitalism. And their protest was more primitive. These earliest of "rank-and-file revolts" culminated in the Sioux Massacre of 1862. The Sioux had sold 800,000 acres of their land to the government, in return for a portion of which they received an annuity. The remainder was absorbed in claims against the tribe. Early in June they assembled as was the custom for payment. Two months passed and the annuity did not arrive. The tribe waited, angry and starving. "The Indians," records the historian, "with a fine disregard of red tape could not understand why they should go hungry when the flour, pork, lard and sugar which belonged to them was locked up in a warehouse." Finally Little Crow, Chief of the Lower Sioux, spoke: "We have waited a long time, the money is ours but we cannot get it. We have no food, but here are stores filled with food. We ask that you, the agent, make some arrangement by which we can get food from the stores or else we may take our own way to keep ourselves from starving. When men are hungry, they help themselves."

Myrick, the chief trader of the settlement, when Little Crow's words were translated, said: "So far as I am concerned, if they are hungry, let them eat grass." The interpreter refused to translate. A missionary put Myrick's words into Sioux. For a moment there was silence—followed by wild yelling, whoops, and gestures. The Indians disappeared from the trading post. Three days later the last and bloodiest of the Indian wars began in the Northwest. The first white man killed was Myrick, the chief trader. His body was found with his mouth stuffed with grass.

A thousand million dollars in timber has been extracted from Minnesota alone by the lumber companies. Thirty-seven per cent or thirty-eight million acres of the original territory of Minnesota was forest land.

Of all the major conquests of the empire builders, lumbering is perhaps the most directly dependent on the rank and file. In early days the capital investment was little more than an axe and food-fuel for the manpower of the lumberjack. But even later with mechanized lumbering the "labor factor" continued paramount. At all stages in the industry the "manpower investment" had to buy not only elbow grease, but skill, hardihood, and daring. In man's age-long battle with nature, it is difficult to find a more dramatic or heroic chapter than that of the lumberjack who consistently risked his life for thirty dollars a month, cleared the forests of an empire, and stored its wealth in the bank accounts of the timber barons.

The jack's personal exploits compete favorably with those Paul Bunyan legends in which they are fabulously enshrined. Skill of eye and hand made the giant pines of Northern Minnesota fall with a slide-rule precision, and rivermen in the drive combined something of the nimbleness of acrobats with the skill of woodsmen. The drive was the most exciting— as well as dangerous—job in lumbering, and it was the riverman's job to loosen log jams and then save himself by running back over the rolling logs. Like the other jacks he worked from dawn to dark at this job, took frequent duckings in icy water, drank whiskey when he could, and took extra chances just for the hell of it. Each drive cost a few deaths but neither the company nor the jacks held life over dear.

Jack was up in the morning at four with the "bull cook" blowing the camp horn and yelling: "Roll out, daylight in the swamp!" or: "Roll out, tumble out, any way to get out. This is the day to make your fortune!" He worked from sunup to sundown at a kind of labor which in weather of forty below drenched his body with sweat while the frost nipped the end of his nose. The noon meal was out of doors and the beans froze to the tin plate, as well as to his whiskers.

Jack's home was a long low communal shack built of logs, with bunks in tiers and few if any windows. It was like an army barracks—except that its design defied those laws of hygiene respected by the army. Again like and unlike the army, a sort of atomic military dictatorship prevailed in each camp. Rules were strict, and the foreman had disciplinary powers which in some camps, according to lumberjacks, included in practice the power of life and death—without appeal. As soon as the railroad had reasonably opened up a means of transportation into the forests, food in the camps was excellent. The jacks refused to work without it.

All winter in camp the men led a bachelor life, seeing no woman's face from fall until spring, unless there were Indian tribes near whose women could be induced to attend Saturday night "squaw dances." When there were none, the "girls" wore handkerchiefs on their arms to identify them. Evenings the men played cribbage or endlessly told over the Paul Bunyan saga, how, for example, "he logged off the Dakotas by hauling a section of land at a time to the landing, with the help of Babe, the Big Blue Ox." Babe was a very large ox—"twenty-seven axe handles and a plug of tobacco between the horns." No old-timer ever cracked a smile in the telling or the listening.

The rank-and-file empire builders, however, developed not only a lumberjack saga but a language of their own in the woods. A certain top loader had his leg crushed in the drive and explained it later to his nurse at a Catholic hospital: "Well, Sister, it happened this way. I dropped in at one of the Sawyer Goodman Company's camps and . . . as . . . the *push* needed men he put me to work *skyhooking*. The first thing the *ground hog* did was to send me up a *blue*. I hollered at him to throw

BUNKHOUSE IN THE NINETIES

"Lumbering is . . . directly dependent on the rank and file . . ."

"The wheat fields of Minnesota built the Empire"

© *International News Photos*

a *Saginaw* into her but he *St. Croixed* her instead. Then he *gunned* her and the result was I got my *stem* cracked."

Wages in the camps ran from $15 to $30 a month in good times, and from $6 to $12 in bad. On the drive, jacks got $2 a day. They worked Thanksgiving and New Years, but Christmas was a holiday. Efforts to turn this into a working day met with mutiny.

The whole tenor and character of life in the lumber camps was beautifully calculated to lead to a wild blowup when Jack got to town after the drive. He frequently dropped his winter's wages in a week of "likker and wimmen." Moralists of the day wrung their hands over Jack's immoral ways, and as a sober historian of Minnesota sums it up: "Instead of putting their money in the bank or *investing it in good securities* [italics mine], they spent most of it on liquor."

Life in the railroad camps in the great era of railway construction was not far different in point of hygiene, hardship, discipline, bachelorhood, and wages. Often when the drive was over, and his money gone or "socked away"—as sometimes happened—Jack took up railroading until the next season or waited till the harvest for a job on a bonanza wheat farm. Most of the buck privates of the imperial army had taken a crack at all three professions and some cultivated them in rotation as "migratory workers." When iron was discovered in the Vermillion and Mesabi Ranges, mining added a fourth profession for the rank and file. Life for the miner did not differ much in cultural meagerness from that of the lumberjack and shovel stiff. (No one had combed either the old world or the new for the "appointments" or refinements of civilization to "grace" his home.) In Hibbing, the mining metropolis of the Mesabi, throughout the Golden Age the streets were unpaved and unlighted, each building in the business district had its saloon, and the sex problem was solved by prostitution. The overwhelming majority of males in the city's population indicated the rarity of married life.

Our American city became the mecca of the lumberjack, shovel stiff, and harvest hand during the hiring season, when they swarmed about its employment agencies and into the city's flop houses. As late as 1915, a resident recalls seeing several thousand men sitting along the curb in Bridge Square —near the employment offices—"so close together you couldn't put a newspaper between their elbows!"

The employment of these shock troops of the empire was seasonal; this and other factors added to the chronic uncertainty of life. To the higher ranks of the empire builders, the cyclical panics which visited the United States in the nineteenth century and the twentieth seemed minor slips in an ever ascending economy. They "recovered" from each depression with a larger measure of prosperity than before. For the buck privates in the imperial army, however, and the middle-ranks, depressions meant a clean sweep in a life's savings and often acute starvation. When timber disappeared and the lumber barons were seeking new fields for conquest, the lumberjack found it hard to find another job for himself, or— after ten or fifteen years as a "migratory"—to adjust himself to one if he got it. The displaced migratory worker added to the increasing army of the empire's unemployed.

Innumerable official biographies, personal memoirs, and public-school histories have made familiar to Americans the lives of the chief empire builders. Little or nothing has been written or preserved of the lives of individual rank-and-filers. The Paul Bunyan saga is a collective folk tale of an epoch, but there is little else. I shall tell briefly the story of one typical buck private in the imperial army as related by himself. He was a Swede named Karl who came direct from the old country to Minnesota toward the end of the Golden Age. He is alive today at the age of fifty, an active member of the truck drivers' union in Minneapolis. Karl came from one of the most backward parts of his native country. His father was a serf. A husky young immigrant in his twenties when he arrived, Karl started his American life in the railroad camps of northern Minnesota, helping to lay ties for the Northern Pacific. The railroad let out the work to a contractor who made his own wage scale, and the less he paid the more he made for himself. The worker was paid only once—when he quit. Meantime he ran up a credit at the company store. This usually reduced the total to a scale of $15 or $20 a month— in check form, again redeemable in goods at company stores, or cashable for a fee at a company railroad office. To Karl the two things which stand out in his memory about Minnesota railroad camps are not the bad living conditions which most immigrants recount with bitterness, but the arbitrary powers of the camp boss and his own immigrant's inability to "answer back" in English.

"The foreman in the camps had autocratic powers. [This was as late as 1912.] Anything he told us to do, we had to do it. If he shot anybody, that was all right. I couldn't talk English to him, but, of course, when you couldn't stand it any longer you could fight—that can be understood in any language. Or you could quit. There was always work down the line—in those days. You'd pack up your little stuff in a bundle and walk, thirty miles or so to the next camp."

From railroading, Karl got into lumber, first through building railroads for the lumber companies, and later in the woods as a lumberjack. That was in 1914, after steam skidders had displaced horses. A steel cable was run back into the woods, maybe to a thousand yards from the steam engine, and attached to the logs by cable men. Karl was a cable man, then a hook man, riding the logs and keeping them in place as they were "steam skidded" out of the woods. Finally life as a lumberjack ended for him when a pine tree fell and crushed his foot. He bled steadily for three hours before they could get him back to camp. Three days later at the nearest hospital he was operated on without an anesthetic. His constitution pulled him through but he lay in bed nine months. The company paid him $170.

Recovered and having learned English, he got an inside job as checker for the Pullman Company in Minneapolis, then worked himself into the mechanical department, qualifying in 1919 as a first-class mechanic.

This was a good job and he kept it until the great railroad strike in 1922. He had been a member of the shopmen's union and when the strike was smashed they set up a company union. Karl wouldn't join it. But he had been getting $225 a month. He didn't drink, he had no family, he had saved his money. A thousand dollars out of his savings he gave to the shopmen's strike, the rest he lived on until he got another job.

In a year or two he drifted into the coal yards as a truck driver, and for nine years, up to the time of the Minneapolis truck drivers' strike in 1934, he worked as a "coal heaver" for the same boss. His career from 1934 we shall recount in a later chapter. Karl's life has been luckier on the whole than that of many of his fellow workers. At least he thinks so.

Far earlier than Karl's day there were strikes on the railroads, in the lumber camps, in the iron mines, and in the mills. The majority, like the shopmen's strikes of 1922, were smashed, but some won concessions from the empire builders. In the generation before the war the Industrial Workers of the World successfully organized thousands of lumber camps throughout the empire, as well as harvest hands and miners. Wage concessions and a clean-up of some of the worst camps were achieved, but the frank class philosophy and militant methods of the Wobblies frightened and enraged the lumber interests, as well as respectable "leading citizens" in our American city. Under cover of the War hysteria, the empire builders struck a blow at the Wobblies from which they never recovered.

In the Twin City capital of the empire, but especially in Minneapolis, the city workers both native- and foreign-born, with a strong sense of their "democratic rights," established unions and for a time won concessions from factory owners. More politically minded than in most sections of the country, they combined political with economic struggles, and in 1916, as we shall see, elected Van Lear, president of the machinists' union, mayor of Minneapolis. Both the political as well as the economic revolts of the rank and file were later to be crushed temporarily by the "patriotic" persecutions of Wartime. Typical, however, of the rank and file's factory strikes against the owners of the empire in the latter part of the Golden Age were those of the flour mill workers of Minneapolis.

The issue of the eight-hour day to replace the twelve-hour one with no reduction in pay swept the mills in 1902 and 1903, culminating in a general strike of the three largest flour companies in Minneapolis. The unions proposed to arbitrate, with the mayor at the head of a committee, but the mills refused to listen either to strikers or mayor. The Washburn-Crosby Company built a stockade around its property, established a kitchen and sleeping quarters for scabs, and brought in "as many practical millers as they could obtain, augmenting these with University students and High School boys." The strike was broken and the union decimated. The men went back to work at the terms of the mill owners who had previously conceded the eight-hour day for part of their employees, but insisted on a pay reduction. The official historian of Washburn-Crosby comments on the victory as follows: "The mill owners were put to much trouble, anxiety and great expense by reason of the strike, but the results they gained were well worth the cost."

A few years later, after the World War, a union in the Minneapolis flour mills still existed—but at one of the meetings it was discovered that all its members were agents of the employers or of one or another labor detective agency. This Utopian condition freed the employers from anxiety if not from expense for many years.

So "well worth the cost" did the elimination of all trade unions and other organizations of collective action by the rank and file seem to the empire builders and their descendants that a few years after this episode, as a result of a machinists' strike, the employers of Minneapolis set up a special engine for breaking strikes and eliminating unions from the city's economic life. It organized one of the most complete under-cover spy systems in the United States and fought every major strike in Minneapolis for thirty years. As a result, Minneapolis acquired a national reputation among employers as an "open-shop town," and with labor as "one of the worst scab cities in the country."

The story of the discovery of iron ore in the Mesabi which gave an iron crown—"worth all the gold in California"—to the empire's Golden Age is part of the history and biographical record of rank-and-filers and buck privates of the empire, not of the emperors. The turning up of ore in the Mesabi was the result of a conscious and systematic effort, requiring large drafts of knowledge, sacrifice, and resource and which extended over a period of three generations. The story has all the drama, thrill, and "moral" of a Fenimore Cooper novel or of the school texts of frontier adventure and virtue which Americans are taught particularly to associate with the West. But none of the leading empire builders or their agents participated in it. The search was initiated and the discovery made by a family of "bushwacking" lumberjacks, sailors, and woods cruisers, named Merritt, who for thirty-five years had one obsession—the pursuit of iron ore in the Mesabi. Geologists and experts who had been all over the range thought the Merritts were cracked—on this one point only. In all else they were admired as intensely practical woodsmen, lumber-jacks, and explorers with exploits almost the equal of a Bunyan legend.

Lewis Merritt had left Ohio in the sixties and come to work at his trade of millwright and sawmill man in that "God-for-gotten corner of the Northwest, Duluth," by the shores of Kitchi Gammi—the "big sea water" of Lake Superior. It was Lewis who first came to believe that there was iron in the Mesabi, and who initiated his sons in the search for it. His fourth son Leonidas, called Lon, became the leader of all the Merritt brothers—there were seven of them—in their annual scourings of the Mesabi hills for iron.

Several of the brothers took up timber claims for themselves, and at times made quite a lot of money, especially Lon and Alf. It is easy to imagine they might have become Saginaw lumber barons, and respectable citizens of Duluth. But instead, driven by the indefatigable Lon, they salted back every cent into exploratory expeditions to the Mesabi, and came back to begin again the next year, "skin poor." The rocks they toted back in their packs year after year brought from the assayer the report: "lean magnetic iron ore; not merchantable."

On November 16, 1890, this suddenly changed forever. Against his will, Lon had persuaded an expert German miner to dig into some soft red dirt on the south side of the Mesabi where his father had always said the iron lay. *The ore was there all right,* but "no proper mine," no veins of ore in a rock—only enormous quantities of fine purple earth. A Cornish miner whom Lon brought to look at it said emphatically, "This ca-an't be a mine!" Anyhow, if it *was* one, how could one sink a shaft into the soft ground to get the iron out? It was the Merritts who evolved the theory that the ore lay in vast shallow "basins" and that the best way to mine it was with steam shovels! No shafts, no timbering, no expensive air compressors. Shovel it out as fast as you can—the furnaces of Pittsburgh are waiting!

The Merritts bought up the ore basins wherever they could with their savings. And Leonidas lobbied a law through the Minnesota legislature framed on the principle of allowing the land to be taken up by rank-and-filers with a little money and not "all bought up . . . by some rich syndicate." This was, of course, a thoroughly romantic rank-and-file idea, which only served in the end to enable the "syndicate" to buy more of the Mesabi at a lower price. But it indicated what was to become increasingly apparent with the passage of years, that the Merritts, for all their faith in the empire, their courage and resourcefulness, lacked the indispensable tactics of acquisition which distinguished the true empire builder.

That they did not lack business enterprise or skill in organization is attested by the fact that they organized and built in the face of the difficulties of a frontier economy and no capital the first railroad from the ore beds to Duluth. But as financiers and imperialists the Merritts were flops. Among those who took advantage of the law for a democratic ownership of the Mesabi was Henry Oliver, manufacturer of plowshares. When the Oliver Mining Company became a subsidiary of United States Steel a few years later, Oliver's shares were sold for seventeen million dollars.

The Reverend Mr. Fred T. Gates, former pastor of the

Central Baptist Church of Minneapolis, who had been called to "higher spheres of usefulness" as the administrator in New York of Mr. Rockefeller's charities, found a way in 1893 to introduce Leonidas Merritt to John D. Rockefeller.

The history of the Mesabi in the next half dozen years resolves itself into a devious story of financial transactions between the Merritts, their claims and their enterprises on the Mesabi, and Mr. Rockefeller. The upshot was that Mr. Rockefeller sold his share of the iron ore in the Mesabi which he had obtained from the woods cruisers to the United States Steel Corporation for sixty-eight million dollars—and as he concluded in later years—was cheated at that. Lon Merritt returned from New York, not only broke, but in debt, to begin over again the search for iron deposits in the Mesabi.

Did Mr. Rockefeller steal the claims to iron ore in the Mesabi from the Merritts who discovered it there? In 1893 the Merritts owned millions of dollars worth of stock of the Lake Superior Consolidated Iron Mines Company. Mr. Rockefeller, as the Reverend Mr. Gates explained to Lon, was a very conservative financier and could not be expected to take anything but bonds in the company he was forming with the Merritts. With the panic of 1893 and money tight, deuce take it, it was hard for the Merritt boys with all their millions to get enough hard cash for groceries. Little by little they put up most of their stock with Mr. Rockefeller to obtain loans and keep work going in the mines. Leonidas Merritt was a poor business man, that is undeniable; Mr. Rockefeller was a good one. Leonidas did not even know whether the loans were time or demand notes! He had left all such matters to the friendly Mr. Gates.

Lon was a good woodsman but he knew absolutely nothing about finance. He had written a *poem* to help raise money for his railroad to the Mesabi!

"Put some cash in the Mis-sa-be,
Lend a helping hand to others,
Others who are working for you.
Let us bind with bands of iron
The Mis-sa-be to the Zenith . . ."

And his testimony eleven years later at the Congressional
hearing proved his ignorance and confusion in financial questions. "I could not conceive," he said, "that I could have gone
down [to New York] with millions, absolute millions of my
own and my brothers' money—I could not conceive how in
hell, within those few months, without ever spending a cent
above my board bill, I could have gone to New York and lost
all those millions. . . . I had no money even to go home."

There is little question that—under Capitalism—the Mesabi
has been far more efficiently operated by the United States
Steel Corporation, the final beneficiary of the Merritt discovery, than it ever could have been by the Merritts. They
possessed extraordinary courage and persistence, skill, culture,
and the qualities of personal leadership, but they lacked both
the instinct and the tactics for large-scale acquisition. These
essential qualities of the empire builders Mr. Rockefeller brilliantly displayed.

Nor have the descendants of the Merritts these invaluable
attributes. One of Alf's sons became a daredevil aviator; another fought in France, won the Croix de Guerre and a
Congressional citation—and returned a private. Two of Lon's
sons dredged the Mississippi and worked in the harbors of the
east coast, and Lon has a grandson who is a geologist hunting
minerals in Africa. A pair of sons of another brother are
farmers in Montana. John E.—one of the third generation who
participated actively in the hunt for iron—is known today not

as an empire builder but as the founder of a co-operative creamery in Aitkin, Minnesota.

No, there was more enlightened—or unenlightened—self-interest in Jim Hill's little finger than in the whole Merritt tribe. Their qualities, wherever they turn up, are invariably technical skill, doggedness, courage and a certain fatal social instinct of fair play—that is all. Although their discovery crowned the Golden Age, they have no place in history and would want none beside Jim Hill or the empire's chief beneficiaries. They belong in spirit and in fact with the men who laid the ties for Hill's railroads, cut the timber for Weyerhauser, ground the grain for the Washburns—the anonymous legion of the rank-and-file empire builders.

The farmers of the Northwest were also rank-and-file builders of the empire; in fact they were not only its most numerous, but economically its most basic division. Their "stake" in the country was visible and taxable. As primary producers they were admonished and admired by economists and as units of the great farm vote they were courted by politicians. In distinction from the other divisions of rank-and-filers, they were "little capitalists," and worked not for wages but a profit.

It might be supposed that the empire builders would have been persuaded or compelled to grant a special status to this division of the rank and file and possibly to accord them a greater share in the fruits of the empire. But the millers and railroad owners found they could control the farmer and his share of the imperial income as effectively as that of their other subjects.

The railroads dictated the freight rates by which the farmers' grain was taken to market. And in Minneapolis, the millers took charge of it, elaborately determining the price and grade. In the free-for-all days of nonregulated railroads, the farmer became the primary victim of extortionate and discriminatory rates.

There is a saying attributed to the farmers of the Northwest in the palmy days of the railroad empire: "First we had the grasshoppers—then Jim Hill." And in 1890, in a letter to J. P. Morgan, Jim Hill wrote, "There is an epidemic craze [here] among farmers and . . . those who receive wages and salaries." It was a reference to the Populist movement which broke out during the Golden Age. But he refused to permit the "craze" to affect his policies. The railroads' control of the state legislatures and of Congress as well continued to offer the farmer a bitter lesson in "practical politics."

As to the miller, the farmer isolated the "main enemy" with some precision in the Minneapolis Chamber of Commerce. The farmer charged, and subsequently proved through legislative inquiry, that the elevators which the Chamber controlled were guilty of false gradings, of the dockage-and-screenings racket, and of false weights. When a weights-and-measures law was finally passed, sixty per cent of the elevator scales in the region were found to be false or defective.

The farmer turned for redress of his grievances not only to the ballot but to the co-operative movement, which he fought for against all odds. The odds included fraudulent law suits, refusal by the railroads to ship grain to co-operatives, and even open violence. When the Equity Co-operative Exchange was organized, enraged Chamber of Commerce representatives broke up an Equity meeting by force. In spite of all opposition the movement has grown lustily and provided the farmer with a powerful economic weapon against his enemies.

None of the farmers' efforts, however, were sufficient to "solve" his problems, and most of the "dirt farmers," who worked the farms with their own hands and those of their sons and who literally plowed back what profits the millers permitted them, found themselves bankrupt at the end of the "wheat era."

In the days before Capitalism, empire builders customarily achieved power by a literal conquest at the point of the sword or the spear. But as we have seen, the leaders of an industrial society resort to military force only as a last resort, substituting as a general rule the chicanery of the courts, corruption of the electorate, sharp trading, or open theft.

The archives of the empire are full of illuminating illustrations of these "principles." In the lumber companies' efforts to secure the right to denude Indian lands guaranteed by the government to the "Indians and their heirs and assigns forever," the lumber lawyers devised an original theory that the trees standing on land were not included in the grant of the land itself. This "issue" was actually fought through the courts for several years—while the lumber companies went ahead cutting. It is estimated that the railroads in Minnesota received a total of fifty-one million dollars from national and state governments in land, bonds, and grants—or more than enough to pay for all the railroads in the state. The Northern Pacific— later incorporated, land grant and all, by Hill in his network— was granted in all fifty-seven million acres of the public domain, which included valuable forests in the Pacific Northwest and mines in the Dakotas and Montana. A vast agitation spread over the country in the second half of the nineteenth century, demanding that government lands be given to workers and farmers, and not exhausted in grants to the "big syndicates." Petitions were brought to the Congress of the United States, and division of the public lands among those who could cultivate them was a major plank in all the Peoples' and Labor-party movements of the century.

Congress at times threw open sections of the public domain to homesteaders on easy terms, but long before this happened the greater part of the most valuable farm land was sold to settlers by land companies, railroads, and timber interests at a good profit. Despairing of the action of Congress, some rank-and-filers took land for themselves by "squatting" on it. The militant Farm Holiday Association of today, with its original and direct methods of preventing farm foreclosures might claim as ancestor the associations of pioneer days formed to defend the lands from speculators and land companies. "Though distinctly extralegal in purpose, the claim associations were organized with constitutions and officers and paid solemn attention to parliamentary procedure. When the lands had been surveyed and were open to government auction, the usual technique was to select one member to make all bids, then to attend the auction in a body, each member armed with a club as a warning to speculators not to interfere."

In this fashion the rank and file, in the struggle against the acquisitional methods of the empire builders, occasionally devised sharp and effective weapons on their own account.

As to the mechanics of transfer into the empire builders' pockets of the wealth built up by workers and farmers, the methods used were manifestly those of Capitalism the world over. But again, due to the rough and ready life of the frontier and to the swiftness and turbulence of the empire's development, these time-honored methods were exercised with a crudity which made them easier to detect and their victims readier in protest. As we shall see later in this narrative, the modern city of Minneapolis still reflects in this respect something of the Golden Age tradition.

The farmers were the basic empire builders of all. Upon them everything else in the economy of the empire rested, including the power and wealth of the emperors. For redress of grievances they turned in the first instance and instinctively to the ballot. And the "agrarian revolts" of the Northwest throughout the nineteenth century became the axis for all insurgent political movements in the United States. To the rank-and-filers on the land, the workers in the cities finally turned as allies against a common enemy. Personifying this revolt and one of its leaders was Charles August Lindbergh, father of the aviator. To his story and that of the parties and movements of which his story is a part we now turn.

CHAPTER IV

POLITICAL REVOLT AND THE WAR

THE life of one family of Minnesota immigrants has been curiously and provocatively identified with the fortunes of the rank and file from frontier days to the era of post-War prosperity. That family is the Lindberghs, father, son, and grandson. August Lindbergh, the grandfather of the most famous of all aviators, came to Minnesota in the middle of the nineteenth century from Sweden. He was of sturdy peasant stock and he cleared the land, fought the Indians, and made a home for himself on the American frontier. His son, Congressman Charles A. Lindbergh, in a long public career became one of the most indefatigable and best hated enemies of the empire builders. His life was spent fighting the methods and mechanism of "big business" and defending the interests of the rank and file.

At a time when the war and its aftermath had already crushed or emasculated the political and economic organizations of workers and farmers everywhere, Charles A. Lindbergh, Jr., made his historic flight and became the national hero of America. This was the era—not only in the Northwest but nationally—of American financial ascendancy and of the triumph of large-scale capitalist control. The so-called "Money Trust" which Lindbergh, Sr., named, hated, and fought for thirty years, easily triumphed over all its enemies at home and abroad. And Charles Lindbergh, Jr., became identified both in his personal and professional life with the interests who had been his father's bitterest enemy. Today big business has quietly appropriated for its own ends the matchless physical courage and seriousness of purpose which were young Lindbergh's family heritage. And to the "average business man" this is as it should be in America. The farmers and workers of Minnesota, however, think otherwise. When the son's name is mentioned they change the subject.

The scope of this book cannot include more than a brief review of the political revolts whose philosophy the elder Lindbergh lived by; but their origin, their political ebb and flow, and the relative potency of the movement on the eve of the city's modern history, are essential to this story. The successive waves of "agrarian radicalism" which swept over the Northwest in the nineteenth century and into the twentieth had one purpose—to rid "the people" of the abuses of "monopoly" and restore to the worker or farmer his "inalienable rights" under an American democracy. In that sense the authors of the movement did not look upon themselves as radicals but as restorationists. The most generalized formula of the movement is found in the name of its first political party in Minnesota, the Anti-Monopoly party of Ignatius Donnelly. First off they were against monopoly in wood and coal, so vital in the economy of the Northland. Negatively they were against monopoly of the farmers' grain through elevators owned by the railroads and the Minneapolis millers, and so positively for state-owned elevators. They were against monopoly in land and so for a policy of turning over public lands by Congress to workers and farmers. The much derided Greenback movement was an effort of workers and farmers to combat "monopoly in money" by eastern bankers. Of course they were against political monopoly, and for breaking it down through the initiative and referendum. Indeed, nearly every plank or slogan can be traced to the restorationist principle. They were reformers of abuses and puritans of Jeffersonian democracy. Above all they

were against the imperial monopoly of the railroads and their
"radicalism" gyrated about this issue for some forty years.

The most famous and ubiquitous of farm organizations, the
Grange, was started by a group of philanthropists to bring
culture and sociability into the lonely life of the prairie. It
swept the country but the moment the farmers became sociable
they cursed the railroads and the grain speculators—and talked
politics. The Grange in spite of itself became the forerunner
of the Anti-Monopoly party in Minnesota and of similar political parties elsewhere. It was replaced by the Wheel and the
Farmers' Alliance—also not a political party but spawning one
in 1892, the People's Party or Populists (farmers plus Knights
of Labor)—until Bryan with his "Cross of Gold" speech captured the Populist electorate for the Democrats. The movement
exhibits a bewildering variety of political blocs and alliances
with the "two old Capitalist parties." For a time it veered
toward "independent action" and then back to a capture of old
political machinery. The Populists in their first campaign
formed alliances with the Democrats in the North and the
Republicans in the South. And a Democratic-Populist bloc in
1898 elected John Lind, Governor of Minnesota—one of the
three times between the Civil War and 1930, that the Republicans lost control of the chief executive.

Charles August Lindbergh breathed in the political ideas of
these movements along with the fresh air of the Minnesota
frontier. He was not a revolutionist but a passionate believer
in "American democracy," which he defended to the day of
his death. He and his fellow pioneers did not picture for themselves a workers' commune on the Marxian model, but an
agrarian democracy, for which the schoolbook version of
American government supplied the texts. These ideas were
later combined with the aspiration for an industrial democracy
as well.

Charles Sr. worked his way through Coogan's Academy by hunting and trapping, and then in order to enter the law school at Ann Arbor went to work on a gravel train to get money for clothes and transportation. Within a few years after graduation he had not only made himself a successful lawyer but won a unique place in the community. He was one of those highly dependable persons to whom everyone turned, whether for a loan of seed, legal aid, or advice on personal problems. He was an unusual moral and physical specimen even among the hardy homesteaders of the frontier. When Charles Jr., the aviator, was three years old, his father used to swim the Mississippi—with a current twice as swift as a man could walk—with the little boy on his back. It was not long before the little boy could swim it alone! Lindbergh taught his son to drive an automobile when he was almost too small to reach the pedals. And there is a story of how once, descending a long hill with a freight train at the bottom of it, the brakes failed to function. The father sat tight and waited to see how his son would handle the car. Charles Jr. promptly and efficiently ditched it at the side of the road. That was O.K. When the machine was taken out and repaired, the son resumed the wheel.

In 1906, Lindbergh Sr. ran for Congress and was elected. When Charles Jr. grew up he accompanied his father on political campaigns, distributed leaflets and dodged the mobs of vigilantes which business men of Minnesota at the time of the War, organized against the elder Lindbergh and his fellow candidates.

Here are some of the views Lindbergh defended in a ten-year career in Congress, gleaned from his speeches and from his three books, which later, when his son became an all-American hero, were carefully removed from many libraries.

The farmers must be organized exactly as every business is

IGNATIUS DONNELLY
He fought monopoly

LINDBERGHS, FATHER AND SON
"Charles, Jr. . . . . accompanied his father on political campaigns . . .
and dodged the mobs of vigilantes . . ."

organized. There should be an adjustment between producers and consumers. Interest rates can and should be reduced to a reasonable scale. What the people pay for the service of transportation can be cut down. Uneconomic competition is an economic burden on all.

On labor: In the past, labor has been figured as a commodity, treated as such, and converted by many employers into great fortunes. Labor should not be competitive except in skill and quality. "The day is near at hand when those who furnish the energy of the world's progress will govern."

He was against monopolist control of all the natural resources of the country, but the fight of his life was against "banker control" of American economic life. In an era of trust busting, Lindbergh concentrated on the money trust. As events were to prove, this fight—except for its "educational" value—was conspicuously unsuccessful.

Lindbergh transferred to the halls of Congress the same habits of hard work and personal modesty which he displayed in Little Falls, Minnesota. He rose every morning at five and went to work. When he was asked for a personal sketch for the Congressional Directory, he submitted the briefest note ever published in that self-advertising volume. "C. A. Lindbergh, Republican, Little Falls." Summing up his career, a politician of his district said, "Every effort has been made to suppress him, bottle him up, choke him off, ignore him, squash him and discipline him. . . . Indeed, Mr. Lindbergh has won distinction by having it so persistently refused him."

On war, he had said, "War is paid for by the people," and when the World War broke, he infinitely enhanced his unpopularity by remarking, "It is my belief we are going in as soon as the country can be propagandized into the war mania."

Meantime, with Lindbergh in Congress, some startling developments were occurring on the rank-and-file front in the

Northwest. The farmers' Non-Partisan League, founded by Townley in 1915, began to put the principles of agrarian radicalism into practice with a vigor and success that outdistanced all its political ancestors. In North Dakota, where the League started, it captured the lower house of the legislature and all state offices except that of treasurer. For its part, Minnesota had a membership by 1918, of 50,000 dues-paying members. In fact, in a short two years the League had become incomparably the most powerful expression of rank-and-file agrarian revolt the Northwest had ever known.

On the economic and labor front, these same years recorded enormous growth by the I.W.W. The headquarters of its agricultural unions were in our American city and it sent organizers among the harvest hands, to the great "bonanza" farms, and into the lumber camps and iron mines of the Mesabi. In the minutes of a meeting of Local 400 of the Agricultural Workers Industrial Union (I.W.W.) is the following statement by Arthur Le Sueur: "If we can come to some understanding with the Non-Partisan League of North Dakota, it will mean that *the balance of power* will be shifted from the state government to the Industrial Workers of the World and the Non-Partisan League!"

This "understanding," however, was never reached; and soon both organizations found themselves fighting for their lives against a frontal attack of patrioteers and big business.

With the entrance of the United States into the War, the empire builders and their successors grasped a golden opportunity to smash all their enemies under cover of the patriotic emergency. In place of indirection, bribery, and persuasion, they were successful in establishing an open military dictatorship over Minnesota. The state was at the heart of the antiwar sentiment in the Northwest, and the Minnesota legislature voted dictatorial powers to a seven-man Commission of Safety.

"Armed with extraordinary powers," writes William Folwell, the state's leading conservative historian, "and granted an ample appropriation ($1,000,000) . . . the commission proceeded to exercise functions *the like of which the history of American law has never disclosed* [italics mine]. . . . If a large, hostile army had already been landed in Duluth and was about to march on the capital of the state, a more liberal dictatorship could hardly have been conceded to the Commission."

Under its "liberal" powers this little band of seven dictators turned their hand to everything from ordering women out of saloons to eradicating barberry bushes and fighting forest fires, but their major activity, under cover of a drive against disloyalists, was a systematic wrecking of the Non-Partisan League as well as the workers' organizations of the Northwest. Said the chairman, Judge John F. McGee, testifying in Washington: "A Non-Partisan Leaguer is a traitor everytime. . . . Where we made our mistake," continues this defender of the War for Democracy, "was in not establishing a firing squad in the first days of the war. We should get busy now and have that firing squad working overtime."

A "home guard" was created which did yeoman service in breaking a Twin City street-car strike in 1918, and on the agrarian front, Townley and other Non-Partisan Leaguers were jailed for "conspiracy." The League had officially announced: "While giving our utmost energies to the prosecution of the World War for democracy, we are not unmindful that there are enemies of democracy in the homeland. . . . Cheerfully acquiescing in the fixing of the price of wheat, the farmers ask that prices of other necessities be regulated to eliminate exorbitant profits." Under the tutelage of Judge McGee, the farmers found their most heinous crime was not disloyalty but trying to make the War into the kind of one it pretended to be.

Having dealt a blow at the farmers' organizations, the Commission shifted its artillery to another front. They decided to smash the Industrial Workers of the World. To the disappointment of the Commission's counsel, the United States Department of Justice could find "no federal statute warranting action." The counsel, undismayed, found a solution for this technical difficulty. The emergency was pressing because the Wobblies at that moment were succeeding with their demand for increased wages of harvest hands. The counsel finally convinced the Department of Justice, according to the Minnesota historian quoted above, "that an immediate paralysis of the I.W.W. activities by the arrest of leaders was more important than their ultimate conviction." (!) Accordingly, on September 28, 1917, a general raid from coast to coast was made upon the I.W.W. One hundred and sixty-six, including Haywood, were arrested in Chicago, where the counsel of the Minnesota Commission was on hand. After a year in jail, 101 were convicted of violation of the penal code and the Espionage Act and sentenced to terms of imprisonment ranging from three months to twenty years. Similar trials took place in Sacramento and Wichita, for all of which the Minnesota Commission of Safety took due credit.

In these days of war hysteria, Charles A. Lindbergh entered the primaries in a race for the governorship of Minnesota. He was endorsed by the Non-Partisan League and by labor, still unorganized for political action. His daughter wrote urging him not to plunge into the uneven fight, but he answered: "It is a principle for which I fight. . . . Now I want you to think it over and put on your Lindbergh grit. Now really would you not be ashamed of your father if he crawled into a hole and pulled the hole after him? Just think of me—you know me—how could I do it?"

Lindbergh, like the League, once the United States was in,

supported the War but he was against its profiteers. He advocated "conscription of wealth," taking the profits out of the munitions industry, and other such formulas as are common in liberal discussion today. One is tempted to ask: How will their advocates fare in the next war? For these views in 1918, Lindbergh was stoned and barely escaped lynching. "Going over the top," he remarked, "isn't half as bad as being on the bottom of a war mania."

His fellow campaigners were mobbed, tarred and feathered, and repeatedly threatened with death. The "war mania" was at its height and throughout the campaign Lindbergh remained at the bottom of it. Coming out of one of his meetings, Congressman Lindbergh had to rescue the driver of his car from a mob which had already beaten him semiconscious. As the two drove away the mob started shooting. "We must not go too fast," said Lindbergh, "they'll think we are afraid of them." Through most of the campaign, his son Charles Jr., the future aviator, accompanied him, distributing leaflets, keeping account of campaign expenses, and driving his father's car. Lindbergh received 150,000 votes, losing to his "patriotic" opponent Burnquist by 50,000.

The tactics of the League were not to become an independent political party but to capture the Republican nomination through the direct primary. The defeat of the Non-Partisan League in the primaries left workers and farmers with no choice but to vote for their "bitterest enemies" in the fall elections or to put up an independent candidate of their own. In July, 1918, the State Federation of Labor held its convention in Virginia, Minnesota; a resolution was offered and passed that a labor political convention be called. It met in August with 125 delegates from labor unions all over the state, and appointed a conference committee to confer with representatives of the Non-Partisan League with a view to putting up a state ticket in the fall. This they did under the name Farmer-Labor party. Thus the Farmer-Labor party, which was to play a crucial role in the history of Minnesota (and—twelve years later—of our American city), was born in the sharp struggle of wartime conflict. The party's first candidate, David Evans, was, however, to go down to defeat.

The struggle continued into the nineteen-twenties. In spite of violent and bloody opposition, the labor movement, both in the trade-union and political fields, continued to grow until it culminated in the national third party of La Follette in 1924. La Follette's defeat, plus a drastic "red purge" in the trade unions as well as the rising tide of "prosperity," brought an ebb in the national movement. But in Minnesota the rank and file as a whole could never again be brought entirely under the sway of the party of the Minnesota Commission of Safety. The War had proved a profound catalytic of all the cumulative revolt in Jim Hill's empire. Out of the whole post-War movement the Minnesota Farmer-Labor party remained the sole organizational survivor. From the Non-Partisan League and the trade-union political conventions the movement had taken shape by 1924 as the Farmer-Labor Association, with dues-paying members in ward, village, and township clubs, and with trade unions affiliated and paying dues on a *per capita* basis. The Association remained alive through the Coolidge era, and continued to run candidates, although with no major successes except to keep Henrik Shipstead in the United States Senate on the Farmer-Labor ticket.

In the years that followed the War—not only in Minnesota but throughout America—business, particularly big business, climbed into the saddle. The country "kept cool with Coolidge" while the new crop of American millionaires broke all previous records. Symbolically, the president appointed Andrew Mellon, "the richest man who had ever gone into politics," secretary of the Treasury. In Minnesota and in our American city, although a basic decline had begun, it was obscured by what seemed to be a new Golden Age everywhere else. Workers' and farmers' organizations reflected the times by entering into an epoch of decline if not decay throughout the world. Not until 1930, when the depression had begun and the rank and file had elected the first Farmer-Labor governor in the United States, did the workers and farmers of the empire again seriously challenge its rulers.

To this briefest of reviews of "radical politics" in the Northwest it is important to add the role of the Marxist left wing of the rank-and-file revolt. Although the Socialists as such were numerically a handful, they participated actively from the earliest days to the time of the Non-Partisan League (which was largely led by professing or ex-Socialists), and more and more leavened, if they never captured, the movement's political philosophy. Besides, the Socialist party (and De Leon's Socialist-Labor party) repeatedly ran candidates of their own for state and municipal offices, succeeding in 1916 in electing Van Lear, head of the machinists' union, the first—and the last to date—Socialist mayor of Minneapolis.

The distinguishing feature of rank-and-file politics in Minnesota is that in the ebbs and flows of "radicalism" in America, Minnesota found herself for the most part on the left of the movement. When the Socialist party, after the War, was split and its left wing throughout the world declared for the Communist International, almost the whole of the Minnesota Socialist party was found in the left wing and went Communist. In 1923 this revolutionary group played an active part in the politics of the Farmer-Labor party until they withdrew in 1924.

A second split occurred in the world revolutionary movement in 1928. The Left Opposition of the Communist International led by Leon Trotsky was expelled from the Communist parties in all countries. Once more the majority in the Minnesota party were found to be in the left wing and, crucially for this history, the wing included several of the ablest trade unionists in the labor movement in America. In later years, these men were destined to play a decisive role in the economic life of our American city. This group of so-called Trotskyists in Minneapolis, as in other cities, in the spring of 1936 entered the Socialist party, where they have since been active in the left wing of that movement.

The segment of history we have just reviewed, as indeed the whole history of the empire, may be regarded in one sense as an educational process—particularly for the workers and farmers—an "intensive short course," so to speak, in the economics and politics of the American system. The educational method was, of course, not didactic but empirical. And the learner was educated almost entirely by a series of mistakes, often tragic ones, paid for in suffering and disillusionment. Both the workers and farmers, armed with the idea that natural forces plus the American system would give them opportunity and freedom, had flocked into the Northwest throughout the nineteenth century. The early conquistadores and the economic system they governed knocked such ideas out of the rank-and-filers' heads. They began, therefore, a series of repair jobs on the empire through the old political parties. But the empire builders captured the party machines and again "educated" the rank and file. Still hopeful of reform, but one step to the left, the electorate tried independent political action and also drafted a blueprint of an ultimate cooperative commonwealth." This is the stage of education Minnesota is still in. And it still promises painful though valuable "lessons" for the workers and farmers of the Northwest.

Incidentally, it is the stage to which the rest of the country is just catching up.

On the other hand, the bankers and business men who were the engineers of the system, have also been educated—to block interference by the rank and file. They have not only devised a series of checkmates, but have more and more clearly come to understand their own prerogatives as a class. After all, both the rank and file and the generals had been taught the same schoolbook texts of American democracy, and both had to rid their heads of it before they could deal with the real world.

To the student, the history of the Northwest is an almost classical treatise on these matters. Americans, with all their demagogy and proverbial "idealism," have lacked the genius for compromise and muddle of the British. History has not permitted them time. This treatise which the Northwest has written is a primer rather than a textbook. But that does not lessen its value. The methods of a Jim Hill, of a Commission of Safety, of a Citizens' Alliance, are blackboard illustrations. And the pupils begin to show, through the Farmer-Labor party, the Farmer Holiday Association, and the militant trade unions forged in the nineteen-thirties, that they have learned their lesson.

Singularly few liberal ameliorists and compromisers among "business leaders" have been produced amid the clashing forces of Capitalism in the empire. If one believes that the final solution lies in the direction of "reasonable compromise" for the good of all, such an omission by history is a tragedy. (In the modern city of Minneapolis, there is a well-defined group drawn from both contending classes which tardily but patiently is attempting to introduce this solvent of the empire's ills.) If one believes, on the other hand, that Capitalism cannot with impunity be tampered with but only abolished, their absence has served to clear the air and write historically a more clarifying text.

Beneath the surface of post-War prosperity which lasted up to the crash of 1929, certain hidden forces were preparing an explosive change in the empire's fortunes. On the economic side they were the empire's gradual decline and above all the depressed state of agriculture, which Coolidge prosperity had never succeeded in rescuing from the slump of 1921.

These and other factors were to assist the Farmer-Labor party to power in 1930, and four years later in Minneapolis to bring a violent and successful challenge by city workers to the empire's status quo.

CHAPTER V

THE FARMER-LABOR PARTY IN POWER

IN 1930, the first Farmer-Labor governor in the United States came into office in the state of Minnesota. When, in that year, Floyd Bjorsterne Olson entered the race for the governorship his prospects were far different from those in 1924 when he and his party had suffered a smashing defeat. Six years as district attorney of Hennepin County had brought Olson popularity and political sagacity. And at thirty-eight, he had no intention of becoming the perennially defeated candidate of a crusading third party. Nor did he misjudge the political scene or his own strength. He won by a good margin.

Several factors contributed to the Farmer-Labor victory in 1930, or more accurately, to Olson's victory. For although the Farmer-Labor party increased its representatives in the legislature, a majority of both houses remained conservative. First of all, profound economic forces ever since the War had been setting the stage for dramatic explosions. The "magnificent era" of post-War prosperity, as we have remarked, had done little or nothing for the workers or farmers of the Northwest. Agriculture had remained profoundly depressed since 1921 and the farmers maneuvered through the boom years by increasing their mortgages and striving to step up production to make up for the drop in prices. Malevolently faithful to economic law, the prices dropped still lower. The boom years were only a little less harsh on the city worker. For the country as a whole, money wages rose between 1921 and 1929 11.3%; for Minneapolis they rose only 2.1%. In the same period, cost of living in Minneapolis remained relatively higher than for the country as a whole.

The boom years were characterized the country over by an unprecedented concentration of capital. And the Northwest participated in this national phenomenon. Chain stores everywhere invaded Minnesota, or increased their influence, and the opening of retail branches of the big mail-order houses not only smashed the business of the small retailer but also impinged upon the small manufacturer. In finance, huge holding companies became the order of the day. The Northwest Bancorporation and the First Bank Stock Corporation, to the dismay of small but rugged individualists, set up a system of "group banking." Small business men, and small bankers as well, became alarmed at this open concentration of financial power and raised voices of protest. The Farmer-Labor party promptly welcomed these new rebels and measurably widened their electoral base.

But aside from economic forces, or rather adding to them, was the state of the Republican machine, which had held power uninterruptedly for sixteen years. Even with its own electorate, Republican morale was at low ebb. The logic of this political situation offered the Farmer-Labor party a golden opportunity to play on the traditional psychology of the American electorate: "Turn the rascals out!" In fact, one of the campaign slogans—the broadest the party had ever offered to the Minnesota voters—showed it had not neglected the opportunity. "Elect Olson," it read. "Minnesota Needs a Change!"

Capping and encompassing all, most observers are agreed the victory was due to the personality and political acumen of Floyd Olson. The youthful governor had fought his way up from an impoverished boyhood to be the youngest district attorney in the history of Hennepin County. In office with a spectacular "campaign against corruption," he sent a number of city officials to jail, and had been re-elected by the largest majority ever won for the district attorney's office. This experience, coupled with lessons he had drawn from his earlier defeat, had endowed him with political wisdom beyond his years. His worst enemies admitted he was a brilliant lawyer. And as a campaigner he displayed both courage and imagination combined with an unusually acute sense of how much radicalism the electorate would take. With these gifts he tied his standpat opponents into knots, and dealt no less effectively with critics from the left within his own party.

Olson refused to accept the 1930 nomination without obtaining a promise that he was to have a free hand in the making of appointments. Though the party convention agreed with little discussion, the pact laid the foundation of a patronage controversy which the rank and file of party was to wage with increasing bitterness through the next six years. "All-Party Committees for Olson" were organized to gather in the dissenters from the ranks of the old parties. And in October, the *Farmer-Labor Leader* announced that many thousand Republicans were openly declaring themselves for Olson, because "they are patriotic enough to know the best interests of Minnesota require a house-cleaning at the State Capital."

The platform of the Farmer-Labor party in 1930 was careful not to make it difficult for these new allies, and stressed only the mildest reforms. Sensitive both to political logic and the "mood of the masses," Olson was to move left in succeeding years in seven-league strides till in 1934 he was to declare: "I am not a liberal, I am what I want to be—a radical." But in 1930 the whole effort of his campaign was to prove him safe and sane, and the party's organ announced: "Olson is not a bitter radical and theorist, but a well-balanced progressive."

The campaign was rich in humorous as well as instructive

episodes. Chase, Olson's Republican opponent for the governorship, took up the cause of Farmer-Labor purity!

"Once it [the Farmer-Labor party] represented a splendid
band of men and women," he began. "Today the Farmer-Labor
party is only a husk of the party of 1920. Then it was aggres-
sively progressive. Now in its platform there is little that is
worthy and less that is progressive, little that is honest and
nothing that is sincere. . . . Political history records no more
audacious attempt," he concluded, "to defile a political party
than the present attempt by political pirates to scrap the life-
giving principles of the Farmer-Labor party and make a job-
hunting band wagon of its corpse!"

Farmer-Laborites were not slow to point out that the "auda-
ciousness and insolence" of Mr. Chase's speech had registered
a new high in political hypocrisy. They reminded the Republican candidate that he had participated in Governor Preus's
"Smash Socialism" campaign against the Farmer-Labor party
in 1920, and at that time had spoken of the "splendid band of
men and women" as "bolsheviks," "enemies of the home,"
"free-lovers," "rats and vipers." Their "life-giving principles"
he had hailed in print as "disloyal and pro-German." It is not
surprising that with political sagacity of this order governing
his opponents, Olson won the election with relative ease and in
January, 1931, became the first Farmer-Labor governor in the
United States.

Why did the electorate choose the Farmer-Labor chieftain
as their governor, and at the same time elect Republican state
officers and a conservative legislature? The answer is, I think,
the inevitable conclusion that Olson—more than the party
itself—won the 1930 election. The whole campaign had led
up to this result. And the fact became significant for the party's
later history, for it emphasized that Olson was more important
to the movement than the movement was to him.

The new governor's inaugural address followed the mild Farmer-Labor platform closely. "Impatient extremists," said the *Leader*, "will doubtless express disappointment and will criticize Governor Olson for not advocating more radical measures." But from the first it became clear that whatever Olson advocated would have small chance of enactment by a conservative and hostile legislature. And it should be noted here, as one of the problems which inevitably face this type of party, that on every controversial issue there were defections to the conservatives from among the Farmer-Labor-endorsed senators and representatives.

In February, patronage, which had already caused rumblings in the Farmer-Labor Association [The latter is the permanent membership organization of the Farmer-Labor party and in common parlance, as in the pages of this book, the terms are used interchangeably.] came sharply to the fore in the appointment of Mrs. Wittich, prominent Republican and chairman of the Minneapolis "All-Party Committee" to the post of commissioner of budget and personnel. This was the key patronage post within the gift of the party, and suggested that Republican support of Olson had perhaps not been wholly disinterested.

As loyal Farmer-Laborites, who had fought for an unpopular cause for many years, saw their Republican enemies—at times the bitterest enemies of the movement—receive new jobs or retain old ones, their confusion and bitterness grew. Many of them as the depression deepened needed the jobs for themselves, and argued that those who had sacrificed for the cause— not the enemies of the very principles of the Farmer-Labor movement—should profit from the victory. Olson replied by a counter attack against selfishness, proclaiming his intention of appointing the man or woman whom he felt best fitted for a position no matter whose toes he stepped on. But as appointee after appointee came along with no qualifications for office other than vote-getting for Olson, and as these were given important, policy-making posts, the most strenuous protests came from defenders of Farmer-Labor principles against whom the charge of office-seeking could not apply.

A notable instance was the situation in regard to the state board of education. This board has a rotating membership and each incoming governor appoints two members. Olson's first policy was to reappoint the conservative incumbents. Under pressure from the Association and particularly from the Farmer-Labor Women's Federation, he finally made some Farmer-Labor appointments to the board. The new members of the board succeeded in securing the resignation of the conservative commissioner of many years' standing and appointed in his stead Dr. John G. Rockwell. Through his efforts the Farmer-Labor party has been primarily responsible for a progressive system of education in Minnesota, and for liberalization of state aid which tends to equalize educational opportunity.

Early in 1931, the line began to be drawn—and year by year it grew deeper—between "Association people" and "All-Party people." The former were those who regarded the party as a worker-farmer movement energized by principles of reform, the latter were the "practical politicians," with the state employees as a nucleus, who depended on the governor for jobs and looked to him and not the Association for leadership. Even such division oversimplifies the issue. There were numbers of state employees who were devoted "Association people," and the Association on the other hand—even its protesting left wing were not insensitive to political expediency, and were apt to do "what the skipper wished." The line of struggle continued, confused, unclear, shifting, but it was there.

By 1932 the party's platform shifted sharply to the left. This was not surprising. The depression was approaching its all-time nadir in the winter of '32-'33, and a flood of sentiment against "Hoover Republicanism" was about to sweep Roosevelt into office in the same election which gave Olson his second term.

The governor's second inaugural address reflects the mighty political, as well as economic, shift which had occurred in the two years since his first:

"We are assembled during the most crucial period in the history of the nation and the state," he began. "An army of unemployed, some 200,000 homeless and wandering boys, thousands of abandoned farms, etc. . . . are evidences not only of an economic depression, but of failure of government and our *social system* to function in the interests of the common people. Just beyond the horizon of this scene is rampant lawlessness and possible revolution. *Only remedial social legislation, National and State, can prevent its appearance.*" [Italics mine]

The 1933 session is significant as the only one in which the Farmer-Laborites, through an alliance with "the liberals," organized the Minnesota House. The Senate was still conservative. None of the proposals which Olson recommended to the legislature of Minnesota could be construed as "revolutionary" or, in view of the economic emergency, even as "extremist." All of these measures, however, met with iron resistance from the Tory Senate.

As to foreclosure, the issue of the hour, a rising tide of farm revolt had already organized itself into the Farm Holiday Association, which was coping with the foreclosure problem in its own way. Following its strikes for "cost of production" in the summers of 1931 and 1932, the Holiday began to halt foreclosures, sometimes by "Sears-Roebuck sales" (seeing to it that nobody bid over a dollar, and then turning the farm back to the owner), sometimes by assembling a crowd so large and compact that physically the sheriff couldn't get through to the Court House steps to make the sale! In neighboring states the situation was moving toward violence, and on February 24 Governor Olson declared a moratorium by proclamation. Foreclosures were halted until May 1, by decree, to give the legislature time to pass the proposed law. The proclamation was unprecedented, but such was the temper of the country that even a conservative press offered little by way of criticism.

In these chaotic days Olson added to his reputation as a Farmer-Labor governor and as a radical, not only in Minnesota but throughout the country. Roosevelt had called a "conference of governors" on March 6, and although Olson did not attend he stole the national headlines by his message to Roosevelt, in which he proposed: "If the so-called depression deepens, I strongly recommend to you, Mr. President, that the government take over and operate the key industries of this country. Put the people back to work. If necessary to relieve public suffering the government should not hesitate to conscript wealth."

In the spring, with the legislature still hesitating over the moratorium, the Farm Holiday decided that a little direct pressure was good for any government—Farmer-Labor or otherwise—and thousands of Holidayites demonstrated at the state capitol. While in many nearby states, similar demonstrations were being greeted with clubs and violence, Olson promptly invited a committee into his office, apologized for not having room for all, and arranged a joint session of the legislature to be addressed by the demonstrators.

From the tribune of the legislative chamber the Holiday spokesmen minced no words to their senators and representatives. "Much worse than the Boston Tea Party will happen unless farmers are given relief from debt and tax burdens," said one. "If we find any old senators who are not going down the

FARM-HOLIDAY

". . . coping with the foreclosure problem in its own way"

© *International News Photos*

AT THE STATE CAPITOL

To the unemployed the Governor said, "I hope the present system of
government goes right down to hell"

© *International News Photos*

AT THE STATE CAPITOL
Dramatizing the feed problem

© *International News Photos*

"If we find any old senators who are not going down the line with us,
we know what to do with them"

line with us," shouted J. W. Kester from Odessa Township, "we know what to do with them. . . . We won't stand for any more monkey business. This House is handicapped by the Senate."

"I'm glad you've come," said the state's highest executive to them. "If you had come sooner that dignified body known as the Senate might have acted quicker for the public welfare."

A bill for a farm-mortgage moratorium was introduced in the House the same day.

Still the session wore on and the Senate refused to support any of the governor's measures. Public meetings of labor, the unemployed, and the Farmer-Labor Association vigorously protested. Finally, on April 13, Olson in a speech from the steps of the State Capital to the unemployed threatened to declare martial law and take what was needed if the legislature failed to provide relief. He added amid the applause of his listeners that if Capitalism could do nothing to prevent the recurrence of present conditions, "I hope the present system of government goes right down to hell."

This speech made the front page in most of the newspapers of the country. Shortly afterwards, the Senate capitulated in part by passing an income-tax law, the farm moratorium, and certain relief bills.

The 1934 convention of the Farmer-Labor Association opened with the heartening announcement that all eighty-seven counties had functioning Farmer-Labor bodies. This convention was to represent the high point of Farmer-Labor radicalism. Olson made the keynote speech: ". . . should not the government own all those industries which have to do with the obtaining of raw materials and transforming them into necessary products . . . mines, packing plants, grain elevators, oil fields, and iron mines? . . . Why should not the State of Minnesota operate her own iron mines? [The state still owns a considerable number of iron ore deposits which are leased to private companies.] . . . I am speaking of these things as merely touching upon the ideals of this movement, of an ultimate co-operative commonwealth. . . . Now I am frank to say that I am not a liberal. . . . I am what I want to be—I am a radical. I am a radical in the sense that I want a definite change in the system. I am not satisfied with tinkering, I am not satisfied with patching, I am not satisfied with hanging a laurel wreath upon burglars and thieves and pirates and calling them code authorities or something else. . . . I want, however, an orderly constructive change, I don't want visionary things any more than the hardest Tory or Conservative wants them . . . it must be gradual . . . the ultimate co-operative commonwealth." Immediately after his speech, Olson left the convention to take the train for Washington. Friends and enemies seem to agree that he was appalled on his arrival to be handed newspapers with the Farmer-Labor 1934 platform (written after he left) demanding the co-operative commonwealth!—idle factories for use of the unemployed, and public ownership of all banks and factories.

Whether Olson had been carried away with his own oratory as many Farmer-Laborites suggest, whether he for once misjudged the political temperature and the national capital abruptly restored his balance, I do not know; but it was not long before he was on the radio "explaining" the platform. The explanation showed the governor at his politically most skillful; he never repudiated any part of it but he did a masterly job of pulling its punches. To begin with, he allowed that if the proposal to take over idle factories was Communistic, then the Red Cross, the Twin City Community Chest, and Mrs. Roosevelt were all Communists, since they had proposed, and in some cases were practising, the same thing. He quoted Woodrow Wilson, Pope Pius, and the Presbyterian Church to show that the platform was really less radical than any of them. Paragraph three calling for the public ownership of *all* banks and factories was something of a stickler, but he called his legal training to the rescue and asserted that later paragraphs modified these so that they did not really mean what they seemed to say. The Farmer-Labor politicians were worried nevertheless, and later an official "analysis" was issued to "clarify" the platform.

In the election of that year Olson lost over fifty thousand votes from his 1932 plurality. But all the rest of the state ticket gained votes for the Farmer-Labor party. It is frankly conceded by Farmer-Laborites that they forfeited the business men's vote and a section of the more prosperous farmers who had been persuaded that the Farmer-Labor platform meant nationalization of the land. On the other hand, a gain in the working-class vote in the three large cities—Minneapolis, St. Paul and Duluth —plus the radical farmer vote saved the election. The electorate had voted in 1934 more nearly on class lines than ever before, and the radical Farmer-Labor platform had resulted in a net gain for the party.

After all, the platform itself was the product of the same forces which were stirring workers and farmers all over the state in 1934, which had already broken out in militant strikes, and which before the fall elections were to culminate in virtual civil war in Minneapolis. Olson, as succeeding chapters will show, was to try very hard to maintain a precarious balance between the conflicting forces of class warfare. But even his skill was to prove insufficient.

The best defense of the Farmer-Labor party of Minnesota— and probably of most other labor parties—from the viewpoint of the real interest of farmers and laborers reveals itself, I believe, in a study of the indictment of its enemies. The main counts registered against the party in Minnesota by its political opponents are these:

1. Corruption and graft.

2. Extravagant use of public funds.

3. Stands for an overthrow of the American form of government.

4. Turns class against class by fostering radical labor unions and farm organizations.

On point one, with all the will in the world the perennial investigating commissions of Republicans have been able to make a very poor showing of actual malfeasance in public office. When a Republican legislature in a burst of partisan zeal voted an investigation of graft in various state departments, the investigation yielded surprisingly small fruits. Disillusioned Farmer-Laborites suggested the reason was that the Republican probers found nothing but Republican office holders to investigate.

Regarding the governor's personal character, the Republicans have charged drinking, "getting mixed up with women," and nefarious connections with the underworld. As one Farmer-Laborite close to the governor said to me, "Olson is no Coolidge," and it was entirely possible for the Republicans to discover deviations from the Lutheran code of morality in his conduct. But they entered into a campaign of vilification which passed all bounds of fact or decency and scored a new high in mud slinging for the West. Regarding "connections with the underworld," this allegation became perennial with the Republican machine and was to culminate four years later in the charge that he had murdered Walter Liggett to protect himself. Liggett was a newspaper man who had once been pro-Olson, but turned against him before the fall election in 1935. He informed Republicans that he had proof of elaborate underworld tie-ups implicating the governor. Liggett was murdered before the election. A flood of rumor spread through Republican circles accusing the governor of "political murder." Newspaper men in Minneapolis with whom I talked expressed their conviction that Liggett had been "bumped off" for personal reasons by the underworld itself. (Liggett's connections with that "world" were well understood in Minneapolis.) The governor in the face of his opponents' charges promptly sent a special message to the legislature, asking for investigation of the Liggett murder. He suggested that the Republican Legislature have complete charge, that they summon "G-men," utilize private detectives, or use any other means they desired to uncover the truth. The legislature declined to make the appropriation or to take any other action. In view of the virulence of their political hatred of the governor in 1935, it seems reasonable that they would have accepted his offer had they felt there was truth in the charge. By the spring of 1936, although rumors of the "political murder" lingered in Republican circles in the East, in Minneapolis even the governor's enemies ridiculed the charge.

That there is graft in the party machine is unquestioned. But in comparison with the record of other parties and particularly the oft exposed record of the Minnesota Republican party, the history of the Farmer-Labor party so far as graft is concerned is a model of public virtue.

But the heaviest Republican and Democratic artillery has been trained against Farmer-Labor extravagance. Here two points can be made. The Farmer-Laborites cheerfully accept responsibility for the five-million-dollar relief bill and other measures for increased relief appropriation. Again, the governor's veto of the bill to reduce the salaries of state employees—a Republican "economy measure"—is considered an achievement of the Farmer-Laborites and not an indictment of the party's extravagance. On the whole, although plenty of inefficiency and bureaucracy can be uncovered by political opponents—and has been—the actual record of a *lower state budget* under Farmer-

Labor administration than under preceding Republican ones, is a convincing if not final refutation of the "main charge."

In the matter of conspiring to overthrow the American form of government, we have an entirely different category of indictment and one calling for different treatment. Dismissing for the moment such campaign charges as that the Farmer-Labor commissioner of education has "sovietism" taught in the public schools—which no one takes with any seriousness—how much is there in the charge that the Farmer-Labor party of Minnesota is an imminent threat to our present form of government? Unfortunately for the earnest believers in the cooperative commonwealth, not much. The less informed and more gullible reactionaries find "no difference" between Olson and Stalin. But the more sophisticated and practical business men have been able to get along tolerably well with the "soviet" state of Minnesota.

As to the fourth charge of fostering trade unions and farmer organizations, the Farmer-Labor party—as we have seen—chalks this up as its major achievement. If "class hatred" is engendered as a result, the Farmer-Laborites simply name the reactionaries as the chief engenderers.

In a word, on points three and four, the efficacy of the charges is dependent less on the factual record than on the critics' point of view.

What is the co-operative commonwealth toward which the Farmer-Labor party strives as an "ultimate objective"? It isn't Communism as the Marxist defines it. It's what Lindbergh Sr. or many other Northwest agrarians would conceive as a reasonable American economic Utopia—achievable through democratic parliamentary process and not by "Red revolution." It envisions the basic and monopolist industries owned and operated by the government: steel, oil, textiles, grain elevators, mills, railroads, etc.—the big banks also. The small business man is guaranteed his property and the right to a "reasonable" profit. Co-operative enterprises are expanded, the farmer enjoys the right to private property and land and receives a reasonable return for his labor as does labor everywhere. An economy of plenty replaces an economy of scarcity, and "production for use," production for profit. This social ideal, passionately held by thousands of workers and farmers, accurately reflects the deep yearning for social and economic justice which the imperial history of the Northwest has implanted in them. As one farmer said to me, "The more you think about it, the more you wonder why we can't get there some day." Roughly, half the voters for the Farmer-Labor ticket believe in the justice and practicability of the co-operative commonwealth. Another half do not lift their eyes either from practical politics or the "immediate reforms" which they hope these politics will bring about. Many thousands vote Farmer-Labor with no decisive convictions pro or con on the co-operative commonwealth, but because they believe simply that Farmer-Laborites "are on the side of the common people." A minority, including members of the Communist party, looks on the Farmer-Labor party as a present defense against Fascism, as an instrument for immediate reforms, and as a transitional stage to *bona fide* Communism. Is it?

One hundred and fifty years have built in the United States an electoral and administrative apparatus called American democracy, by no means in isolation, but on the contrary, organic with Capitalism. In both the economic and political spheres of "capitalist democracy" there are conditions and rules in obedience to which victory is possible. In the sphere of politics one of them concerns a ratio between electoral success and campaign funds. The most serious charge which "pure" Farmer-Laborites make against their party machine is the acceptance of contributions from business and financial interests to its campaign war chest—in return, it is implied, for positive political favors or at least immunity from attack. The late Governor Olson was, in particular, bitterly attacked by certain Farmer-Laborites for yielding to this political weakness. More significantly perhaps, he was also defended. One high official of the Farmer-Labor administration whose personal integrity is beyond question and whose conduct of his own office has been both honest and faithful to Farmer-Labor principles, said to me, "Hasn't the Farmer-Labor Party achieved real gains for the farmers and workers of Minnesota? How would that have been possible without winning elections? To win elections, money is necessary. That money can only be obtained from those who have it in sufficient quantities. Governor Olson was able to secure that money for the party and I have no doubt that certain political concessions were made. In my mind they were entirely justified." The Farmer-Labor critics of the governor and the party on this point have offered me no documentary evidence—and I have none to offer.

But the tie-up between success at the polls and a war chest is only one of the many rules. They all go back to a close relation between American democracy and the economic system it is intended to support, energize, and regulate—Capitalism.

There have been isolated instances of tourists breaking the bank at Monte Carlo, but, for consistent winning, it is far better to be the croupier himself because the system is devised for the house and not the tourist. In the game of capitalist democracy—American, or any other kind—the revolutionist has consistently maintained that the cards were stacked against the outsider, *i.e.,* against those whose interests were not the croupier's. He therefore proposes bluntly to change the rules. Parliamentary Socialists in England, People's Front supporters in France, as well as Farmer-Laborites in Minnesota, have on the other hand, by and large, accepted the rules and merely asked for a few amendments. Like the occasional tourist at Monte Carlo, they have sometimes approached the table with a promising system, but the croupier is well fortified against them. Implicit at least in this analogy is the author's appraisal of the nature and prospects of the Farmer-Labor party.

There is no escape, I believe, from this dilemma. Partial reforms are of course possible, but on every basic issue, unless the party in power—Farmer-Labor or otherwise—is ready to substitute a new economic system, it must see to it that the one in existence works. Examine any concrete Farmer-Labor reform and the dilemma presents itself. When a mortgage-moratorium law was passed in Minnesota, left-wingers pointed out that it was *not* a *genuine* moratorium. They were right, of course. A genuine moratorium on farm mortgages would not only have prevented future loans to the farmers, but also wrecked the financial structure of savings banks and insurance companies. Such a law if carried out could only bring collapse and chaos *unless* the party taking such a step were prepared to go beyond it to a revolutionary change in property relations.

Radical idealists have long been emphasizing that any national labor party must be a "real one" not like the Minnesota makeshift run by politicians who compromise its principles. But any national Farmer-Labor party will inevitably be a replica—in all fundamentals—of Minnesota's. It will offer the same advantages and suffer the same limitations. Minnesota's specimen after all is as "real" a one as we are likely to see. The party was born of a solid alliance between trade unions and the most militant farmers' organization of the day. And one cannot question the sincerity or courage of its founders, many of whom were tarred and feathered for their convictions. Any subsequent loss of control by the base over the top is not, as the aspiring architects of a "real Farmer-Labor party" believe, an "avoidable mistake." On the contrary it is an inherent trait of a party which must submit to compromise with the system under which it lives. If Farmer-Labor principles are to be written into statutes, the immediate business of the party must become the winning of elections. The candidates, as in the case of the winning candidates after 1930, promptly assumed control over the party. Organizers, speakers, ideologists, theoreticians of the cooperative commonwealth who had built the Association deferred now, of necessity, to the new "tops," the actual office holders. In a crisis even the "purest" of the rank and file deferred as well. In a thousand ways the transfer of power was exemplified. If a ward club of the Association objected to a defection from campaign promises or Farmer-Labor principles, and threatened to bolt, the "tops" held after all an indispensable whip of power: "Your criticisms are a tacit support to reaction. If you don't vote for Candidate Smith the Republicans will win." To a Farmer-Laborite nothing further need be said. There is a saying in Minnesota that the "pure Farmer-Laborite is the man who tells you in private that Olson should be shot and Shipstead hung and then goes out and works like the devil to elect them both."

"The Association should control the candidate and not the candidate the Association," insist the most active and conscientious of the membership. "We shall see that it does." The problem of control over office holders, however, is one that has baffled the Social-Democrats of Europe and every reformist party since the invention of the ballot.

Summarizing this brief résumé: the primary business of a Farmer-Labor party is the capture of office, which explains both its nature and its limitations. In this the Farmer-Labor party of Minnesota or any Farmer-Labor party which might be created on a national scale in the United States would not differ basically from all the labor or reformist parties of Europe. Accordingly, it can hardly, in the author's opinion, be expected to establish either Communism or even the co-operative commonwealth, which presuppose a basic change in the rules of the game. Significantly, however, it has a dual nature and its base in the rank and file movement of the farmers and workers not only encourages and strengthens these organizations themselves, but also makes the party subject to their pressure. Its dual character—with a left foot in the proletariat and a right foot in politics—is a characteristic, not accidental but basic, and is destined to play a leading role in the new and violent phase of the city's history to which we now turn.

CHAPTER VI

1934: CITY OF TENSION

"CITY welcomes New Year with gayest, most carefree celebration in years," ran a Minneapolis headline on the first day of the year 1934. Minneapolis entered her year of greatest tension and of civil war a city of substantial optimists. In the dark winters of 1932 and 1933, the gloomiest tales of bankruptcies and even of "impending anarchy" had swept the drawing rooms of the empire builders. One family, when gold fled the country and banks failed throughout the land, had gone abroad to await the collapse of the American economic system. That family was now back home enjoying the "normal recovery" which had actually begun. The depression had not hit Minneapolis manufacturers, it was said, as severely as it had a dozen other Middle Western cities. This was true. And now the increasing use of black ink over red in year-end balance sheets produced a definitely exhilarating effect. There were other reasons for optimism. Minneapolis had weathered the storm of the depression; but what's more, she had weathered four years of the Farmer-Labor party which some of her citizens feared even more than the world crisis. Big business still feared it but had learned nonetheless successful tactics of self-protection. Most encouraging of all, the New Deal and its "crackpots" had operated for nearly a year, Capitalism had survived, and Minneapolis business in particular had enjoyed rather more of its benefits in the form of subsidies, and less of its "costs in labor unrest" than most cities. For the long future of the empire and the prosperity of its twin capitals there was more to hope than to fear.

As early as Thanksgiving Day, 1933, the new note of optimism could be detected, though it was unsteady and still mirrored the long "winter of discontent."

"Thanksgiving brings new courage to many in the city," editorialized a Minneapolis newspaper. "Of things worthy of a devout pause," the writer continues, "Minneapolis found many, turkeys for example, an increasing number of jobs and a public spirit quickening to the thought that some of these things really ought to go, *on occasion, to nearly all* [italics mine] of the world's citizens. Perhaps the most thankful of all were the sixty-one hundred men and women who have been assigned in the last few days to something they haven't had for a long time—jobs—and the sixty-one hundred more who will join them the day after Thanksgiving."

By the New Year, sturdier optimists mobilized reasons and dollars as the preface to a new day. After an evening of cheerful New Year's Eve parties in the big houses on Lowry Hill and the bigger ones near Lake Minnetonka and hilarious celebration in the city's cafes, the Minneapolis press martialed a substantial argument for all the city's gaiety and quoted "everybody" on the upturn.

". . . employment has increased twenty per cent in the past four months . . . post-office receipts better . . . farm prices higher . . . Christmas shopping up twenty per cent. . . . While Minneapolis and its trade territory have not measured any tremendous *strides in the march toward old time prosperity* [italics mine], conditions are definitely, unmistakably better than a few years ago."

It is a comment on the mutability of human opinion that a year and a half before the leaders of Minneapolis' business were to denounce with unanimity the New Deal, they led a pæan of praise in 1934 for the government's spending program. According to the Minneapolis *Tribune* (January 8), "Leaders in business and industry in Minneapolis joined Sunday in an enthusiastic belief that the inflow of $626,753,343 (!) of Federal funds into the Northwest in 1933 to '34 has had a definite effect already *in starting the territory on its way back to old time prosperity*" [italics mine]. ". . . the new crop of money, nearly double the entire farm income of the four states in 1932, will benefit the people of both towns and cities."

Robert F. Pack, president of Northern States Power, praising the government's program, said, "Its results are certain to be beneficial on a really impressive scale and . . . will give the Northwest a very definite start on its way back to sound business and farm conditions." Mr. Owen, president of the Minneapolis Chamber of Commerce, and a circle of other "leaders of business" echoed his enthusiasm. Horace Klein, copublisher of *The Farmer* and *The Farmer's Wife* told one thousand members of the Minneapolis Implement Dealers Association, "Uncle Sam has plenty of money and wants to play poker. We all have good cards, let's play the game with him."

A January 12 editorial buoyantly asserted, "The C.W.A. has had many critics but few so hide-bound that they cannot admire the speed and precision with which the hastily conceived relief undertaking is being carried out. . . . Mr. Roosevelt's program, in short, is working out exactly as he indicated it would."

Of all the enthusiasts for the government's spending program, Mr. A. W. Strong, Republican and leading spirit in the conservative Citizens' Alliance, who was to play a leading though losing role in the approaching summer of civil war, alone inserted a note of mild skepticism, allowing that the "benefits" from it all would be "at least temporary."

But if there was not a dissenting voice in Minneapolis on Mr. Roosevelt's spending program, business with a sounder and more sensitive class instinct had scented "danger" in the labor provisions of the NRA. "Although the effects of the NRA have been good," said President MacFarlane of the Manufacturers' Association of Minneapolis, "industrial unrest . . . has been a disturbing and expensive experience." And with refreshing ingenuousness Mr. Charles L. Pillsbury, executive of Munsingwear, unwittingly laid his finger on one of the causes of civil war in Minneapolis four months before it happened, by saying that collective bargaining is all right, but "labor leaders have interpreted it to mean that collective bargaining can come only through belonging to a union." This was to be the interpretation which not only Minneapolis labor leaders but tens of thousands of underpaid workers were to give to those provisions in the two years to follow. From this Mr. Pillsbury concluded that the NRA contained "real dynamite."

Except for these occasional doubts, however, the city's outward life was bustling and optimistic. "Color was the keynote in recent fashion showings of clothes for the South" to which many substantial citizens, after issuing their statements of optimism for the New Year, repaired to escape a freezing Minnesota January. In Minneapolis, itself, the issue which competed in discussion with government spending was the new liquor law, a vital matter after an age of drought and prohibition. The new temper of confidence made itself felt variously. On January 10, "Horseback riders at the Pastime Arena turned back the clock Wednesday night and made merry. . . . Sixty-five riders in costume went through a series of maneuvers before an audience that filled the huge arena." But perhaps the subtlest and surest sign of renewed faith in life was the disappearance of "depression stories" in social circles. In 1932 it was fashionable to repeat anecdotes of "jumping suicides," and to boast of poverty. In 1934 it was not. On the whole the members of the Citizen's Alliance and other business men felt more confident in the restoration of a Golden Age to the empire than they had since the fall of 1929.

There was one dramatic eruption out of the historic past in the early weeks of 1934 which disturbed the civic pride of Minneapolis citizens, if not their economic optimism. That was the sudden blazoning of the Twin Cities "as the crime center of the nation." St. Paul became known to the outside world as the home of a vast kidnaping ring. This episode deserves a word of comment.

It is inevitable, I suppose, that in America under our loose social economy a second and third generation of men should arise inferior in constructive vision, with less economic good luck, but with equal passion for quick wealth to that of the first predatory giants of the nineteenth century. Not endowed with a progressive role in history, they nonetheless shared with the earlier looters of the country a sound belief that force, bribery, and theft, if they were ingeniously applied, would yield results. They differed from the empire builders in relying on these methods without legal coverage or without admixtures of more constructive elements. These men were, of course, the American gangsters. Some immigrants, some native-born Americans, the types in St. Paul and elsewhere possessed a determination not to be caught as "suckers" like the millions of rank-and-file empire builders.

Significantly, for a generation or more, they had operated with immunity in the city of St. Paul. In return for police protection within the city, they confined their looting to outside jobs. The first citizens of that city, the actual inheritors of the empire, displaying indifference if not actually denying their existence, were content to have them plunder its surrounding territory providing they left the capital and its inheritance intact. In 1934 this tradition of a pact between the underworld and the authorities which had kept crime out of St. Paul for a generation snapped—like so many others in that year of tension. The gangsters turned on their own hideout.

The nation knew of the broken pact only when Mr. William Hamm of St. Paul was kidnaped. Soon it was learned that a nationally known railway executive and the president of a St. Paul bank were "next on the list." The United States Department of Justice hastily rushed investigators to St. Paul. On January 19, Edward Bremer of St. Paul, brewery magnate, was held by kidnapers and the newspapers carried an advertisement that the ransom money was ready for the kidnapers. On February 16, Attorney General Cummings "took an interest in the Twin Cities." The press reported, "The Twin Cities, Thursday night, found themselves thrust into the national spotlight as 'breeding grounds for criminals' and as 'the two cities in the country that really needed cleaning up.' "

For the first time in a generation scions of the empire builders in St. Paul, under the ægis of a crusading editor and with a host of G-men, opened a heavy drive on the underworld. Kidnaping was too much! In the meantime Minneapolis resented her share of "unfavorable publicity" and declared it wasn't her fault if the city across the river offered hospitality to the underworld.

For a time these scandalous items competed in public discussion with government spending and the new liquor law, but the business community concluded in the end, and correctly, that they were no cause for losing faith in the empire.

Several important items, however, had been left out of their analsyis of the city's economy by the New Year's optimists. The first was the aftermath of the world depression on business, and on the living standards and mood of the rank and file. In 1932, eighty-six per cent of the manufacturing plants in Minneapolis were operating at a loss. In the same year cost of living in the Twin Cities had dropped twenty per cent but pay rolls had gone down thirty-five. By February, 1933, flour production and meat packing had dropped to sixty-five per cent of normal, although for the country as a whole food production had fallen but ten per cent. Minnesota's mining index reached ten per cent of normal in May, 1932, and twenty per cent of normal in March, 1933. The building index touched twelve per cent in March, 1932. By the spring of 1934 unemployed and dependents constituted almost a third of the population of Minneapolis and Hennepin County.

A socially minded scion of the timber kings once told me he thought that Minneapolis' destiny was to become the "greatest peasant capital in the world." His words imply both a rural and an urban decline which, I think, is unwarranted by the facts; but however that may be, it is certain many Minnesota farmers touched or dipped below the "peasant level" in the depression years and their losses affected sharply the economy of the Twin Cities. Total farm income from 1924 to 1929 averaged about $370,000,000, but in 1932 it had dropped to $160,000,000. But net cash income fell much faster than gross. Unable to pare down the irreducible minimum of taxes and interest, net income fell from an average of $177,000,000 (1924 to 1929) to $11,000,000 in 1932. On a per farm basis, sixty dollars a year—on an average—for the farmer to spend on clothing, groceries, fuel, amusements, medical services, etc.

To the rank and file, these economic phenomena had been concretized tragically in the lives of individuals. Many thousands of families were on a subsistence dole. Of those still at work, there were textile workers supporting a family on six and seven dollars a week, skilled upholsterers receiving twenty-five cents an hour, warehouse men working for nine dollars a week. In the trucking industry toward the end of 1933, men supported families on twelve to eighteen dollars a week and put in from fifty-four to ninety hours a week for it. The influence of organized labor was at its nadir. Minneapolis had a national reputation among business men as being a one hundred per cent open-shop town. With the advent of the NRA, many workers who began to join trade unions lost their jobs.

Objectively considered, although the depression in Minneapolis was severe it was nevertheless not as disastrous to business nor as onerous on the working class as in scores of other American cities. But the second item that none of the New Year's optimists reckoned with was the city's decline *before* the depression. Beneath the surface of New Year's confidence and recovery were all the contradictions of a dissolving empire which we have drawn together in a preceding chapter. Without the depression Minneapolis would have perhaps muddled on for another ten years, her problems mollified by amelioratives and sedatives and her contradictions irritating to her vitals but invisible to the world. The depression rapidly ripened these historic difficulties in a space of three years for an explosive dénouement in the spring of 1934.

In 1930 the Farmer-Labor party, as we have seen, had won political power—of a sort. For any challenge to the business interests of the city this was a point of vantage on which the rank and file counted heavily and the empire owners in their year-end diagnosis largely ignored. A rather startling contradiction in the arena of class forces existed in Minneapolis between the years 1930 and 1934. Labor by joining hands with the farmer had won a measure of political power. But meantime labor's economic power lagged. The labor movement in Duluth and St. Paul was weak and Minneapolis had the reputation of being "the worst scab town in the Northwest." Who, then, had put the Farmer-Labor administration in power? The farmer, of course, the small business man, and organized labor (what there was of it)—but also *unorganized and potentially organizable* labor in the Twin Cities. Here was a contradiction which did not escape the leaders of the rank and file in the spring of 1934. Significantly, Governor Olson in a mass meeting held in April in the Shubert Theatre urged the truck drivers to "organize and fight for their demands." History does not record any other governor of a sovereign state committing a similar indiscretion.

How far the Farmer-Labor governor of a capitalist state was to be able to help his truck-driving constituents in the midst of open civil war is another question. One rank-and-file truck driver was to tell him to his face that "he was sitting in the middle" and that middle was a "picket fence." But that is part of a later story.

In the spring of 1934 the Citizens' Alliance of Minneapolis appeared to all observers to be one of the most powerful and efficiently organized employers' associations in the United States. Neither the business men, the workers, nor the "average citizen" had any doubt of it. It had long been criticized as reactionary and stupid but it had outlived its critics. In the primary matter of maintaining the open shop in Minneapolis it had a record of almost unbroken success. With a permanent and well-paid staff, a corps of undercover informers, and a membership of eight hundred business men, it had for nearly a generation successfully fought and broken every major strike in Minneapolis. Its former president, Mr. A. W. Strong, boasted to the author of this book that through its influence even the building trades in Minneapolis were for a time largely open shop. If in the days of prosperity and a relatively expanding economy the Alliance had successfully smashed union labor, it was likely to defend that conquest with even greater ardor in a time of shrunken markets and diminishing profit.

Although rank-and-file leaders knew the strength of their antagonist, here again the economics of the empire played a trick on the New Year's optimists. A successful challenge is never made against a ruling group while it is historically young, powerful, and progressive. One remembers the commonplace of history that feudalism was not overthrown until it had ceased to be either progressive or functional. The sons of the empire had neither the actual power nor that sublime confidence in an economic mission which had been theirs in the Golden Age. Consciousness of unassailable power for a generation with a slow decay of its substance left them not as persons but as an economic group both arrogant and a little stupid.

In the spring of 1934 two strikes in the trucking industry broke out in Minneapolis. As a distribution center dispensing her own and other cities' manufactures to an agricultural empire and receiving food products in return, transportation is a strategic key to the city's commercial life. And in the third decade of the twentieth century an important share of that transportation went to the motor truck. The strikes of truck drivers, which succeeded in paralyzing the whole commercial life of the city, were to constitute the first major challenge for a generation by the rank and file to the empire builders.

Private thoughts and acts of individuals are conditioned if not controlled by historic trends. But individuals also embody trends themselves and occasionally change them. As historians are fond of pointing out, the most trivial of personal episodes may have a place in "the history" of empire. One morning in the fall of 1933, Karl Skoglund, a coal driver, was told by his employer that unless he stopped talking about a union for the truck drivers of Minneapolis he would lose his job. Skoglund was the typical Scandinavian immigrant whose life we sketched briefly in a preceding chapter. As the reader knows, he had a strong predilection for unions and by 1933 had become both a labor organizer and a political revolutionist of record. In spite of the inference, Karl had not been too successful in organizing the truck drivers in Minneapolis. But——

"After that I said to myself, I got to put on my fighting clothes and organize a union here. If I don't, I lose my job in about a week. Even if you are a revolutionist and know what it's all

about, you're apt to put things off. Well, right now I couldn't,
or I'd be out on my ear."

With such immediate and personal impact, general economic
forces were driving other individuals into action in the trucking
industry of Minneapolis. The primary impulse arose from low
wages and long hours, but this impulse had been strengthened
by the advent of the NRA. Workers by law were declared to
be free "to join unions of their own choosing." The prehistory
of the first successful revolt of the city's rank and file can be
conveniently enlivened and filled in by turning to Bill Brown,
who drove a truck in this strategic industry between 1919 and
1933. "For some reason or other the teamsters' council gave
me the job of international organizer in 1933, so I decided to
work with a few men in the union who knew *how* to organize.
They were the Dunne boys, who were working in the coal yards
at the time, and Karl Skoglund. Conditions were lousy and
there was plenty of sentiment for the union. When the bosses
threw our demands into the waste basket, we went to the teamsters' council for permission to strike. I said, 'Hell, if we lose,
we're no worse off than we were. This is no union we've got
now anyway, but if we win it will be like a red flag to a bull.
The workers will come to us and we can organize the whole
damn industry.' So they gave us permission. I wrote Daniel
Tobin, international president of the union, for an O.K. Two
days after the strike was over, he wrote back that we couldn't
strike. *By that time we'd won and had a signed contract with
increased pay.*"

This somewhat personal monograph of the president of the
truck drivers' union touches on most of the organizational es-
sentials of the prerevolt period. The men to whom Brown turned
for organizational help, the Dunne brothers and Karl Skoglund, became the leaders and strategists for the rank and file

in the wider and more significant revolts that followed the first skirmish.

The coal strike itself, except for the briefest newspaper mention, was successfully ignored by the New Year's optimists. In their own best interests this was a mistake. They should have studied its leadership, its method, its final objectives, and above all its "militancy." For in microcosm, it embodied all the elements which in the civil war of July no one in the Northwest found it impossible to ignore. First of all, preparation had been surprisingly detailed and painstaking. A map of the coal yards of Minneapolis was prepared, and mimeographed instructions were issued to picket captains *before* the strike. Within three hours sixty-five coal yards out of sixty-seven, covering an area of ten square miles, were closed up "as tight as a bull's eye in fly time." This had been Skoglund's and Dunne's work, but it was the rank and file coal heaver who thought up the original tactic which won the strike itself. That was the militant use of "cruising picket squads," a tactic which in later years came to be copied in labor struggles throughout the United States.

To the five or six factors touched on in this chapter which pointed toward a rank-and-file revolt and offered a basis for its success in the spring of 1934 and which were omitted in the diagnoses of New Year's Day, there should be added another: the type of leadership which was brought to the approaching civil war. Several of the union leaders were members of the Communist League of America (Trotskyists). If no attempt was made, during the general truck drivers strike which followed, to establish a "soviet in Minneapolis" as the employers charged, certain definite traits characterized the strikes—beginning with the successful coal skirmish—which can be laid to the revolutionary training of the leaders:

   1. Militant picketing—termed by the employers "lawlessness."

2. Skepticism in all negotiations—based on a frankly work-ing-class point of view—of the good intentions of the employers, the police, or the government.

3. Infinitely painstaking preparedness for any action under-taken and speedy audacity in its execution. This, as much as any other factor, irritated the Minneapolis employer. Nearly any business man will tolerate a revolutionary—popular tradition to the contrary—if he is impractical and Utopian. The quality that was to render the union's leadership intolerable to the truck owners was its efficiency.

4. And lastly, the ability to distinguish between a city-wide strike and a revolution. It turned out that it was the employers and not the union leadership who were constantly confusing these two distinct social phenomena.

Bill Brown, the president of the truck drivers' union, had made a sound prediction in the spring of 1934. The success of the coal strike meant that workers flocked into the union by thousands. In the face of the blossoming of union buttons on the overalls of truck drivers—three thousand by April—the rep-resentatives of the empire builders, inside the trucking industry and out, held a strategy meeting at the West Hotel. It was the first of its kind since their decisive victory in the teamsters' strike eighteen years before. The session was distinguished by buoyant confidence, a reliance on old-time Citizens' Alliance tactics, and a complete refusal to compromise with the union. A Citizens' Alliance representative stated that the 1916 drivers' strike had been smashed at a cost of twenty-five thousand dol-lars and had been well worth it. This present affair could be flattened out locally and with little expense. But to the employ-ers' disgust, when the owners met with the drivers' representa-tives to feel them out, the latter insisted on discussing three points only: Who did the employers represent; the demands of the union; what did the employers propose to do about them? The raising of the first question at a meeting designed to prove, if possible, that the union represented *nobody,* irritated the truck owners. The conferences—there were two in all —followed an old Minneapolis pattern and ceased.

At a mass meeting shortly after, the rank and file of the major industry of Minneapolis voted to strike unless their demands were met. With the possible exception of the half dozen strike leaders, no one in Minneapolis realized that this was to mean the first serious challenge in a generation to the status quo of the empire.

CHAPTER VII

THE FIRST CHALLENGE

ON the day before the strike of truck drivers paralyzed the life of the city, and eight days before a citizen army hastily recruited was to battle openly with pickets in the market place, life in Minneapolis exhibited its usual reassuring normality and bustle. Mr. Totten Heffelfinger, nephew of Yale's All-American guard, who was to declare before 2000 business men in a few days that a "mass movement" might be necessary to save the city, sat quietly at his desk studying prices on the grain exchange. Mr. Arthur Lyman, for many years attorney for the Citizens' Alliance, found himself considering an invitation to the council meeting of the Minnesota Diocese of the Episcopal Church. The meeting was to be held in Rochester in a few days. No one could have told Mr. Lyman in those quiet days that his last-minute decision to exchange the office of diocesan delegate for a deputy's badge was to cost him his life on a curbstone in the Minneapolis market. Of those closer to the dispute, Mr. Neil Cronin, chairman of the Regional Labor Board, entertained and expressed the highest hopes that "differences" in the trucking industry could be adjusted. Universally the newspapers exhibited optimism.

Even among workers, betting was prevalent that the deadline would pass without a strike. Shrewdly the employers had raised wages in key companies and for key workers' groups. It was a fair guess that the drivers who had been picked out for wage favors would be divided from those who had not. The Employers' Committee, who were principals to the dispute did not alarm themselves, and only attended meetings of the Regional Labor Board when they chose. Accused of this by the Labor Board itself, they denied it vigorously, and asserted that on the occasions of their absence they had been unable to assemble their members. Strike or no strike, they had no intention of recognizing the right of the union to speak for their employees, *or of granting any of its principal demands*. As Mr. Strong, founder of the Citizens' Alliance, said to me, "I can conceive of dealing with a conservative and responsible labor leader, but certainly *not with any of the A. F. of L. leaders* in Minneapolis, or with the leadership of Local 574 [the truck drivers' union]." Mr. Strong's remarks, reflecting the principles dominant among Minneapolis employers, indicated that a responsible labor leader might turn up in the next world but not in this one—or in Minneapolis. Among the workers, plenty knew there'd be a fight but few anticipated its bitterness or scope. A few persons, however, as they say in Minneapolis, "knew what the score was." For the most part they were on the union's organizational committee, and had taken part in the negotiations. They had in fact been "keeping score" for over a year. "We knew," one of the leaders said to me, "that the bosses would never recognize the union. Their record proved it. Nor would they grant the workers any concessions unless we forced them to do so. We prepared *at the very beginning* for a fight which we knew was inevitable." Here is one key at least to all the events of the summer of 1934 in the city of Minneapolis. At no point before or during the strike, as the record shows, did the union leaders "kid themselves," or miss the implication of their actions. At several points the employers did, at all points the government negotiators succumbed to this human weakness. Somewhat more personally Karl Skoglund said to me, "We discussed very carefully the May decision. Only by all the sections of the trucking industry *acting together* did we have a chance to win anything for any one of them. We knew very well that would tie up the city. And although what we were striking for was the right of collective bargaining guaranteed to us by law, we knew that if we failed the Citizens' Alliance would succeed in pinning prison sentences on all of us. It was a real decision." It was. Once made, there could be no turning back. And there was none.

Prestrike negotiations, like the diplomatic parleys on the brink of war, are conducted in part "to prevent the war" and in part to win allies for a potential battle. The public, a useful ally, leaned favorably to the employers' charge that "the sole issue in this strike is the closed shop." That issue, "like the domination of Wall Street," automatically wins applause from the public gallery. The employers were ahead. Then shortly before the strike, the union abruptly withdrew the closed shop and substituted the most modest demands, and the truck owner's diplomats lost their moral footing and never got it back. The union asked that the employers sign an agreement binding themselves to abide by the provisions of Section 7A of the NIRA. That was a hard one to beat. They asked for no discrimination because of union membership, and for seniority in layoffs and hiring. The Regional Labor Board promptly indicated its approval and the public saw no reason whatever for civil war in Minneapolis. But the employers refused to accede to these demands. From then on the diplomats of the coal heavers, the piano movers, etc., were ahead in the peace parleys.

On the eve of the strike, the Regional Labor Board issued a statement "for the information of the public," containing this sentence, "No conciliatory move of any kind whatsoever at any time was made by the employers—they even avoided meeting with the board on Friday and Saturday."

The employers returned a statement which beneath the studied language of industrial diplomacy indicated a temperature well over the boiling point. After elaborately and resentfully denying "avoidance" of the board, they repeated the modest demands listed above and stated that the union refused to discuss wages and hours, "until or unless the employers signed a contract . . . with Local 574." They added, ". . . we promptly notified your board that *such demand was improper* [italics mine] and would not be acceded to by the employers as there is no requirement of law that any employer enter into any written agreement of any kind or nature with any organization, whether a labor union or otherwise."

Stripped of diplomatic trappings to the hard bones of class interests, negotiations to date had meant simply this: the employers were against the smallest atom of union recognition, direct or indirect; the workers were for any kind of recognition, direct or indirect. Reason the same in both cases. A follows B. Any recognition, even signing an agreement to do what they were legally bound to do anyway—respect 7A, meant "economic demands" later. The employers' opposition to the union's most modest demands, to which neither the public or the Labor Board had the slightest objection, was not an abstract prejudice, as it appears in the diplomatic parleys. It was based on the coldest calculation from their own experience, that in the long run *any sort of union recognition* means higher wages, and "interference." Indeed, the employers deserve every respect as logicians if not as diplomats. The union's modest demands were likewise based on the coldest calculation that any sort of union recognition is a beginning, and that only union recognition is worth a damn in securing—in the long run—better working conditions and economic security.

Given the thesis that union recognition is bad, the employers' statements were sound, but their diplomatic White Papers were notably poor propaganda. They were far too honest. The "principle" they were fighting for was visible to the naked eye at a

hundred yards. Had the employers been better diplomats instead of honest antiunion employers they would have concentrated on "racketeering in the union," inconvenience to the
public, Communism, or some other theme which would have
distracted the public from the actual issues of the controversy.
Better advised, they did so in the next strike.

The inflexibility of the truck owners in these days of negotiation was underestimated by the Regional Labor Board. (And
by the governor and by the public.) Unlike the Citizens' Alliance, its members failed to associate original sin with organized
labor. They all hoped and expected a settlement. Only the union
leadership had no pacifist illusions, and on the evening of May
12, in a mass meeting at Eagles' Hall, upon their recommendation the truck drivers voted strike. The vote in Eagles' Hall
followed swiftly on the heels of the last joint meeting of the
Regional Labor Board which, a few hours earlier, had been
shattered to bits by the refusal of the employers to sign any
agreement whatever with the union.

In the next eleven days the strike ran the whole gamut of
class warfare in a sharp curve upward from steady picketing to
a virtual general strike and the threat of civil war. The first
three days found the city peaceful and paralyzed, picketing
efficiency about ninety-five per cent. The Minneapolis *Tribune*
listed the following "businesses hit by the strike": general and
department stores, groceries, bakeries; cleaners and laundries;
meat and provision houses; all building materials; all wholesale
houses, all factories; gas and oil companies, stations and attendants; breweries, truck, transfer, and warehouses; all common carriers. "Ice wagons, milk and coal companies, being
unionized, are excepted."

On the second day of the strike:

"With nearly 3000 picketeers blocking every entrance to the
city and massed about the gates of every large fleet owner, they

succeeded in halting most of the ordinary trucking movements. . . . In the central market [strategic concentration point for the union on account of lowest wages, and the practice of chiseling, admitted even by the Employers' Committee] the tie-up was particularly effective. No trucks were allowed to come in with farmers' loads of vegetables. . . . Newspaper deliveries Wednesday were made by police escort. . . . Large fleet owners were playing a waiting game."

After the strike the union leaders described these days as follows: "We had very little trouble in the first few days except from outside trucks coming into the city, and from the gasoline stations. There were many finks among the gas-station attendants, who after being persuaded to close down, would open up an hour or two later. We determined to see that they kept closed and on the second day sent out a hundred picket cars for the purpose."

Residents describe the sight of one angry group of pickets lassoing the station pump of a stubborn strikebreaker and hauling it bumping down the street. But except for clashes at gas stations there was little show of violence on either side.

The sheriff described the situation to me as follows: "They had the town tied up tight. Not a truck could move in Minneapolis." To the average citizen, "Minneapolis seemed like Sunday," and in a Sunday mood he was disposed, since the provision markets still had food to sell, not to get excited. Workers at factory windows stopped work to give the picket cars a cheer as they passed by. The farmers alone at this period were fighting mad as their loads of vegetables and produce were turned back by pickets at the city's gates. This story of the farmers' role in the truck strikes is highly significant and we will return to it again in this narrative.

There were two primary reasons for the strike's effectiveness in these days of peaceful paralysis of the city's life. The first was that several of the largest truck companies had deliberately ordered their trucks off the street—awaiting a more strategic moment for open battle. The second was the military precision of the strike machine. "If the preparations," writes the *Tribune* on May 16, "made by their union for handling it are any indication, the strike of the truck drivers in Minneapolis is going to be *a far reaching affair, covering all the city and all its business and industry.*" [italics mine]

The heart of the strike mechanism was the headquarters at 1900 Chicago Avenue. Here several hundred men from the cruising picket squads ate and slept and were dispatched with military precision to the "front." And here the picket strategy was literally mapped out and put into motion.

The "Strike Headquarters of General Drivers' Union Local 574"—emblazoned in foot high letters on a banner before the headquarters—was an old garage hired a few days before and remodeled to fit the strike machine. It served as barracks, commissary, hospital, auditorium, squad-car assembly and staff headquarters for the strike committee. The brain core of military operations was the dispatchers' room, formerly the front offices of the garage. Men stood all day at four telephones which poured forth information to them and registered calls for strike help from every corner of the city. Picket captains were under instruction to phone every ten minutes from a known point, such as a friendly cigar store in their picket district, or a bar, or a striker's home. "Truck attempting to move load of produce from Berman Fruit, under police convoy. Have only ten pickets, send help." Or, "Successfully turned back five trucks entering city at — Road North. Am returning Cars 42 and 46 to headquarters." The messages were in all cases written down by the man at the phone and passed to the dispatchers, V. R. Dunne and Farrell Dobbs. All disposition of pickets was in their hands, hourly decision on strike tactics theirs, all instructions to picket captains written by them. The actual mechanism for dispatching cruising cars to the front was as follows: a messenger took the selected car numbers from dispatchers to a man at a microphone; he called out, "Calling Cars Number 2, 7, and 9. Proceed!" The cars rapidly assembled their pickets from reserves of strikers in the building. Night or day, never less than 500 men hung around headquarters. A dispatcher's window opened from the garage office onto the runway before the main exit, and as the squad car passed the window, the picket captain received written and secret instructions from the dispatcher. None of the motors were started in the garage, to keep the building—which after all was a hospital and a dining room too —free of carbon monoxide. The pickets pushed their own squad car till it reached the street, when the switch was turned and the motor started. Picket captains alone received the written destination and instruction for the squad cars, and reported back to the dispatcher after each operation was over. This was a precaution against stool pigeons.

After three days police tapped the telephones and thereafter strike information came in and went out in code. Police radio instructions over the air "Arrest rioting strikers corner Seventh and Nicollet," etc., were in turn picked up on a low-wave-length radio at strike headquarters.

In addition to phone calls, the dispatchers depended for tactical information on a motorcycle squad of five who cruised the streets day and night, reporting trouble. They carried strict instructions to engage in no picket battles, themselves, with police, finks, or special deputies—no matter how hot or critical they looked—but immediately to request headquarters to send aid. Pickets guarded some fifty roads entering the city with instructions to turn all trucks not having union credentials back where they came from.

"Most strikes are lost," said one 574 leader to me, "because the strikers lose touch with the strike. They sit at home watching the food give out and reading newspapers telling them the strike is lost anyway. Lack of chow and the lies of the boss press finally drive them back to work. We never let these things happen in the truck drivers' strike."

Between four and five thousand persons ate at strike headquarters and slept in or near it for the strike's duration. Fourteen or fifteen hours of the day they were on the picket line, while at night they listened to the news of the strike, the status of negotiations, the bosses' latest move, etc., which were reported in detail over the microphone. It is hard to find a strike in which the two strike fundamentals, food and morale, were more carefully provided for by the leaders than in the truck strikes in Minneapolis. The main interior of the garage became an auditorium, with a platform erected for speakers and musicians. About two thousand men and women assembled nightly inside, and as high as twenty to twenty-five thousand in adjoining streets to listen to the loud speaker.

In an elongated near-extension were located a kitchen, eating counters, hospital, and auto-repair shop. The kitchen was the car-wash section of the garage, whitewashed now and with a dozen stoves and boilers and a sink in it. A crew of 120 women under the direction of two chefs from the cooks' and waiters' union worked in two twelve-hour shifts for eleven days. Food was served day or night. It was estimated that at the peak of the strike as many as ten thousand people, men, women, and children—most strikers brought their families—ate in strike headquarters in a single day.

The hospital—located in another wing of the garage—served the strike not only in the obvious sense of first aid to the wounded, but it played what might be called a military part in the class war. Anyone familiar with strikes knows the role that hospitals are called upon to play in breaking a strike. The

most militant and active strike leaders are those most often
attacked by the police and most often injured. Taken by am-
bulances to the city hospital, they are invariably held for police questioning and jailed till the strike is broken. To the employer this is a legitimate use of city institutions. To the striker
it is strikebreaking. In this fashion an ordinary strike loses the
pick of its fighting forces through a system of hospital incar-
ceration. But in the big truck drivers' strikes in Minneapolis
the loss was avoided. Of the hundreds of strikers' hospital cases
in the May strike only two went to a regular hospital—and one
escaped. The others were treated at strike headquarters, where
two physicians and three trained nurses sympathetic to the
strike were in constant attendance. Equipment included surgical instruments, and out of the scores of cases treated no case
of infection developed before or after the strike.

In addition to treatment of wounded pickets, it was equally
necessary to the strike's efficiency to keep the hundred odd
trucks and squad cars in repair. A machine shop at headquarters with fifteen auto mechanics looked after this job. As evidence of the strike's popularity, $15,000 in applications were re-
ceived in the first three days of the May strike. This sum and
more was spent in the eleven-day warfare. A donation of $2000
was made by the milk drivers' union to the strike and lesser
sums from other unions. Governor Olson contributed $500.
Food and gasoline consumed the major portion. It was a common charge of the Citizens' Alliance that the union's money
was squandered by the strike leaders in riotous living. In point
of fact none of the actual strike leaders—the Dunnes, Skoglund, Dobbs, etc.—were put on the union payroll until the conclusion of both strikes, and then at the going truck drivers'
wage of $26 a week.

Commenting on the building above described, the *Tribune*
remarks: "The strike headquarters . . . are everything but a fort

and might easily be converted into that should occasion come."
Occasion never did, but the union took heavy precautions
against raids by the police or vigilantes, which were daily threatened. One man was made captain of the guards, so to speak,
and maintained two to four guards on duty in shifts at each
door of headquarters. By him were designated other workers
who policed the interior of headquarters, watched for stool
pigeons, kept order, and broke up fights. Four watchmen kept
a day and night vigil on the roof of headquarters and were
equipped with tommy guns.

The city divided for and against the strike. For, some ninety-
five per cent of the workers, or sixty-five per cent of the city's
population; vaguely sympathetic, neutral or against, the other
thirty-five per cent. In another day or two, thirty-five thousand
building-trades workers were to declare a strike in sympathy
with the truck drivers. Ten thousand street-car operators considered a joint strike. On the second day all the taxi drivers in
Minneapolis walked out in sympathy. And in another week,
the Central Labor Union endorsed the strike. The majority of
Minneapolis employers, possibly two-thirds, supported wholeheartedly the diehard stand of the Citizens' Alliance; a minority,
while against the strike, were likewise against the "inflexible
and unreasonable" stand of the Alliance toward the issues. The
majority of the farmers were against the strike—though not all.
The Farm Holiday Association made substantial contributions
to the union's commissary.

The other side of the controversy likewise had its strike headquarters; in fact, in a few days, it was to parallel 1900 Chicago
Avenue, with its own barracks and commissary and its own
staff headquarters for a "citizens' army." At first, however, a
suite of rooms in the Radisson Hotel sufficed the Employers'
Committee as headquarters. One of the active strategists in
this other strike headquarters described his activities as follows:

"We worked night and day. I'd sometimes sleep on a cush-
ion in the office. There was the whole question of publicity
statements for the press, full-page advertisements to be written telling the truth about the strike. Then all day long business men would phone us, or rush in desperately for advice—
a new problem for this factory or for that truck owner. The
matter of keeping in touch with our membership [the members
of the Citizens' Alliance] telling them what to do in this or
that emergency"—*there were many*. "And the negotiations—
with the governor, with the federal mediators, with the strikers,
the preparation of briefs, the conferences with our own lawyers.
In fact, for a time, the Employers' Committee sat day and night
in almost continuous session." It was war, all right—between
two economic classes, and with neither side offering the public
much in the way of disguise.

While the two headquarters operated, each in its own way,
negotiations continued—and came to nothing. Toward the end
of the era of peaceful paralysis, Governor Olson summarized
the stalemate in a published statement to the employers:

"The Union agreed this morning to withdraw its demand
for a direct contract. By your letter you have refused to agree
to the creation of a board of arbitration. It is not for me to pass
judgment upon your action, but I confess I am grievously dis-
appointed because of your refusal.

". . . It seems inconsistent to me for you to state in one sentence that you will agree to bargain collectively with your employees [which the employers had done through professing adherence to Section 7A] and in the following sentence to state
that you refuse to sign a written agreement with the Union. One
who is willing to make a bargain is usually willing to bind it
by written contract."

He thereupon threatens the calling of the National Guard
if an agreement is not reached:

"If that becomes necessary, the military department will take complete charge of the distribution of commodities, which the citizens of Minneapolis desire to purchase; it will commandeer such equipment and conscript such manpower as is necessary to bring about that distribution and maintain law and order. If these steps do not accomplish the end desired, further steps, consistent with military occupation of the city will be taken. ... In view of the public interest involved, I hope you will see fit to renew your negotiations with the strikers and reach an agreement over Sunday."

An ultimatum—and as the governor's statement would indicate, the temperature of all parties (including the governor) was rising. Indeed, on the fourth and fifth day the strike entered a new and ominous phase. "The city's food supply," writes the *Tribune,* "began to feel the pinch of the strike ... a general shut down of bakeries is estimated to be only a day away. In groceries similar conditions existed. ... The market gardeners have organized against the strike." Having failed to establish their case with the Regional Labor Board, or the governor, the Employers' Committee nonetheless sensed a shift of public sentiment to them with the drying up of the food supply. A "Citizens' Committee of Twenty-five," named at a mass meeting of business men, was entrusted with seeing "that the city's commercial transportation system [was] not indefinitely paralyzed by the strike, and to lay plans to move trucks through the picket lines if necessary." The Committee of Twenty-five promised the bakeries heavy convoys of special police, and instructed them to show their public spirit and move food. The bakers took a look at the picket lines and left their trucks in storage. The employers' strategy committee went into secret session. The moment had come for an offensive. With the governor and the Regional Labor Board pressing hard for settlement, with losses in business volume mounting into millions, with the city "faced

by starvation," a settlement would have to come soon, or it
would be the union's victory. But whereas in the first days of
the strike, public sympathy had been with the union, it was
now veering against them. The average citizen, whatever the
merits in a labor dispute, does not stand by and see bread taken
out of his mouth without protest. The "correlation of forces,"
as the military experts say, had changed. The union knew it;
they also knew that the food supply was not as low as adver-
tised. And they knew also that if the bakery trucks moved,
and the market gardeners, on their heels, piano trucks, factory
trucks, taxicabs, and everything else would move too. So they
stuck to their picket lines. At the meetings of business men
and other more neutral citizens as well, speeches began to be
made about "Communists capturing our streets. . . . Minneapolis brought to its knees by a handful of agitators," etc. The
truck owners of the Citizens' Alliance joyfully joined with their
new allies in patriotic denunciations of the "Red Dictators"
who are out to "starve our city into submission."

In secret session, however, they became more concrete. They
proposed to move a *Tribune* paper truck as a decoy to attract
pickets, falling upon them with a heavy reserve of armed guards
and police held at first in ambush. Once in action the guards
and police could beat the pickets into a pulp at their leisure.
To execute such a plan was not easy. The strike machine at
1900 Chicago Avenue refused to allow pickets to expose themselves to armed guards without the shield of numbers. They
had actually withdrawn picketing from the *Tribune* alley, suspecting a trap. To carry out the plan, treachery was required
inside the union. A stool was accordingly sent in by the Minneapolis police, and the plan carried off with success. Two or
three truck loads of pickets, including women as well as men,
under instructions from the stool pigeon were dispatched to the
alley near the *Tribune's* office. They were there surrounded and

roundly slugged by the Minneapolis police force and by special guards. It was the first serious defeat suffered by the union. On the same day the *Tribune* appeared with the following headline:

500 Additional Police
Trucks Try Defying Pickets
Convoys To Be Protected

The offensive had begun.

The story of the *"Tribune* Alley Plot" from the union's viewpoint was given me by Grant Dunne, strike leader and present in headquarters when the picket cars were dispatched by the police stool pigeon:

"A man came to us recommended as an active worker in one of the Farmer-Labor wards, who wanted to help the strike all he could. We took him in and he worked hard at all kinds of jobs. I used to watch him and think him one of our best men. He was there twenty hours a day, and always busy. Somehow he got onto the mike one night for announcing cars. And I heard him stop the speaking program and announce, 'Calling three cars'—he gave the numbers—then he said, 'This is a little job we have to do tonight, and some of you women pile in there with the men.' There were always a lot of women around and looking for a little excitement; they got in. Then somehow, he or an accomplice got over to the dispatcher's window and gave the picket captain instructions to go to the *Tribune* alley. Within ten minutes we got word that the three cars had been blocked into the alley and both the men and women unmercifully beaten with saps and night sticks. In another five minutes, the first car of the women showed up back at headquarters. Some of the women were unconscious."

From this point the narrative can be taken up by Skoglund, who was present when all the wounded arrived, and remained with them through most of the night.

"I remember the night. They brought the women in, and the other pickets from the *Tribune* Alley, and laid them down in rows in strike headquarters. All the women were mutilated and covered with blood, two or three with broken legs; several stayed unconscious for hours. Saps and night clubs had been used on both the men and women. When the strikers saw them lying round with the nurses working over them, they got hold of clubs and swore they'd go down and wipe up the police and deputies. We told them no, the Alley was a trap. 'We'll prepare for a real battle, and we'll pick our own battleground next time.' That night, all next day, and the next night, fellows began to collect clubs. They'd gone unarmed before that. Now they got sticks, hose, and pipe. You'd see men all over headquarters making saps and padding their caps for a battle. One picket would crack another over the head and say, 'Does it hurt?' And he'd say, 'Yuh, I can feel it. I'll put in some more.' That's the way it went, the fellows were wild there for a couple of days."

Dunne relates that the man who had urged the women into the picket cars appeared as usual the next morning. He was immediately seized for search and questioning. On him were found membership cards in half a dozen unions in Minneapolis, and in several Farmer-Labor clubs. "In his car we found a Burns detective badge and credentials. Begging for mercy, he confessed that he had worked for a time with the police lining up special deputies, and was afterward sent by the police as a stool to strike headquarters." *

* A full account of the use of espionage in this instance by the Minneapolis police and the Citizens' Alliance was given by Grant Dunne before an investigating Committee of the United States Senate. See: "Violations of Free Speech and Assembly and Interference with Rights of Labor," Hearings Before a Subcommittee of the Committee on Education and Labor, United States Senate, 74th Congress, Second Session. on S. Res. 266, p. 44.

Following the *Tribune* Alley episode and the open declaration of an offensive by the employers, the strike entered into a phase of virtual civil war. A mass meeting of two thousand business men had been held on the previous day in the Radisson Hotel, in which patriotic speeches were made in denunciation of the strike. Mr. C. C. Webber, who presided, declared that "the strikers are run by a handful of agitators, local and imported," and that "our job is to see that we are not dictated to by a mere handful." The merits of the dispute were not discussed. Totten Heffelfinger declared that a "mass movement of citizens" may be necessary to end the strike. "There may be five thousand men on strike in Minneapolis," he shouted, "but not five thousand or ten thousand, or twenty-five thousand people can bring the citizens of Minneapolis to their knees!" It was this mass meeting which named the Committee of Twenty-five mentioned above, charged with "laying plans to move trucks through the picket lines if necessary." The Committee met promptly and decided it was *necessary* to begin the movement of trucks on Saturday morning. At the same mass meeting the organization of a "citizens' army" was begun. A Major Harris declared that he had had a "good deal of experience in handling mobs," in similar situations, and it could easily be achieved "without any bloodshed whatever."

This army of peace was rapidly recruited in the next few days. It was composed of doctors, lawyers, business men, insurance salesmen, clerks, and a few workers. It included scions of some of the oldest families, and the "socially prominent" of Minneapolis. Still another "strike headquarters" was established to house the recruits of the new army, consisting of barracks, a hospital, and a commissary at 1328 Hennepin Avenue. "It is planned," the newspapers reported, "to keep the men there during the strike."

I have talked with a good many of the members of this "citizens' army" since the "war" was over. Some said, "We didn't know we were to be used to move trucks. We joined solely to preserve law and order." Innocent children! Others thought they were to be used to "convoy food trucks only." Others knew they were recruited to "smash the truck drivers' strike," and entered into their duties heartily. Confusion about the objects of a "war" is true of recruits in any army. The Employers' Committee, however, had no doubts as to the utility of their new allies. They would be used to convoy trucks, and when trucks moved, the strike could be smashed.

At 1900 Chicago Avenue, as well, great clarity existed as to the issues of the coming battle, for a battle was on the order of the day, which both sides candidly admitted. Dobbs, strike leader, expressed it this way, "Both sides were preparing for a battle and we decided we would pick the battleground ourselves, this time. We selected the market where there would be plenty of room."

The employers centered their attention on the market as well. That great area of warehouses and market stalls, whose whole existence depended on trucks, was the natural heart of the strike. On Saturday, members of the new army deputized as special police assisted in the convoy of market trucks. And on Saturday the police and the specials gave the strikers a second defeat. Pickets were still unarmed and some forty of them were severely beaten by the police. The strikers, however, retired in good order, carrying their wounded. The union was not yet prepared for the test. For several days, however, the allies of the trucking union had been growing. The whole labor movement of Minneapolis was now on the defensive. They sensed that a decisive defeat for the striking truck drivers meant the beginning of the end for organized labor in Minneapolis. "Five or ten delegations a day of twenty to thirty men from all kinds of unions showed up at headquarters and said: "Use us, this is our strike." The unemployed organizations came solidly behind the truck drivers, the building-trades union thirty-five thousand strong declared for them, and the Central Labor Union shortly after voted their endorsement of the strike. One striker described activities at headquarters on Sunday, May 20, as follows: "Nobody had carried any weapon or club in the first days of the strike. We went unarmed but we'd learned our lesson. All over headquarters you'd see guys making saps or sawing off lead pipe, with a hacksaw. The Clark Woodenware Company was manufacturing wooden saps for the deputized guards, but we highjacked the truck loads of clubs and brought them into headquarters. I remember one day an old man came into strike headquarters and asked if we thought the spokes of bannisters would be any good as clubs. We said sure, and by God in two hours he came in with an armful. He'd torn out both flights of stairs in his house and brought in the spokes."

CHAPTER VIII

BATTLE IN THE STREETS

TO the historian in retrospect, the "Battle of Deputies Run" as an episode in class warfare, appears clearly as a two-battle and not a one-day engagement, in spite of the fact the second battle was the more sensational and has received the widest fanfare of publicity. Monday's battle was the more interesting and well ordered as a strictly military engagement between two forces of armed men. Tuesday's battle, though it completed Monday's work and in effect ended the war except for minor engagements, was tactically speaking, both a rout and a riot.

A story of the Monday battle as seen from the viewpoint of a union leader follows:

"We built up our reserves in this way. At short time intervals during an entire day we sent fifteen or twenty pickets pulled in from all over the city into the Central Labor Union headquarters on Eighth Street. So that although nobody knew it, we had a detachment of six hundred men there, each armed with clubs, by Monday morning. Another nine hundred or so we held in reserve at strike headquarters. In the market itself, pickets without union buttons were placed in key positions. There remained scattered through the city, at their regular posts, only a skeleton picket line. The men in the market were in constant communication through motorcycles and telephone with headquarters. The special deputies [citizens' army] were gradually pushed by our pickets to one side and isolated from the cops. When that was accomplished the signal was given and the six hundred men poured out of Central Labor Union

113

headquarters. They marched in military formation, four abreast, each with their club, to the market. They kept on coming. When the socialites, the Alfred Lindleys and the rest who had expected a little picnic with a mad rabble, saw this bunch, they began to get some idea what the score was. Then we called on the pickets from strike headquarters who marched into the center of the market and encircled the police. They [the police] were put right in the center with no way out. At intervals we made sallies on them to separate a few. This kept up for a couple of hours, till finally they drew their guns. We had anticipated this would happen, and that then the pickets would be unable to fight them. You can't lick a gun with a club. The correlation of forces becomes a little unbalanced. So we picked out a striker, a big man and utterly fearless, and sent him in a truck with twenty-five pickets. He was instructed to drive right into the formation of cops and stop for nothing. We knew he'd do it. Down the street he came like a bat out of hell, with his horn honking and into the market arena. The cops held up their hands for him to stop, but he kept on; they gave way and he was in the middle of them. The pickets jumped out on the cops. We figured by intermixing with the cops in hand-to-hand fighting, they would not use their guns because they would have to shoot cops as well as strikers. Cops don't like to do that.

"Casualties for the day included for the strikers a broken collar bone, the cut-open skull of a picket who swung on a cop and hit a striker by mistake as the cop dodged, and a couple of broken ribs. On the other side, roughly thirty cops were taken to the hospital."

The Minneapolis *Star* gives the following account of the same episodes in Monday's battle:

"Two brief but heated clashes between police and a yelling throng . . . resulted in dispatch of nearly one thousand special officers [the citizens' army] and regular police to the area.

"Although the truck operators had announced they would move perishables, *no attempts were made* [italics mine] after the first outbreak near the Gamble Robinson Company, 301 Fifth Street, N."

This was the strikers' first offensive described above.

"Clubs, pipe, rock, and in one instance a knife were used by the crowd after police watched two truck loads of strikers enter the district and unload. A third truck drove up, bearing the sign, "All organized labor help spring the trap. Rid the city of rats!"

"The men jumped from the truck at Third Avenue, N. Some hundred police armed with sawed-off shotguns . . . attempted to halt the advancing group."

This is the honking truck of shock troops mentioned above.

"Advancing while approximately 1500 others turned up, the pickets dared the police to halt them. An arm rose, wielding a club. One policeman went down.

"Other police leaped into the battle, using their night sticks in retaliation. Rocks hurtled through the air. Half a dozen police dropped. One policeman was stabbed on the back of the neck with a knife. Strikers and others in the crowd fell to the ground. The crowd then retreated, taking with it its injured.

"Several of the injured police were taken into packing houses for emergency treatment, and later to various hospitals.

"Nearly an hour later, a second battle broke out at the corner of Sixth St. and Third Ave., N. One of the crowd tossed a club at Patrolman Wm. Mealey. Three policemen were lying on the ground when reserves pushed back the crowd. Several strikers were injured in this battle.

"The crowd cheered as the injured officers were loaded into an ambulance, and taken to General Hospital."

At no time did the bystanders—the bulk of whom were not strikers—show sympathy with the police or the deputies.

"The crowd grew. At the same time, additional special police and special deputy sheriffs, one wearing a football helmet, arrived. One of the special deputies was Alfred Lindley, Minneapolis sportsman and mountain climber. He was dressed in polo jodhpurs, and wore a polo hat. The crowd jeered Lindley constantly. One picket reached out a club and flicked Lindley's hat to the street.

"When reports of the disturbance reached Johannes, he ordered the night shift of regular officers back to duty. . . . Ass't Inspector Georgan ordered the deputies to form a line and marched them back to headquarters. . . . This move brought cheers from the crowd."

John Wall, the sheriff of Hennepin County, commented to me on these episodes. "It was a mistake," he said, "to use men without uniforms. You see," he explained, "the strikers regarded them the same as strikebreakers. But the chief of police was hollering for more men so we tried it."

The events of the next day were to amply justify the sheriff's analysis that the strikers regarded the deputized business men as "the same as strikebreakers," and to them somewhat more detestable than the police who at least were paid for it. In fairness it should be said that a considerable number of the "deputies" neither anticipated or relished the role they were called upon to play.

Despite the ferocity of Monday's battle, and the fact that the union had succeeded again in halting the movement of trucks, and that many police and special deputies, as well as strikers and bystanders, were seriously wounded, the employers saw no reason for either halting or modifying the character of their offensive. Negotiations for a settlement of the costly and bloody warfare continued after the battle for fourteen hours up to three o'clock the next morning. The Minneapolis-St. Paul Regional Labor Board summarizes laconically the results:

"Monday's battle was a military engagement"

". . . roughly thirty cops were taken to the hospital"

© *International News Photos*

The battle was reported over the radio like a football game to listeners
in all parts of Minnesota

© *International News Photos*

"The strikers regarded the deputized businessmen the same as
strikebreakers"—*Sheriff Wall*

"The employees demand that a written contract directly with the union be entered into. This the employers positively refuse to do."

Employers' strike headquarters in the West Hotel, in collaboration with the army which was still gaining recruits at 1327 Hennepin Avenue, still had its heart set on settlement "without the intervention of the union." They prepared to throw even greater forces into the market place. Chief of Police Johannes, despite Monday's slaughter, encouraged them. "It was a religion to Mike Johannes," remembered an officer of the Citizens' Alliance later, "to keep the streets of Minneapolis open."

On the day of the Battle of Deputies Run, the newspapers reported, "By late today there will be nearly 1700 police including special officers—an additional 500 are being sworn in for active duty." The strikers too were gaining recruits. Nearly every worker who could afford to be away from his job that day, and some who couldn't, planned to be on hand in the market. No one had announced a second battle, but twenty to thirty thousand people showed up in the market place on the morning of May 22.

As Dobbs, who is strategically minded, put it to me a little regretfully, "A planned battle was almost impossible on that day." The two sides were simply there in force, and fought it out. Men and women, boys and girls, crowded windows and stood on roofs above the armies waiting for it to begin. The news photographers were all ready, the movie men present, and a radio announcer for KSTP right in the middle of things to report the battle like a football game to listeners in all parts of Minnesota. The newspapers had reported that morning, "several large produce houses are . . . to move perishables into their warehouse; other trucking operations are resuming on a small scale." This was the issue of the battle: Will they move the trucks or won't they? And the crowd knew it. Will the strikers lick the cops and the business men or the business men and the cops lick the strikers? They were all waiting for the kick-off.

Finally it came—a trivial incident. Some petty merchant moving some crates of tomatoes—and a striker throws one of the crates through a window. The shattering of that glass was enough. The two sides joined battle, hand to hand, sap, blackjack, lead pipe, and night stick. It was actually over in less than an hour, with the police and the citizens' army back in their headquarters, or hiding out, or in hospitals, and the strikers in control not only of the streets of Minneapolis but for the moment "of the situation."

No succinct account of the battle was written or could be, least of all by the reporters with deadlines to meet who found it impossible to be in fifty places at once—or rather a hundred and fifty, for the battle with the deputies and police in retreat spread to all corners of the city. As late as ten o'clock that night the pickets continued to mop up, or to settle individual accounts in alleys and bars. Nevertheless the individual episodes were so lively and significant, and the individual emotions engendered so various and heated, that it is worth while recording a few from eye witnesses on both sides.

One of the leaders and organizers of the citizens' army records his side of it as follows: "There came news that there was going to be trouble in the market district, and Colonel Watson [the military leader of the special deputies] agreed to help with these men. We had long conferences beforehand with the sheriff and with the chief of police; everything was mapped out and organized. I didn't go to bed for three days at the time of the trouble. Well, on this day, we were ordered to be in the market place at four A.M. Everyone was divided into sections and it was agreed there would be a uniformed policeman with each section.

"Once in the market we were in touch with our headquarters constantly, with the sheriff and the chief of police. Our men, you understand, were not armed except with a small stick. Colonel Watson had refused to arm them, a good many having no military experience whatever. He was undoubtedly wise. Well, the police did not hold the crowd back. They simply held up their hands to their shoulders and allowed themselves to be pushed till the crowd entered the market. Then unexpectedly the police on duty were relieved and a new detail appeared, which as far as we can discover had no instructions whatever regarding our outfit. There were two or three trucks to be moved that day, to be convoyed. Well, after the trucks had been moved and had gone out, suddenly these strikers and bystanders rushed in, thousands of them, the police hung back, and you know the rest. The strikers were armed with lead pipes, baseball bats with barbed wire around them, and every other goddam thing. Arthur Lyman was killed and there were a great many serious injuries. Colonel Watson, Major Harrison, and a few others were in headquarters afterwards. And this crowd came around. They were ready to murder us. We armed ourselves with shotguns and side arms, and went out and stood there facing 'em. Well, when they saw the guns they stopped, and jeered at us. Finally we managed to push our way out. Another incident— a truck load of our men, citizens, were chased all the way from the market to our headquarters. We opened the door, drove the truck in, and shut the door. Our fellows were beaten up and bleeding and in a terrible condition.

"After the trouble in the market, I carried side-arms and arranged for special protection for my wife and children. I carried a gun in the office or anywhere I went for three months.

"When the battle was over we tried to keep the men together for a while, but they fell away. *They refused to be exposed to the slaughter when the police offered them absolutely no protec-*

tion. And besides there was no more need for them; the strike
was settled shortly after."

Here, on the other hand, is the battle as Dobbs saw it: "Some
twenty thousand people jammed the market area. The actual
spark which started the battle after several hours of waiting
was a crate of tomatoes thrown through a plate-glass window.
Instantly it became a free for all. Arthur Lyman was killed
while running to cover in a grocery store—between the curb
and the door. But it made no difference who it was provided
he had a deputy's badge or a club. Just to show you how dangerous it was to be a deputy, several of our fellows picked up
the clubs from fallen deputies, and were immediately knocked
cold by pickets. Our boys didn't look in a man's face—all they
saw was the club. Hours after the battle deputies were getting
theirs as far from the market as Nicollet and Twelfth Street."

Bill Brown, president of the truck drivers' union, gives his
experience as follows:

"I went down there with a couple of truck drivers who were
supposed to be my bodyguards, but they kept seeing fights they
wanted to get mixed up in, so that bodyguard stuff didn't work
very long. You know the market—well, imagine sixty thousand
people in there. [Dobbs reports twenty thousand, but Bill's
imagination is at least three times Dobb's in a fight.] People
upon the roofs, a radio announcer, guys with cameras. Everybody waiting for the kick-off. I happened to be quite near where
it started. Somebody brought a crate of eggs or tomatoes or
something out of a little store. And a little blond feller, I don't
know who he was, yelled, 'Hey, there's a fink here, starting
to move goods!' That was enough. They busted everything in
the place. Somebody took the crate and crowned him with it. I
can see him now, standing there with the crate around his neck
like a collar. Then the blond feller yelled: 'Come on, let's get
'em,' and the crowd swept forward against the deputies. A

picket captain yelled, 'Some of you guys get over on this side.' So they completely surrounded 'em. The harness bulls [police] fell back but the crowd went after them. In an hour there wasn't a cop to be seen on the streets of Minneapolis. About six o'clock I rode down Hennepin Avenue—about fifteen blocks from the market—there were no cops; our fellers were directing traffic."

Another striker: "I seen one cop under a car, and a picket poking underneath with a stick to get him to come out."

Another striker: "We brought a bushel basket of deputies' and cops' badges back to headquarters, and two polo helmets. One feller had a captain's badge he was pretty proud of."

Another striker: "Fourteen cops hid in the Armour cooler; they didn't come out for almost twelve hours."

The last tale may be apocryphal; I couldn't say, but my informant is usually reliable.

At all events, it is known when the pickets returned to headquarters they decided that the officers regularly stationed on adjoining streets to watch over the union should be dispersed. The officers were "chased away" by strikers, and police headquarters did not replace them for the duration of the strike.

The list of wounded for the Battle of Deputies Run was a long one, on both sides, and two deputies from the citizens' army were killed. One of them was Arthur Lyman, prominent Minneapolis citizen, attorney for sixteen years for the Citizens' Alliance and vice president of the American Ball Co.

Those personally involved on the side of the employers remember the battle with some bitterness. The average middle-class citizen, however, took it somewhat as a sporting event, and admits when questioned that he thinks "the damn fools who went out as deputies got what was coming to 'em."

At the battle's conclusion a truce of twenty-four hours was declared at the governor's request during which the employers agreed to move no trucks and the union consented to cease picketing—except for "a few strike pickets to see that the truce is really carried out."

Although the Battle of Deputies Run and the truce which ended it, as events proved, was the beginning of victory for the union, the employers' strategy committee continued to run a temperature of fighting fever at the West Hotel. Three ideas, as far as may be judged by events, dominated their councils: (1) Throw greater and greater cordons of police into the field, and move our trucks—at any cost. (2) Arrest and imprison the strike leaders after tricking them into the West Hotel by promise of negotiations. (3) Yield nothing to the governor of the state or the Regional Labor Board, when we do negotiate. They were strengthened in their intransigeance by their closest and most militant ally, Chief of Police Mike Johannes. In the July strike, a public board of investigation was to find Johannes guilty of ordering unprovoked attacks on pickets which cost the lives of two strikers and the wounding of forty-eight, an episode which won him the epithet from Minneapolis citizens of "Bloody Mike." In the May strike, even before the expiration of the governor's truce above mentioned, Johannes heartened the warlike Citizens' Alliance with the declaration, "Even if peace efforts fail, all normal trucking operations in Minneapolis will be resumed at nine P.M. today. . . . Any truck owner who wants to move his trucks can do so at nine P.M. with the full protection of the police department and the military forces. . . . I have asked the owners to move in fleets as much as possible to facilitate in protecting them." The strikers countered by announcing a resumption of picketing at nine P.M. "to halt any attempted truck movements."

Meantime a huge open-air mass meeting of strikers and sympathizers demonstrated the scope and depth of the strike's support. Representatives of labor for whom a lifetime of "safe and sane" leadership had demonstrated to everybody their opposition to Communist agitators pledged their full support to General Drivers 574. Cunningham, president of the State Federation of Labor; Urturbees, president of the Building Trades Council; Roy Weir, state representative and organizer for the Central Labor union, and Lieutenant Governor K. K. Solberg praised the courage and endorsed the justice of the strikers' cause before the victors of the Battle of Deputies Run.

The governor decided that a first-rate emergency existed and at the request of the mayor he ordered a mobilization of 3700 National Guardsmen, likewise requesting extension of the truce for another day. "The extension was agreed to after eleven men, representing ten unions including Local 574, appeared before the governor with a demand that the National Guard be demobilized."

For the forty-eight hour truce and a day or two after, the battle shifted from hand-to-hand encounters in the streets to endless parleys in the Nicollet Hotel. But before the parleys opened a significant episode illuminated the temper and purposes of the contending parties.

The union negotiators, "taking no chances with the bosses," proceeded to the peace conference with four picket cars in front of their leaders and four behind. The precautions were not without justification. Arriving, they found a hundred and fifty uniformed police, detectives, and guards flanking the peace palace. Walking up to Mr. Samuel Levy, attorney for the Citizens' Alliance, who was "out in front" to welcome them, the union representatives quietly delivered an ultimatum: "We refuse to meet with you or discuss any settlement, unless you take the cops off our neck." (That afternoon the papers reported this ultimatum verbatim in headlines.) The police and guards were withdrawn. It is significant that they had been sent to the hotel with warrants for the arrest of each of the union's negotiators. Had the latter been of a more trusting nature and entered the hotel without protest, this last-minute ruse would have succeeded, the strike might possibly have been broken and the union smashed. Long experience, however, had taught the leaders that employers do not consider "diplomatic immunity" part of the ethics of class warfare. Later, on occasion, the union negotiators felt it wise to bring picket guards with them into the peace parleys.

The negotiations, once started, were conducted with elaborate impersonality. "We never saw the bosses during the whole time," reports one union leader. "The employers were in one room, and we in another." The Regional Labor Board, together with a corps of lawyers for the truck owners and a Federal mediator, volunteered to be the diplomatic shuttle between combatants.

Strengthened in their will to victory by the militant statements of the chief of police, the employers yielded nothing in the first proposal they shuttled to their employees. "So we just sat there," explained a union leader present at the peace parleys, "and kept shooting their proposals back to the employers' room. But after a while they began to come better." Early in the game the employers agreed to reinstatement of all strikers, "if not found guilty of any crime." For the union negotiators this meant "the opportunity to frame and convict on false charges any man whom they wanted to get rid of in the union." It was a trick so far as the strikers were concerned which the Citizens' Alliance had used in the past to smash unions in Minneapolis. They refused. The employers yielded. The negotiations moved on into the night. Between shuttles Miles Dunne caught a nap with his head on the telephone book, and V. R. Dunne curled up under the conference table. Now and then a press photographer came in, wisecracked a bit, and took everyone's photograph.

Throughout, the nub and core of dispute was a matter of

fundamental principle and strategy—for both sides—known as "recognition of the inside workers." Why were these fighting words in the Nicollet Hotel, and worth another Battle of Deputies Run for either side? To the employers, the "banana men, the chicken pickers, and the pork picklers" who worked inside their warehouses were outside the jurisdiction of a truck union. But why did they care so much? They cared because their inclusion meant that a kind of industrial union would be set up in the trucking industry of Minneapolis. Without the inside workers, they would be dealing with a pure and simple craft union of truck drivers, weaker in bargaining power, easier to maneuver and smash. To the union the issue of "the inside worker" meant the same thing, a step toward industrial organization, a strong union. In addition they pointed out that the inside workers were exploited like the rest, that they were already in the union, and had struck with the others. The employers stood adamant. The union said, "All right, we give you an hour. Then the fight is on, truce or no truce." This ultimatum aroused both panic and audible furore among the mediators, whose job after all was peace at any price—or nearly so—at this stage. The two labor representatives of the Regional Labor Board, Mr. Miller and Mr. Alexander, trained in a more respectful and less militant school of negotiation, protested and poured all the oil which their organisms could exude and muster on the militants. None of the oil was absorbed, and a little later the union representatives walked out of the hotel and back to 1900 Chicago Avenue. An hour or so later, the governor's car and chauffeur arrived at strike headquarters with a message requesting resumption of negotiations. The strike leaders returned to the Nicollet Hotel in the governor's car.

The "inside worker" Gordian knot had now been rewritten into a paragraph called Section 8, almost as famous in Minneapolis' history as NRA's 7A. And the governor assured the union that it included all the men over whom the union claimed jurisdiction. Ambiguously worded, the employers thought it didn't. But the union, on the governor's word, agreed to sign. Still cherishing their interpretation, the employers signed too. The agreement won by the union guaranteed in addition a minimum wage, reinstatement, no discrimination, arbitration for future wage changes, seniority in hiring and layoff. But above all a recognition of the union—not direct, but via a Labor Board stipulation, and capable of development, later on, into a series of direct contracts with the employers' signatures thereon. It was a modest victory indeed, but it was a victory—and a beginning.

The union leaders walked out of the hotel to strike headquarters, where that evening a membership meeting ratified the settlement. That meeting of striking truck drivers was a boisterous and heated one. The rank and file of the union hotly debated the settlement. The leaders frankly presented the Labor Board stipulation as a compromise, "but on no fundamentals," and urged acceptance with all the force they could muster. Some of the crowd were for no compromise and back to the picket lines. Had the leadership been what the Citizens' Alliance had long been publicly protesting, "irresponsible agitators," bent on bloodshed and a Russian soviet in Minneapolis, they would have called for an insurrection, and certainly gotten one, or at least a continuation of the strike. Instead, desiring a trade union and not a revolution, recognizing the need for recoupment and consolidation of actual gains as a basis for future struggle, the leadership urged acceptance.

"There's no question," Bill Brown, president of the union, said to me, "that we could have taken over the city after the Battle of Deputies Run. We controlled it. All that would have been necessary 'to seize power' would have been to urge a few thousand strikers to capture the Court House. They would have done it." He smiled. "Yah, sure, the union might have made me soviet mayor, huh? and Skoglund over there commissar of police." He laughed. Then, "That's just what the Citizens' Alliance had been screaming for days that we wanted to do, make a Russian soviet in Minneapolis. But we happened to want a truck drivers' union in Minneapolis. And some of our leaders were revolutionists enough to tell the difference between a militant strike and a revolution."

The Communist party of Minneapolis, none of whose members were either in the leadership of the strike or members of the union, denounced the settlement violently as a sell-out to the Citizens' Alliance; maintained that the leaders could have had a general strike if they had wanted but had sold out to reaction. Throughout both strikes the Communist party violently attacked the union's leadership. The Communist party today still maintains that the union leadership was tactically wrong in not continuing the May strike till a better settlement could have been won. But the accusation that the leaders had "sold out" the union, and that they were followers of the most corrupt and reactionary racketeers in the labor movement, they regard now as a mistake. The party officially endorses the union as such today.

At the membership meeting which ratified the union's modest victory, and ended eleven days of the fiercest class warfare in the history of the Northwest, an officer of the Citizens' Alliance listened in. In an old slouch hat and a raincoat on the edge of the crowd, he followed with emotions which can only be guessed at the turbulent progress of the meeting. Later on he undertook to describe to me his impressions. "There were thousands and thousands of bums and hoodlums and Communists there. Agitators worked the crowd up to the highest pitch of mob fury. They shouted, sang, and yelled. It was really horrible. I felt like slipping away, getting out of Minneapolis onto a farm somewhere, and never coming back."

The "mob" however had different emotions. They felt that Minneapolis in time might be made a tolerable place in which to live. The next morning that portion of it which had been organized into Local 574 went back to work under the modest terms of its union contract.

CHAPTER IX

PERSONAL LIVES

I N reading the story of important events one assumes auto-matically that contemporaries were aware of them. As a rule, of course, the opposite is the case. Individuals pursue their own ends passionately with as much indifference to historic change as possible. Even the most dramatic and violent social upheavals permit a good deal.

I have selected a half dozen personal lives at random from the ranks of Minneapolis citizens, none of them protagonists of recent events, and in this chapter have written about the city through their eyes. Their personal lives I have put in the fore-ground as they do, keeping history on the sidelines, so to speak, showing where it touches their lives, how often it passes them by and how, on occasion, it absorbs them for its own purposes.*

On a July day cocktails were served on the porch of the Far-rand house in Wayzata. It was a semi-Colonial countryish house built to be livable and modern. A hedge and land enough to be isolated from the road without being an estate. Not a house like those of some of the empire builders around Minnetonka— with a gate-house, etc.—though the Farrands had inherited some of the empire themselves. A lot of people in Wayzata admired Bert Farrand. His father had been a corporation lawyer

---

* Although I believe the picture drawn is an accurate one of the inter-action of social forces and personal lives in the city of Minneapolis, the names and characters are fictional.

in St. Paul in the days of Jim Hill's empire, and Bert had done what few sons of leading families in St. Paul had ever done—moved to Minneapolis and gone into politics!

Janet, his wife, owed the fact that she had gone to Vassar where Bert met her (Bert was Yale) to her grandfather, who had accepted a piece of land in the Mesabi for a bad debt. When the Merritts discovered iron ore the bad debt had made a wealthy man out of him. Janet's beauty and her warm but practical personality she would have had anyway even without the Mesabi. That afternoon she had packed off her eldest son to camp just before the cocktail party. Bert arrived from the tennis court with his shirt off (the thermometer had been at ninety-five for four sets). Before changing, however, he made his guests a second round of cocktails. There was an amazing kitten turning somersaults on the porch in pursuit of a tennis racket among the guests, and the twins (aged six), who were serving cocktails stopped passing them in order to dance and scream. Conversation became gay and ridiculous. It was a very casual and civilized heightening of personal lives compounded of animal spirits with a dash of talk and liquor.

The notorious heat of Minnesota summers invades a July conversation. It is sometimes impossible to talk about anything else.

"Why don't you put in a pool, Bert?"

Janet remarks that a small diving pool can be installed for $775. Bert winces.

A guest says she "hates all pools!"—in fact any kind of water that isn't salt. She objects to there being no ocean in Minnesota.

Donald Carter—Yale, handsome, and flour-mill ancestry—thinks he might invent a way to saltify diving pools.

The lady guest says, "The idea is a gold mine."

So Donald develops it. "A bit of the Atlantic on your Wyoming ranch! Imagine the advertising possibilities—We guarantee that after-glow: Carter's ocean pools." Donald accepts a Martini dividend as he talks, and stands easily like a diver himself with the cocktail in his hand. He is young and tall with fine shoulders (crew at Yale), and there is as much balance and swing in his voice and ideas as in his body. The guests looking at him as he talks compare Donald with the other Carters. He is not as wild as one of them nor as conventional as another, and is perhaps the most disarming. Indeed, Donald Carter is a very healthily sane young man, sophisticated—without being too much so. Donald's father came to Minneapolis from New England, helping to make Minneapolis the flour-mill center of the world. Donald went *back* to New England to school. He went to Groton. The "construction of *ocean pools* for inland peoples" he describes with a fine mixture of fantasy and technology. After Yale, he attended Massachusetts Tech—and to this day, though reabsorbed into flour and the dynasty, he has a real passion for steam engines.

Across the porch Janet and Anne (Don's wife) are telling the Caldwells what a handsome job they did on the horse show this year. The Caldwells' annual horse show isn't a big all-city thing for the public. It's a comfortable private affair, élitish, but round a homemade track on their "farm" and for friends. As a matter of fact they have two horse shows a year. And to the one in the fall all the farmers round about are invited in. They ride their own farm horses and the Caldwells give them beer afterwards in the big barn. Jock says the German farmers in his neck of the woods are a fine thrifty lot and make good neighbors. What goes on at the Caldwell horse show is the nearest approach in Minnesota to Devonshire or Kent.

Anne Carter and Aline Caldwell talk horseflesh, and Donald throws in a kidding word now and then. He likes a good horse himself, and Polly and he have a stable of their own, but horses are far from a passion with him. Neither is the business of making flour in Minneapolis, nor the business of making money anyway, nor the business of being a Carter. His life lies by welcome chance and design as completely outside of history as possible, though the lives of his forebears were historical enough. He combines a socially sophisticated life which befits a Carter with a lively interest in engineering design and a real though not pressing urge to chuck the flour-mill industry. "I would like to run a hardware store in a small town. I think that would be fun." At the last Yale reunion, Don found a class-mate who had given up banking and was teaching mathematics in a boys' school. He admits he contemplated the man's even and mildly intellectual career with envy of a sort. The empire builders have bequeathed Donald Carter their most substantial gifts. But the real luxury they equipped him with—which I suspect he knows—is the ability to step largely outside of history itself and afford that disinterested delight in steam engines and a contemplation of the desirability of a hardware store or a pro-fessorship of mathematics.

Nobody meeting Donald or watching him swim would deny that he was "a fine type." But the same can be said of Jock Caldwell and equally of his wife. "We've been haying all day in the peat meadow, both of us—and I adored it," she says, laughing a little with her face alight. Aline looks ten years younger than she really is, with a beauty that is both healthy and glamorous—and somehow isn't rural. He is ruddy and jovial. They discuss the drought, the first crop of timothy which escaped it, the danger to the wheat. Bert kids them about their agrarianism. They go to bed at eight-thirty and rise at six. But for six months of the year they sojourn in London, Paris, and points European. Caldwell comes from a distinguished Twin City family. She had brains and beauty—which she still has—when he married her, but was "nobody."

"You two have the best lives of anybody in the world!" Janet bursts out.

Indeed it is hard to see how the historic tensions of modern Minnesota can possibly impinge on the Caldwells or shake their integrated health and vitality. Only at one point that summer, as far as their friends could see, was a momentary connection made between them and history. After the Caldwell horse show a half dozen guests ate a late dinner at the Woodhill Club. Bert mentioned Floyd Bjornsterne Olson, governor of Minnesota. Aline Caldwell said she had always wanted to meet him. The guests speculated on whether the governor would die of cancer at the Mayo clinic, or live to become the Farmer-Labor senator from Minnesota. "So far as I'm concerned, he can die," said Jock. "Why?" asked Aline, her lips parting. Jock's ruddy face got purple. "He stands for everything I'm against, doesn't he?" said Jock angrily. "Soak the rich—" supplied Janet. "Yes," said Caldwell, "and all the rest." "I didn't know you were rich, darling. Are you?" said Aline, smiling, and putting her hand on his arm. But Jock refused to laugh. The party died and broke up.

The next day was Sunday and a scorcher. The thermometer topped a hundred and four by a fraction. In the morning the Farrands gave a "sprinkler party," concentrating all the fountains from the wide lawns back of the house and in relays leading the house guests through them in bathing suits. It was a game that especially appealed to the twins. (Afterwards there were gin fizzes for adults.) In the afternoon it hadn't cooled off a bit and Bert suggested they go to the Platt's pool. Warren Platt, whose father was a utility tycoon in Jim Hills' day and onward, had built a French Chateau in 1929, ten minutes' ride from the Farrands in Wayzata. As an accessory to the Chateau he converted a fairish sized pond into a swimming pool by smoothly cementing the natural basin. The pool lay in the midst of lovely rolling country back of the chateau, and Warren Platt's good taste had omitted any artificial landscaping beyond the cement. Dripping and refreshed, Bert and guests entered the semicourtyard of the Chateau. It was an authentic graveled courtyard with the lofty walls of a real Chateau encircling it. In the heart of Minnesota it convincingly reminded you of Normandy. In fact, when you arrived suddenly from the little Minnesota town of Wayzata, it positively took your breath away. The Chauteau had twenty-seven rooms built of stone of an ancientish look, high Norman walls, and an authentic tower with a pointed Norman roof.

Warren Platt hospitably took everybody in the front door of the Chateau, laughing and offering everybody a drink. An air-cooling system conveniently accommodated Normandy to Minnesota and a modern bar close to the front door perfectly fitted the Middle Ages into Minneapolis.

Warren mixed the drinks himself. He was damn good at it and had had a couple himself before the Farrands barged in. A couple of other Minnesotans were also cooling off and warming up in the bar. Despite the medieval towers, contemporary Minneapolis history actively functioned in Warren's head, far more than in any of the other sons of the empire we met at the Farrands. With a grandfather who was a country banker, and a father who developed a fortune out of the empire, Warren had lost a large chunk of it in the crash. But with characteristic militancy he finished the Chateau anyway, and is now building back both his own fortune and Minnesota's. His intellectual curiosity as well as his conversation practically encompasses human knowledge. And his business interests are almost as wide. They embrace gas, power, the manufacture of airplanes, railroads, automobiles, rubber, and the commercial conversion of peat and lignite. There's a story in Minneapolis that one of his friends—as a gag—asked Warren if he knew anything about the thesaurus. Warren gave a fifteen minute description connecting the family of "thesaurii" with a certain prehistoric species. Then someone gave him a copy of Roget's *Thesaurus*.

Warren is proud in a perfectly self-respecting fashion of his pioneer grandfather, proud of pioneer Minneapolis, and entirely confident of its future. Liquor and relaxation make him rather more conscious of historical forces than otherwise.

"When I was a boy," he recalls, "I remember riding out in the country on my bicycle, stopping at a farm house, any farm house. A fine old German woman with gnarled fingers would give me a glass of milk and some doughnuts. Do you suppose that could happen to you today in Minnesota? No sir.

"But that's America to me. And there's enough of it left, too. When I was in the war over in France, I thought of those old German women with gnarled fingers back in Minnesota, and I said to myself we've got to win this war! This may sound silly to you but I mean it."

And he did. It is easy to smile at regional patriotism, but Warren has a deeply emotional feeling about Minnesota's past which comes to him naturally as the scion of an ingenious and successful empire builder. And he believes that if we can hang on to the ruggedness and the initiative which enabled his forefathers to develop the Northwest, and which gave Warren not only the Chateau but the impulse to help found the Northwest Research Institute and study the conversion of lignite into coal, Minnesota will fulfill her destiny.

Conversation at the bar touched on a lot of things, the movies, Bert Strong, the drought, and Spanish politics. Warren believes that anyone like himself, lucky enough to have pioneer blood, varied business interests, and a Chateau should use his best energies to defend Minneapolis but as a corollary expunge the abuses of Capitalism. Warren is conscious of history, almost self-conscious of it. The trouble is, he says, that Roosevelt and Olson were both destroyers of a fair start toward a reasonable Utopia. He is not a standpatter but an ameliorist. In fact, he uses that word to describe himself.

Somebody who came into the bar of the Chateau that afternoon mentioned General Drivers Local 574. Warren put it up to the truck drivers and the Minneapolis labor movement in general right there in Normandy. He said, "If labor will content itself *with a little less,* then Minneapolis can go on. After all, cost of living is cheaper here for the workingman. If labor insists on higher and higher wages, as the truck drivers are doing, then a lot of business men like myself will simply shut down our factories. We don't have to go on working—we'd prefer to, but most of us have a little farm, *or something,* we can get by with."

Bert asked Warren and Polly over to dinner in a day or two to continue the discussion, but Warren had invited a half dozen guests up to the farm in the lake country for a week of fishing.

History has never unexpectedly impinged on Mr. Canton or surprised him suddenly while pursuing his personal ends. It probably never will for Mr. Canton belongs to a race that has successfully lived their personal lives by compromising with history before it had a chance to compromise them. Mr. Canton is an Englishman by birth and instinct. And like the builders of the British Empire—as against the builders of the Minnesota empire—he has made a practice of taking history in his stride.

Apart from that it is difficult to isolate Mr. Canton's personal life because most of it is spent in making the history of a large Minnesota corporation of which he is president. But last summer Mr. Canton took a vacation in England, aptly combining his personal life with wider interests. First of all he talked to some utility bigwigs in London, reporting back to Minneapolis that England was fifty years ahead of America—in certain respects. He saw St. John Ervine's latest play in London, dropped into the shop of the most famous collector of antique silver in England, learned who had the new brains for the Labor party, went to Aldershot, found Lancashire textiles depressed, and had some talks with key people here and there on the fate of the Empire, including a Lord of the Admiralty. Chuckling, he tells a story of an army officer who said of Ethiopia, "If there had been anything there that England wanted she would have gotten it years ago."

Last summer isn't the only time Mr. Canton has left Minnesota and traveled about, discussed politics. Finding himself in a club of business men in New York on one occasion, he found them attacking imperialism in India and praising Gandhi. He got on his hind legs and made a speech, saying it was all very well to attack imperialism—he didn't like it himself—but, "Let's get practical for a moment." The next morning the business men got together and sent a cablegram to England, which said "Gandhi's wrong, England's right."

The rank-and-file revolt in Minneapolis, in so far as it affects his corporation, Mr. Canton believes he has taken in his stride. He says he makes a practice of talking with everybody who claims to represent his employees, whether A. F. of L. unions or intrashop groups. Mr. Canton posted a notice last year on his bulletin board saying that anybody had the right to join or refrain from joining a union. Mr. William Green, president of the American Federation of Labor, promptly gave him a clean bill of health.

However, Mr. Canton has a cherished plan which he prefers even to the labor philosophy of Mr. Green. It is this:

Assume an employer's wage bill is $500,000, his interest and dividend charges $500,000; wages are to be "fair" and agreed on, the returns to capital "agreed on," and not allowed to exceed a modest amount. "Then the concern earns, we'll say, $500,000 additional. Well, half of this is to go in profit-sharing to employees, half in dividends to stockholders." The employees all belong to a union confined strictly to the industry.

"Suppose the government started meddling or talking about government ownership—why, it would be to the advantage of the men to put it right up to the government and fight all that; they'd have a stake in the industry!"

Mr. Canton is convinced of liberalism with a religious intensity—a broad-minded, practical, British intensity! "You can assume a man is an animal, with nothing spiritual in him. In that case," he continues pointedly, "why not kill off all the unemployed, why bother with insurance, old-age pensions, economic betterment? [Mr. Canton, like England, bothers with these rational amelioratives.] But if you think he has something spiritual in him, then get around a table, and try for an understanding—without rancor or prejudice. That is the hope of civilization!"

The books, news, and liquor of England, as well as its practical liberalism, inhabit the Canton household. Mr. Canton and his family live in a large, rambling, but in no wise pretentious house on a quiet street in Minneapolis. There are ample bookshelves, and on the table a copy of the *Connoisseur,* and the English newspapers. Incidentally there is also a book on "Anarchy," by Emma Goldman, which is a presentation copy. On the fly leaf is the wish that the reading of the book will inspire Mr. Canton "to the ideal of Anarchy as it did the author." It hasn't. But somehow the book rounds the catholicity of Mr. Canton's tolerance.

A circular seat in an alcove around a fireplace is perhaps the most popular center of the house. Mrs. Canton wanted to turn it into a bar but Mr. Canton was opposed, suggesting that whiskey and soda can be served and enjoyed quite as readily without it.

Mr. Canton in person and practice brings some share of the infinite wisdom of compromise by which England has survived into the uncompromising atmosphere of Minneapolis. Naturally he disagrees flatly with Mr. Strong of the Citizens' Alliance, whom he describes as a very kindly man, except for his one obsession on the subject of unions. How much more *practical* for employer and employee alike if Mr. Canton's plan were to prevail over Mr. Strong's!

Mr. Canton and those like him are more liberal than the employers in the Citizens' Alliance—this is my personal opinion—because he is far more sure of himself than most of them. He has an instinctive and deep-seated belief in liberalism. And indeed for Mr. Canton behind it are generations of experiment proving to Englishmen that compromise rather than a head-on fight *will not alter the rule of those of education and ability—* like Mr. Canton—*but insure it.* The other employers in Minneapolis are not so sure.

Mr. Canton has been reading the life of Oliver Cromwell this summer. "He overthrew the autocratic rule of the king for Parliament, then he made himself autocrat *above Parliament.* Till, of course the people called a halt." (The people to whom power was finally restored in England were people like Mr. Canton.) "History moves in cycles, comes around to about the same place in the end." He predicts that Russia will one day be the greatest center of Capitalism and the United States of radicalism.

Ten years ago Ralph Rogers believed all rich people were terrible. Ralph was born in Faribault, Minnesota, and came to Minneapolis when he was fifteen. The self-respecting middle-class circle into which Ralph was born looked down upon, avoided, and under no circumstances ever contemplated marrying daughters of the idle rich. Ralph, after he had lived in Minneapolis, married Agnes. Not very idle and not *very* rich, but enough rich to enable them to buy a roomy house with a tennis court in the suburbs and not live in a duplex in Minneapolis.

It would be hard to find a "better fellow" in Minneapolis today or in any other city than Ralph Rogers. To do business with, for example, to work for or have work for you, to have for a husband or a father, to play tennis with or go fishing. When Ralph meets a stranger he believes he is as good a guy as he is, till he finds out. Ralph Rogers is as fine a type of the "average American" as Henry James or Sinclair Lewis ever wrote about. He knows it and is damn proud of it. By way of instinctive loyalty to Faribault he is a little snooty about the socialites of Minneapolis, of whom he knows a number, as well as of the truck-driving proletariat. The kind of a man he likes is Joe Pine, who built up an independent upholstery business out of nothing, and loathes the mail-order houses—as Ralph does.

The Rogers have five children—or is it six? Every year they go on a vacation at Lake Superior for about a week, and take all the children with them. There is usually some sort of hired man, wood chopper, trapper, or whatnot, to whom Agnes turns over the children. Then Ralph and Agnes go out alone fishing.

Ralph, with his brother, run a cozy little furniture business in North Minneapolis. As you might guess if you knew Ralph, he is really pretty lousy at keeping books, but there is a hidden canniness in him somewhere that enables him to be a pretty fair business man, and he is a marvelous salesman. Old Mr. Rogers was a good salesman too; he spent his life selling stoves and pli-bricko, the lining for furnaces. Neither Ralph nor his brother Al had any feeling for stoves and pli-bricko. They went into furniture—"because there is more romance in it," Ralph told me, selling it from a brief case of photographs for the large wholesale companies. Then they got a display room in a rather factoryish section of the town, and edged over into retail.

Sitting around one day after business hours he told a hardware man who agreed with him that the chain stores had gone about as far as they could. "If Roosevelt stays in, the whole force of the government will be out behind the little fellers."

Ralph has a brother-in-law who is running for the state legislature. One night at his home, some of his friends and his brother-in-law's constituents consumed a great deal of gin in the kitchen. They were good fellows and they swore loyalty to themselves, to the candidate, and to Ralph. Coming back into the parlor, where some of Agnes's friends were likewise having a drink, unexpectedly the conversation turned to the truck drivers' union and Communism. It was at the time that somebody had brought in Chicago thugs to beat up on the truck drivers' union. Ralph stood on his feet and told everybody what he thought of Communism:

"I've worked hard for what I've got. I've been a laboring man, myself. If any of those sons-of-bitches started taking it away from me, I'd fight like hell. These goddam 574 truck drivers have beat up plenty of people in this town. Why in hell should they squeal, now that they're getting it in the neck? That's what makes me sick."

Agnes agreed with Ralph, but said she thought the truck drivers were being misled, and that if someone explained to them the truth about 574 they would drop out and support people like her brother-in-law.

Ralph has plenty of animal spirits left when he gets through with selling furniture at the end of each day, and his friends universally like him. The guy he meets in the smoking car likes him too, his children like him, and his wife adores him as far as I can observe. Ralph likes them all, too. For the most part, through a fortunate combination of circumstances, he lives outside of history in the city of Minneapolis. But occasionally history and circumstance sock him, and when it does he reacts automatically—like most of his countrymen—to the deeper instincts which the history of the middle class in America have implanted in him. (If this were pointed out to Ralph he would be proud of it.)

History started impinging on Ralph really before he was born, when it gave him a Methodist minister for a grandfather, and prepared a small Minnesota town as a place for him to live in till he was fifteen or so. His mother believed neither in cards, dancing, liquor, or riding a bicycle on Sunday. Ralph has emancipated himself on all four counts, and a few others, but usually after his third gin and bitters he exclaims, "My God, I must call up mother!" He rings her up and tells her that the kids are fine. One can't help liking Ralph for doing it, and especially when after that he returns to his fourth gin and bitters.

Ralph went for a year to the University of Minnesota. He had to leave to go to work. While he was at the university, however, he helped pay his way by working as a strikebreaker for the railroad during the national strike in 1922. He was paid $77 a week for strikebreaking. Ralph said he "did it for the experience," but besides he didn't know any other way he could make so much money.

When history closes in on Ralph—which may be fast or slow —depending on such historic accidents as war or revolution, the author of this book, who has no faith in the progressive role of the American middle class (as Ralph has) will doubtless find himself in a fist fight with Ralph. For roused, Ralph will fight like hell against anyone who disagrees with him—enough. I have no doubt he will clean up the author. Ralph is an independent furniture dealer, he is a good American, and an only partially reconstructed Methodist. Dynamite for a skillful political leader to detonate. But it will take a better demagogue than Huey Long, or Father Coughlin, or a fanatical defender of the status quo like Bert Strong, to rouse him. (Ralph, by the way, is against "reaction," which includes the Citizens' Alliance and all its works.)

If the formula can be found—which hasn't happened yet— to appeal to Ralph's Faribault metabolism—he will join a Constitutional army and clean out 574 or anything else in defense of America and Rogers Bros. But history is still a long way from calling Ralph to the colors.

In the same summer that contained the Battle of Deputies Run, Ralph and Agnes did something completely unprecedented with their personal lives. His brother-in-law appeared one day at their home and said he was going to the Kentucky Derby. He asked them to come along. The Rogers had no more thought of attending a Kentucky Derby than of going to Russia for the Theater festival. They said of course they couldn't go. What about the children? What about the furniture business? Suddenly Agnes announced she was going. There was only fifteen minutes to pack.

Ralph and his wife, and his brother-in-law and his wife, arrived in Louisville in the late afternoon. There had been no time to cash a check. Ralph wired a Chicago friend to bring fifty bucks to the train. (He also sent a wire to his mother.) Arriving in Louisville, Ralph found his suitcase contained six pairs of pyjamas, but he hadn't packed a shirt. Recalling the trip afterwards, they couldn't remember half the funny things that happened. The Derby party found rooms at a Mrs. Morgan's. "When we felt at home a little," Agnes relates, "we asked for ice and glasses and had a drink. On the day of the Derby the boys went out, and I stayed with Mrs. Morgan. I had been unwell before I left Minneapolis, but I didn't mind staying with Mrs. Morgan. She was a Southerner and very romantic, and had become engaged to her husband on Derby Day. She wept a great deal, and I found out that her husband had also died on Derby Day five years before.

"The boys were expected back at nine in the evening to meet a friend. They didn't come. Mrs. Morgan kept saying, 'I can't imagine where they are.' And I kept saying, 'I can't either.'" She laughs appreciatively at herself and at Mrs. Morgan in recollection. "Of course I knew all the time where they were. Getting snooted up in every bar in Louisville—for the Derby.

"Finally Donald came in with one of those rubber horses— balloons you know, that they sell at the Derby. I couldn't stop him. He kept hitting Mrs. Morgan on the seat with it, and shouting, 'It's the only horse I've seen in Louisville—the only one.' It was true. Of course they never got to see the Derby. But we had a marvelous time."

There can be no question about that. I have been on a few small parties with Ralph myself. He is as fine a companion as there is in Minneapolis for a party or a trip to Louisville or Grand Rapids or the Taj Mahal, if one has any feeling whatever for lusty cavorting, plus liquor, plus the shrewd and hearty comment of an unqualified American on this cockeyed world.

One day in Louisville, Ralph stuck his fist unexpectedly through a motor car window. The driver was furious. But Ralph was equal to it. He referred him to his brother-in-law as his attorney, and the matter was amicably settled.

I think it was on the same day that Ralph walked up to one of the more obvious Kentucky Colonels loitering on a street corner and said, "Sir, can you direct me to a horse?" This remark, with all its imponderable overtones to Derby devotees, became a legend in Louisville.

Ralph Rogers didn't live through the period of Minneapolis' Golden Age, but he has an idea at the moment for developing a small private golden one of his own. As a matter of fact it's a good idea. Rogers' furniture is actually suffering from the moderate upturn of prosperity in Minneapolis. Sounds funny, but the people who "saved money" by buying Ralph's davenports in that out-of-the-way street across the bridge—where Ralph sold them for less—are now buying them at the "better stores" on Nicollet and Hennepin Avenues. So the Rogers Brothers have just arranged a year's lease on a "volume of sales" basis in the heart of the city. And they're going to take the plunge. It's exciting. Instead, after ten years of business, of only taking a couple of hundred dollars a month in salary out, and plowing back a microscopic remainder, the prospect opens of *real profits!* Not that the Rogers have any desire to live like the Pillsburys or Heffelfingers; they're proud to be like the great American middle class to whom they sell their furniture, *but* after all there are five kids, so far—and it would be a little easier to be snooty to the socialites—for whom Ralph retains a healthy contempt—with the store on Hennepin Avenue rather than on Sixth Avenue, North. With that highly legitimate snooty anti-snoot added to five children, a marvelous wife, gin and bitters, and a tennis court—and a sense that hard work gets you somewhere—there wouldn't be much left to add to life.

Roy Bauman's father and grandfather came over from Germany when his father was fifteen, and settled on a Minnesota farm. Cows mostly, but some hogs and chickens and a little truck gardening. Roy worked on the farm till he was twenty-one, when he went to the city to get a *good* job. Roy's wife has her own explanation of the urban migration. "He didn't like to do the chores and wanted more time to step out." When Mrs. Bauman offers this version, Roy grunts. He doesn't deny it. Since that time Roy has usually had one of the better truck-driving jobs in Minneapolis, different bosses, but for the past nine years for the same company. Mrs. Bauman was brought up on a farm too. Her parents came from Denmark and there is a tinted photograph of her father and mother on top of the piano. Her mother is very beautiful, a serious, sensitive, and yet determined face, black hair, combed back above finely modeled features. She is twenty-two in the picture.

This evening it was twenty-minutes to nine before Roy got back from work—one of the long-haul days. Splashing water over his face in the kitchen, Roy says, "There are the goddamdest people driving automobiles these days." The drivers he hates worst are the women. "They stop when they ought to shoot ahead, or shoot ahead when they ought to stop—just the opposite of what you'd think—the way women do everything—" Putting the steak down on the table, Mrs. Bauman says, "Oh yeah!" (The Baumans have steak about once or twice a month.) There are tomatoes on the table from the Baumans' garden in the back yard. "Besides, I have a few radishes, chard, peas, and beans, but this year the cutworms got most of them."

The Bauman house has three rooms downstairs, and three up, besides a closed-in porch upstairs, and a closed-in porch downstairs. It is shared by two other couples besides the Baumans and their three children. They pay ten dollars together toward the $27.50 monthly rent. There are vines over half the house, a good back yard, and a garage. It is nice, but it costs too much to heat in a Minnesota winter and the Baumans are moving next year to a smaller place without couples.

An extra forty miles with six stops on the route has made Roy hungry as hell. "I was out past Le Grande's place today," he says, cutting a slice of bread. Mrs. Bauman looks at him affectionately. A month ago Roy took Mrs. Bauman on a "honeymoon"—to Le Grande's—to celebrate their sixth wedding anniversary. Mrs. Bauman is as much in love with Roy as she was six years ago when she married him, and brought with her two daughters from a former marriage. He is tall, dark, slow moving, packing a tremendous wallop in his back and arms—not easily roused but a fighter when he is. On the picket line during the strike he was wonderful either against scabs or cops.

Bill Hodson and his wife are sitting in the front room while Roy finishes his dinner, reading the newspaper and talking with the kids. "Can you sleep nights?" asks Bill as Roy comes in from the kitchen. The weather, as I have noted, invades almost any July or August conversation in Minneapolis. The Baumans' flat roof turns the upstairs into an oven in the real hot weather. It was actually over a hundred up there last night. The family distributed themselves, on the front porch, the living-room floor, and in the back yard. "Last night," Mrs. Bauman says, "the two girls slept outside on the grass."

The Hodsons and the Baumans are on mutually visiting terms and they settle down for the evening in the living room. There's a davenport and a piano in the room, a number of colored prints framed on the walls, together with a cornucopia of artificial flowers. Sheets of music on the piano include "Edelweis" and "I Haven't Forgotten You, Kathleen." The eldest daughter plays quite well "if she'd only practice more." She's out now but the youngest (Roy's kid), aged four, somersaults about on the floor between the Hodsons and the Baumans as they drink beer. Mrs. Bauman gave up long ago trying not to spoil her. Roy never tried.

An evening at home with a little beer, or over at the Hodsons' house with a little beer, is getting rather typical with the Baumans. When Roy was single he used to go to the movies nearly every night, but Roy and his wife have only seen one picture this year, Will Rogers in "Old Kentucky." For a night out they prefer a wrestling match and at one time followed the careers of national and local champions with great accuracy. "We'd sit in the gallery," Mrs. Bauman recalls, "and I'd always get very excited." Sundays and whenever he'd get laid off Roy used to hunt quite a bit—pheasant, jackrabbits, and duck. But he's given it up now, mostly, since his gun blew up on him a couple of years ago.

As with most Americans, a great deal of Roy's mental and physical energy, his recollections and his conversation, tie in with his job. He likes truck driving. Quite a lot of variety to it. a long haul one day, a short one the next, different loads, stops, customers, wrangles, and breakdowns. He likes his new three and one-half ton Ford V-8 truck. Today he took it out in the afternoon for a nice forty-mile run into the country, with a "medium load." "Truck driving tires you about equally if you have an empty truck or an overload. If the truck is empty, it jars hell out of you because the springs are so stiff you might as well not have any. Same if it's an overload—jams the springs flat down to the wheel shafts."

Roy tells Hodson that they're not paying overtime at his place and he must speak to Bill Brown at the union about it. "But the fellers just take a little more time on the job so that it evens out."

Mrs. Bauman interrupts to say that she thinks that is wrong. "One ought to play square with your employer!" Roy says, "Sure, I agree with that. Why is he chiseling then on his union contract? He's agreed in writing to pay overtime. I'll play square with the boss if he does with me."

Some breakdowns on the road are tough, especially in the midst of a bitter Minneapolis winter; some are welcome and relaxing. Roy recalls one of the latter for Hodson's benefit. About fifty miles from Minneapolis, his fan flew off and went through the radiator. The super sent out a mechanic and together they made the repair job in about forty minutes. It was after five then, all the truck deliveries had been made, and both Roy's mind and the mechanic's turned to other things. Roy remembered a farmer in the neighborhood who could supply a quart of gin on occasion. They stepped on it and went to see the farmer. He thought the mechanic was a Federal agent at first and shut up tight. But Roy persuaded him. The farmer produced two quarts out of the barn—with one for himself. By two A.M. Roy definitely made up his mind it was time to move. The mechanic wasn't so sure. Their host was against it—he wanted them to drink all night. Roy got into the truck, pulling in the mechanic with him, and started the motor. He pushed his host off the running board.

That night they slept in the truck. When the sun rose at six, they woke up, but the mechanic had left the lights on, and the motor wouldn't start. (Bill Hodson laughed like hell at this point in the story.) Roy told the mechanic to go ahead and crank the car. He refused. "Will you do it, if I give you another drink," said Roy, producing a reserve of the farmer's gin from under his coat. The mechanic started the Ford V-8.

Finishing the story, Roy brought out four bottles of beer, nice and cold from an electric refrigerator he had bought for Mrs. Bauman last winter. Roy had it figured out that it was just as cheap as peddled ice. But the electric ice box worried him one way. He hated to gyp the ice-wagon drivers. He had tried to find a union-made refrigerator. Mrs. Bauman is as militant a union man as Roy is. She worked in the commissary cooking for the strikers during the May strike, and she leaves a copy of the *Organizer* in the milk bottle every week to educate the milk man in the principles of 574.

Hodson is a member of the car men's union, and the conversation got around to union labor and the next president. Some one said that there were a hell of a lot of Lemke-Coughlinites in Minnesota. Roy snorted. The Baumans are Farmer-

Labor in Minnesota and Franklin Delano Roosevelt for the White House.

Over more beer, the conversation somehow connects up with religion. Both Roy and his wife are Lutherans, and all the kids have been christened Lutheran. But there is a book in the house that used to belong to Mrs. Bauman's mother written by a Milleniumist. It has been read till the covers have disappeared and the pages worn thin, especially in the "Seven Seals" chapter. Mrs. Bauman quotes the passages on carriages without horses, and "that men shall fly in the air like birds" to show that the Bible has the dope on modern America. Over more beer she brings up the prophecy about a catyclysm that will mean the world's end. Men will get more wicked and God will chastise them for it. (Though now the world is certainly better than it used to be.) Anyhow, she feels that the final catyclysm will be a world war between the rich and the poor. The poor won't win, but the world will end and they will receive their "inheritance" in heaven.

Upon this general dénouement Roy declines to comment, sits and smokes and looks at his wife, but it suggests to his mind something less metaphysical—the *"next* war." He says he will fight at home, but he won't go to Europe. Besides, "Labor is going to have something to say about the next war and can stop it if they want to."

Roy doesn't spend a hell of a lot of time figuring or talking about world events, political or economic. He does spend a lot, however, figuring the immediate economics of the Baumans. During the depression Roy went into debt. By 1934, he owed $350. Then came the strikes—forty-eight days of them. "Rent kept right on and we had to eat." Roy's total indebtedness to creditors mounted to $500. Today Roy gets roughly $10 more a week than before he joined the union—a 33 1-3% raise. He figures a "strike investment" of $150 has netted him a little over $500 more a year. "I've pretty much whittled off the debts, besides living a darn sight better." Roy says he thinks he could have "beaten" some of his bills, but since the grocer and the doctor trusted him he thinks he ought to pay.

Like the scions of the empire builders and like Ralph Rogers, Roy pursues his personal life as hard as he can, and has always been as indifferent to history as he can afford to be. But his range of personal initiative is very closely knit with the destiny of all the other truck drivers of Minneapolis, and iron workers and machinists and so on. And he is deeply if not explicitly conscious of it. Roy, in 1934, got around $17 a week (he was the highest paid driver in the company). Now he gets $28. He was the best truck driver they had then; he still is. Not personal initiative—except on the picket line—but a collective historical change has modified the concrete setting for Roy's personal life.

It shouldn't be forgotten that Roy, though he differs in some of his conscious and unconscious responses to history from Warren Platt and Donald Carter—and Ralph Rogers and Joe Pine—shares some of them too. He believes in God, and in America, and likes to hunt and to drink. Sometimes the common elements of an American culture make him think the way Warren and Ralph do. Sometimes they don't. When the Reverend William A. Brown addressed a meeting of truck drivers in the summer of 1934 and in the name of God and Universal Brotherhood asked them to call off the strike, Mr. Brown's and Roy's God suffered a split personality.

During the years from 1930 to 1934, history impinged sharply on Roy. He saw a lot of the men he'd been working with laid off. They ate less and less, and there wasn't fuel enough in their homes for the cold Minnesota winters. The children of some of his friends got "flu" and died. Roy was lucky and kept his job through the depression, but in 1932 he was getting $16 a week and in 1934 around $17. With a wife, three children and Mrs. Bauman in the hospital, he just about made it. And for these wages he worked about ninety hours a week in those days. When the union came, Roy was one of the first in his outfit to join; it took a little nerve to join a Minneapolis trade union in 1933.

When the strike came, Roy spent seventeen and eighteen hours a day on the picket line. He felt they *had to win the strike* or he'd lose his job and be even worse off than he was in 1932. Mrs. Bauman worked all day peeling potatoes and making coffee in the commissary, and listening breathlessly to what they said over the mike in the evening mass meetings. Rather more than Roy she felt *the strike had to be won.*

When they brought in the women who had been beaten up by armed guards in the *Tribune* Alley, and laid them out in rows at strike headquarters, Roy went and got himself a club.

A week before, Ralph Rogers and Agnes were playing bridge with three other couples at a neighbor's home. Ted Halsey blew in and said, "How would you guys like to be deputy sheriffs?" Ted owned a middle-sized Minneapolis transfer company and it was a question of moving a paper truck through the picket line. Everybody volunteered, against the protest of the wives. "We all had badges and side arms," said Ralph, "and we didn't have any trouble. It meant a thousand-dollar contract for Ted and I was glad to help him out. That's the way I got into the 'army.' "

George Fisher, who was one of the guests at the Caldwell horse show, and showed up later at Woodhill—when Jock expressed the hope that the governor would die of cancer—took the Battle of Deputies Run far more seriously than Ralph. He had been at the Radisson Hotel when Totten Heffelfinger said, "Not five thousand, not fifteen thousand, not twenty-five thousand strikers can bring Minneapolis to its knees!" Lunching at the Minneapolis Club, the day before, he had seen a picket "directing the traffic on Third Avenue." It had made his blood boil. His grandfather had helped to build Minneapolis, and he felt a wave of patriotic self-defense against the muckers who were taking the city away from him and from his grandfather's memories. He reported for duty with club and badge at four A.M. on the day of the battle.

On the day of the battle of Deputies Run Ralph's personal life interfered with history a little, instead of the reverse. He had an engagement in the middle of the morning and got permission to leave for an hour or two. When he returned, the battle was in full swing. "It was really horrible," Ralph reflects. Ralph has plenty of physical guts, and if someone had hit him first, he would have knocked out a couple of pickets; but arriving late this way and "cold," so to speak, he began to wonder why he was there. "I was glad to help move Ted's truck for him," he thought, "but why should I get my head busted so these goddam kikes in the market can make a dime more or less peddling bananas." He called up Agnes, talked it over with her, and went home. History has not yet called Ralph to the colors in the class war.

George was different. He fought hard for the honor of the city, until the citizens' army was repulsed and scattered. His blood still boils a little when he sees a truck driver.

Roy was at it all day—in the battle and in the mop-up. He fought with a kind of delighted fury, and has gotten a kick ever since out of his memories. He sent three cops to the hospital.

Ralph, George, and Roy, and a lot of other citizens saw each other in the market place for the first time and the last, in the historic battle of May 22, 1934. The next day they retired as quickly as possible—in so far as history would let them—into their own personal lives.

Chapter X

CIVIL WAR IN JULY

SCARCELY two months were to elapse after the settlement of the May warfare, before another strike, even wider in scope than the first and more fiercely contested on both sides, was to break out. The defensive powers of the Citizens' Alliance were enormous and the forces of the rebels not yet strong enough to conserve their gains without new battles. Irreconcilables among the truck owners chafed under the labor board stipulation and chiseled on agreements at all points. In the files of the union are 700 cases of discrimination by the employers following the first strike. Above all, the Gordian knot of the inside workers had not been cut by the ambiguous section written into the agreement by the governor. Jurisdiction over this strategic regiment of the rank and file was still in dispute. The union prepared for struggle in defense of previous gains and added the basic demand of an increase in wages. The employers, on their part, charging that the union, not they, had violated the settlement, "broke off relations."

In the July warfare, in contrast to May, there was no question of a surprise attack by either side. Both leaderships, as well as the class forces behind them, girded themselves and mobilized heartily for the struggle. The secretary of the Citizens' Alliance confided to me that "the employers had been caught napping in May." They proceeded to mobilize in advance, and both in armament and strategy to profit from their mistakes and weaknesses in the past. The mayor and the chief of police went into conference with the Citizens' Alliance. The old policy of "killing the strike by ignoring it" was kicked out the window, and hundreds of full-page advertisements and columns on columns of propaganda attacking the union appeared in the press. As has been indicated, the issues of the second strike were, as before, essentially unionism or no unionism in Minneapolis. The Citizens' Alliance had not changed its spots, but they made no such mistakes as formerly in discussing the actual issues at length in the public press. On the propaganda front the employers hammered essentially on three points: (1) the union had broken its agreement, the employers had kept theirs; (2) this was because the leaders were Communists and primed to incite the misled truck drivers to a red revolution and the establishment of a Russian soviet in Minneapolis; (3) honest rank-and-file truck drivers were entirely satisfied with their conditions—hence the employers urged that they rise up and repudiate their leadership; (4) finally, the strikes were ruining Minneapolis. The last one had cost $1,900,000. The employers posed the question: Would the public again permit its streets to be captured by a handful of alien agitators?

The employers' propaganda machine became a different animal from the sedate and arrogant Citizens' Alliance of the old strike. Instead of the honest but naïve statements which even to the disinterested public meant clearly no recognition of any union under any circumstances in Minneapolis, the Employers' Advisory Committee now carefully distinguished "legitimate" and American-minded trade unions from the terrorist Communist-led Truck Drivers' Local 574. The employers, like intelligent partisans, sought allies in the ranks of the enemy, and easily found them among the most reactionary leaders of the American labor movement. Under the appealing headline, "Must Minneapolis Be Penalized by a Strike to Satisfy a Handful of Communist Agitators Who Plan to Make Minneapolis the Birthplace of a New Soviet Republic?" they quoted Daniel J. Tobin, president of the International Brotherhood of Teamsters:

"Well, we are hearing from the Communists and radicals," wrote Mr. Tobin. "We see from the newspaper that —— —— were very prominent in the strike of Local 574 in Minneapolis. All we can say to our people is to beware of these wolves in sheep's clothing," etc., etc., etc.

For purposes of propaganda, it was rightly considered unnecessary by the copywriter to recall that it was the Minneapolis branch of Mr. Tobin's union, in its eighteen-odd years of respectability—prior to 1934—that the truck owners, ably backed by the Citizens' Alliance, had intransigently refused to recognize.

Not all the truck owners or other employers in Minneapolis approved these tactics of the Citizens' Alliance. They were too honest to do so. But they had formed an industrial union of their own in the face of a common enemy and they "stuck to their leaders." From the tactical, propagandist viewpoint, the Citizens' Alliance was certainly dead right. It is far easier to excite mass support in a struggle against Reds "who plan to make Minneapolis the birthplace of a new soviet republic" than to prove that inside workers should not remain in the union which they have joined. And it is certainly more effective to quote A. F. of L. labor leaders, including the international president of the union in question, against the strike than to show cause why 2½ cents more an hour—the union's demand— should not be paid.

So much for the propaganda front. Even a more important step in preparedness was the accumulation of munitions and armaments.

On Monday, July 16, the day the strike vote was taken, Chief of Police Johannes asked for a nearly 100% increase in his police budget. The budget included the cost of 400 additional men and the maintenance of a police school. The need for a school, Chief Johannes states, was illustrated by the May strikes, which he termed a "disgrace." He asked for $7500 for the school and $33,200 for other equipment. "The police," he said, "must be trained *just like an army* to handle riots." Included in the budget were $1000 worth of machine guns, 800 rifles with bayonets, 800 steel helmets, 800 riot clubs, and 26 additional motorcycles.

The union countered the efforts of its enemy on both fronts, the propaganda front and the preparedness-for-war front. Mass meetings served this double purpose: "to spike the lies about our union in the boss press" and to mobilize deeper and deeper reserves from the Minneapolis working class. Needless to say, the May preparation of a strike machine, with headquarters, picket captains, squad cars, commissary, etc., was repeated— except on a larger scale. When the strike, which lasted thirty-six days, was settled, it was revealed that the leadership had organized their food supply and made other plans calculated to endure a forty-day siege. A remarkable strategic feature of the second strike was the union's plan to win the farmers as allies. On the first day of the strike the union announced that all members of farmers' organizations were free to drive their trucks to town and market their produce. Large numbers of farmers belonged to the Market Gardeners' Association, the Farm Holiday, and other organizations and those who didn't promptly joined. Thus a very practical basis for co-operation between farmers' unions and *labor* unions was laid. The farmers set up their own market in a vacant lot to which retailers came, and the success of the new market was so great that it was continued after the strike. As in the May struggle, the Farm

Holiday Association made substantial food contributions to the strikers' commissary.

The largest mass meeting in the history of Minneapolis was held on July 5, an affair which was organized to combine a street demonstration with a huge meeting in the Municipal Auditorium. It began with a parade of labor unions starting from Bridge Square. Alderman Hudson of Minneapolis, mounted on a white horse, led off as grand marshal of the parade! He was followed by a squad of twelve motorcycles, veterans of the May strike, and followed by the unions of Minneapolis each under its own banner. The truck drivers marched four abreast in formation, with a huge 574 banner in red bunting flying over their heads. The other unions included the building trades, laundry workers, garment workers, machinists, auto mechanics, etc. Some twenty farmers' delegations were present, each with its own banner. In the air, zooming and at intervals swooping low over the parade, were two airplanes with "574" painted on their bodies. They belonged to sympathizers and were later used to take union speakers about the state and especially to the farmers in appeals for food. Banners carried the following slogans—the workers' answers to the employers' full page advertisements: "Down With the Citizens' Alliance!" "Down With the Red Baiters!" "We Support 574," "We Demand the Employers Comply With Their Agreement"; and finally the ominous and prophetic words, "Employers Are Preparing for the Worst Battle of Organized Labor in the History of Minneapolis."

The last part of the parade only left the Bridge Square, a distance of eighteen blocks, as the vanguard entered the auditorium. Urtubees, a conservative and certainly an American-minded labor leader, and Roy Weir, organizer of the Central Labor Union, spoke. John Bosch, president of the Minnesota Farm Holiday Association, pledged the support of his organization to the strike. In general, the meeting denounced the Citizens' Alliance and pledged solidarity with the "just cause" of the truck drivers.

It is estimated fifty thousand words, most of them at high temperature, were used by the employers over the radio; more than thirty pages in paid newspaper advertising, and some two hundred and fifty newspaper columns issued in denunciation of the proposed strike and the union leadership. Why did this barrage of propaganda fail of its desired effect? Partly, of course, because of such counter-actions as the mass meeting recounted above. But also because of (1) a personal relation between the leaders and the rank-and-file coal heavers and truck drivers; (2) the strikers' own newspaper which countered each day the propaganda barrage with salvos of its own.

On point one take the case of V. R. Dunne, one of the arch-Communists* and a revolutionist of record, whom the employers of Minneapolis held up to the truck drivers as leading them to bloodshed and destruction. Probably four or five hundred workers in Minneapolis knew "Ray" personally. Scores had worked with him in the coal yards, talked with him, eaten with him, known his wife, his brothers, and his friends. They formed their own opinions—that he was honest, intelligent, and selfless, and a damn good organizer for the truck drivers' union to have. They had always known him to be a Red; that was no news. Roughly the same situation existed in regard to the other leaders. Or if a worker who did not know the leaders personally was made a little jittery by the upsetting news that

---

* As mentioned above, the small group of Marxists in the leadership were Trotskyists. The employers' insistence on "orders from Moscow" furnishes additional humor for those familiar with the relations between the followers of Trotsky and "Moscow."

he had been led by the nose by Red vipers, he would check up on Dunne, Skoglund, or the others. Before long he would find an iron worker whose brother had worked with Skoglund, or a machinist who knew the Dunnes' father and mother. Daily intimacy with their leaders—Bill Brown had been president of the union for twenty years—and word-of-mouth transmission, was found worth a hundred and fifty pages of paid advertising.

Another antidote to the employers' White Papers was the strikers' daily newspaper, *The Organizer.* For the first time in American history a labor union managed to print a daily strike newspaper. Not a weekly—that would have been next to useless—but a daily which leapt from nothing to a circulation of ten thousand in two days, which in most cases, anticipated each blow from the Citizens' Alliance. It had two outstanding editorial characteristics: an unsparing and quite ruthless analytical style as applied to the issues of the strike, and a gay and ironic humor. Both literary attributes it succeeded in translating successfully into the truck driver's own lingo, and he read it with avidity to the almost complete exclusion of the boss press. Its popularity was so great that it not only paid for itself but began making money for the union.

Before the strike actually broke, another element was introduced into the situation which deserves comment. When the first wave of strikes inundated America during the first six months of the NRA, the administration found it necessary to find a sedative for this largely unexpected ferment in American labor. It devised the machinery of government mediators and Labor Boards. Their record is an amazing one. Two nationwide automobile strikes, a general steel strike, a general coal strike, and innumerable lesser industrial disturbances involving many millions of workers, were scotched before they began. Only slowly did the workers discover that the agreements to which the government mediators asked them to attach their signatures left them precisely where they started. A whole group of men acquired nation-wide fame in the new profession, and were summoned by governors and presidents of corporations on a moment's notice to give first aid to industry sick or dying or labor trouble. The highest in this profession were and are called "ace mediators." It was two of these—the Reverend Father Haas and Mr. E. H. Dunnigan—who were summoned to Minneapolis to administer oxygen, if possible, to the dying negotiations between Local 574 and the truck owners, and to stop the strike.

Mr. Dunnigan's personal participation in the 574 negotiations was so unique not only in his own experience but in that of the average strike of NRA days, that it is worth recording in the words of Farrell Dobbs, who might perhaps be readily conceded as the ace negotiator for the truck drivers. The narrative again illustrates that native truck-driver skepticism which as much as any other quality won the strike for them.

"Mr. Dunnigan showed up in 574 headquarters on the day he arrived by plane, having first slipped in a few moments with the bosses. He burst into headquarters cocky as hell, with a black ribbon on his pince-nez and four cigars showing in the pocket of his coat. While he was waiting to see us, he saw my wife and a nurse checking up on medical supplies in preparation for the July picket line. They sorted out the surgical instruments and made an inventory of the bandages, splints, and medicines needed. This gave him his first education in Local 574.

"Finally, when the meeting was over, he was asked in. He presented his credentials and told who he was. He told how many strikes he had settled, and how as soon as he hit town he always went to the workers first; that he had found nine times out of ten they were right, and the employers wrong. You know, the stuff an ordinary worker would fall for if he didn't know what the score was. Finally he gave us his proposition—that the union make him their representative in all negotiations with the bosses. We said, 'All right, you take our demands to the employers and see what you can do.' He looked at us. 'Of course I'll have to have some latitude for bargaining purposes.' We said, 'No, we'll do the bargaining ourselves. See what the bosses say and report back to us, then we can tell you what to do next.' Mr. Dunnigan left in a huff."

The meeting which voted the strike was held in Eagles' Hall and broke up about eleven-thirty when the membership moved in a body to strike headquarters. It was locked! A final gesture of the employers to balk the strike. The truck drivers battered down the door and took possession. Squad cars of roving pickets got under way before morning.

The history of class warfare, like the history of conflict between nations, often repeats itself. The pattern of the first ten days of civil warfare in July repeated the pattern of May but in a broader circle, embracing wider and wider classes of population, and at a higher level of conflict. Thereafter the calling of the National Guard destroyed the old pattern and introduced new forces and contradictions into the struggle.

If in the first day or two of the May strike—the period of peaceful paralysis—the city was calm before the storm of *Tribune* Alley and the Battle of Deputies Run which followed, the first days of the July strike were calmer still before a far bloodier and more violent storm. The news accounts of the first two days of civil war in July are almost ironical in their triviality. "Strike Front Quiet . . . Two pickets were arrested when police caught them stopping small trucks driven by two men who said they were going swimming." Or two days later: "Strike pickets late Wednesday night in the market district conducted machines and drivers to Temple Garage . . . where contents of the truck, canned peas, were unloaded. The trucks and drivers [from a nearby town] were then escorted out of the city. None of the drivers were harmed, nor was any damage done to the machine. . . . The peas were left at the garage."

But meantime the Employers' Strategy Committee had gone into session with the chief of police to plan an offensive far more deadly than the betrayal of pickets by a stool pigeon and the beating of women in an alley.

Just as the Battle of Deputies Run is inexplicable without the *Tribune* Alley incident which preceded it, so Bloody Friday is inseparable from the "hospital convoy" of Wednesday. Wednesday's episode, from the strikers' viewpoint at least, was comedy or perhaps farce; Friday's, tragedy of a grim order.

On the afternoon of July 19 a small knot of passersby gathered about a handful of photographers and movie cameramen in the market district. Surprisingly enough, they carried in their hands newspapers which gave a full and dramatic account of an episode *which was about to take place.* The paper's headlines announced that the first truck loaded with goods for the hospital had successfully gotten through picket lines under heavy guard. In a moment or two the truck itself arrived—a five-ton one, adorned with banners which said "hospital supplies," containing a few hundred pounds of canned or bottled goods. Guarding it were eleven squad cars manned with 44 police holding shotguns in their hands. They informed the bystanders that they had been instructed to shoot if attacked. Meantime, at the strike headquarters V. R. Dunne called Police Chief Johannes on the phone and asked him what it was all about. The hospital council of Minneapolis had just been thanking the union for making possible "full and regular delivery service to all hospitals." Has 574 ever interfered with hospital deliveries? Dunne asked Johannes. The chief admitted they had not, and finally agreed, at Dunne's insistence, to send a messenger and to call off the convoy. Somehow the messenger got lost. The convoy lumbered on impressively, with the movie men taking its picture, to the Eitel Hospital.

Entire strike headquarters roared all evening over the incident, and the *Organizer,* the strike paper, appeared with the headlines: "Johannes Rolls One (1) Truck—150 Cops Convoy 150 Pounds of Freight in a 5-Ton Truck."

But the employers and the police chief who had planned the episode were in deadly earnest. They had confidently expected that the truck would be attacked, that the pickets would be shot down, that under the wave of public wrath against "the interference with supplies for the sick" other goods could be moved.

"In issuing his orders to his men, Chief of Police Johannes told them, 'We are going to start moving goods. . . . Don't take a beating,' he said, 'you have shotguns and you know how to use them. . . . *When we are finished with this convoy there will be other goods to move.'*" "The Police Department is going to get goods moving,' the Chief said. "Now get going and do your duty.'"

Was the whole episode, however, the chief's own not brilliant but independent effort to carry out his duty? The day before, the press carried this item: "Members of the Employers' Advisory Committee conferred at some length with Chief of Police Johannes and Sheriff Wall. . . . The Committee—not the police—"declined to reveal when the *first concerted attempt* to get trucks moving will be made, but nothing will be done *until arrangements are made to insure the success of the movement.*" [italics mine]

Though treating the episode as farce, the *Organizer* did not fail to draw serious conclusions. "The plan was to provoke a riot so that the cops would shoot down pickets, and Mayor Bainbridge and the bosses could howl for the militia to be brought out to move trucks." With ominous concreteness the

Organizer adds: "The names of the finks who loaded the fake cargo at Jordan Stevens have been turned in to the union by a Jordan Stevens worker"—the union had its sympathizers in almost every organization in the city, who with amazing swiftness checkmated the plans of the enemy—"along with the name of the scab driver of Johannes' circus car. . . . Ten thousand copies of the *Organizer* sold on July 19."

Even to the employers and the police the episode of Thursday appeared as a dud. They followed it immediately with a second offensive—more carefully planned than the first—which was a complete success.

The pickets attempted to stop the movement of a scab truck. Heavily armed forces of the police opened fire and mowed them down. The truck was moved. This was Bloody Friday.

Unfortunately, in class warfare shootings are more delicate affairs than in ordinary battles. They depend on a special correlation of motives and emotions. Without that perfect correlation the battle, whatever the casualty lists of the enemy, is a failure. The "hospital supplies" idea might have saved them. Unfortunately that advantage was absent on Friday. Had the workers been armed, or had the pickets, *first* attacked the police, Bloody Friday might have been a "victory," for the employers. Unfortunately none of those favorable accidents occurred. On the afternoon of Friday, July 20, a truck, accompanied by fifty police armed with shotguns started moving in the market. A second truck, containing ten pickets, arrived and cut across the path of the convoyed truck. The police opened fire. Sixty-seven persons were wounded, including thirteen bystanders; two died. The Battle of Bloody Friday took about ten minutes.

The first newspaper accounts, written by reporters rushing to their typewriters through streets covered with blood, and with the incidents of the shooting freshly in mind, reported starkly that the police had opened fire, *first,* before the pickets moved or even had gotten out of their truck; second, that they opened fire again when the pickets were running—forty-six out of forty-eight wounded were reported shot in the back.

Later editions of the Minneapolis press introduced three new elements, none of which found mention in the first account: (1) it was stated that the police warned the strikers "several times" to disperse; (2) the police "repeatedly fired into the air at first"; (3) they only shot at the strikers after an officer had been brutally attacked and beaten by strikers.

I reproduce below the eyewitness account of a picket who was present and who wrote down his impressions at the time:

"For two hours we stood around wondering what was up for there was no truck in sight. Then as two P.M. drew near a tensing of bodies and nervous shifting of feet and heads among the police indicated that something was up. We were right, for a few minutes later about one hundred more cops hove into view escorting a large yellow truck. The truck, without license plates and with the cab heavily wired, pulled up to the loading platform of the Slocum-Bergren Company. Here a few boxes were loaded on. . . . At five past two the truck slowly pulled out. . . . It turned down Sixth Avenue and then turned on Third Street toward Seventh Avenue. As it did a picket truck containing about ten pickets followed. As the picket truck drew near the convoy, the police without warning let loose a barrage of fire. Pickets fell from the trucks, others rushed to pick up their wounded comrades; as they bent to pick up the injured, the police fired at them. . . . One young worker received a full charge of buckshot in the back as he bent to pick up a wounded picket.

"The rain of bullets then became a little heavier so I and three other pickets hopped a fence and walked back to headquarters. . . . Pickets by the dozens lying all over the floor with blood flowing from their wounds, more coming in and no place to put them. The doctor would treat one after another who urged him to treat others first.

"The Minneapolis papers printed hundreds of lies about what had happened but none was brazen enough to claim that the strikers had any weapons at all."

Eyewitness accounts of any battle, as the historian knows, are notoriously contradictory and partisan. How much more so an eyewitness account by a partisan participant in the class war! However, fortunately for the purposes of this narrative, the storm of partisan public excitement was so great over the incidents of Bloody Friday that a public investigation was ordered by the governor of the state. The conclusions of the commission tallied dramatically with the record which newspaper reporters fresh from the scene had written for their first editions. They are as follows:

"It is very difficult to make a report of the shooting of the strike pickets which has not the appearance of bias against the police department, the conduct of the officers being unbelievable to a person of common humanity."

Of the shooting, the investigators said in substance that a wholesale truck carrying merchandise which could easily have been put in the rear seat of a passenger car moved out into the street under armed police convoy. Pains were taken to let strikers know of the plans. Newspaper reporters and cameramen were present.

"Police took direct aim at the pickets and fired to kill.

"Physical safety of police was at no time endangered.

"No weapons were in the possession of the pickets in the truck.

"At no time did pickets attack the police, and it was obvious that pickets came unprepared for such an attack.

THE FARMERS SET UP THEIR OWN MARKET
As allies they were strategic

FATHER HAAS AND E. H. DUNNIGAN—ACE MEDIATORS
Neither pince-nez nor clerical collar impressed the strikers

POLICE OPEN FIRE ON TRUCKLOAD OF UNARMED STRIKERS

"The truck movement in question was not a serious attempt to move merchandise, but a 'plant' arranged by the police."

Governor's Commission of Investigation

"Neither am I willing to join in the approval of the shooting of unarmed citizens of Minneapolis, strikers and bystanders alike, in their backs, in order to carry out the wishes of the Citizens' Alliance . . ."—*Governor Olson*

"The truck movement in question was not a serious attempt to move merchandise, but a 'plant' arranged by the police.

"The police department did not act as an impartial police force to enforce law and order, but rather became an agency to break the strike.

"Police actions have been to discredit the strike and the Truck Drivers' Union so that public sentiment would be against the strikers."

The day after Bloody Friday the governor charged that Chief of Police Johannes had broken a promise to Father Haas and himself that there would be a truce and stated, "The blood of those wounded and dying is upon the heads of the men who brought about the breaking of that promise." In spite of denials on the part of the Employers' Committee, Johannes naïvely revealed the identity of "the men" when he issued the following statement in his own defense:

"I agreed to take the matter up with the Employers' Advisory Committee and see what action *they* wanted taken. I met the entire committee at the Hotel Radisson. *They turned down the truce proposal. They said they would not accept any truce, and at the same time requested me to furnish guards for the trucks.*" [italics mine]

Tourists who were in Italy during Mussolini's march on Rome were later—in some cases many weeks later—to learn that during their Italian vacation one social order had been violently overthrown and another put in its place. They reported that they had noticed nothing unusual during their stay. It was only natural that during such a minor episode of social struggle as the police shootings of July 20 life for the average citizen of Minneapolis was unaffected and undisturbed. It was only later, when the social explosives ignited by the battle began to detonate, that individuals entirely remote from the controversy found themselves engulfed as partisans on one side or the other.

Meantime, city life showed itself peacefully normal and unfluttered. On the day that Johannes' men were firing over one hundred shots at the pickets on Seventh Street, "Maple Hill held its first sing of the year" with "two thousand people to take part in the songfest." Shirley Temple in "Stand Up and Cheer" was at The Boulevard, and James Cagney in "Here Comes the Navy—A Romantic Comedy-Drama of Uncle Sam's Jacktars" was packing them in at The State. The morning paper reported that the White Sox had beaten the Yankees, that Mrs. Franklin M. Crosby of Ferndale, Lake Minnetonka, had issued invitations for a party Tuesday at the Woodhill Country Club. It was to be in honor of Miss Ella Sturgis Pillsbury, debutante.

In the general news there was, however, a happening on Bloody Friday which gave heart and encouragement to the friends of that battle. The press carried an account of the breaking of the San Francisco general strike by "armed bands of vigilantes." The *Journal* promptly suggested that similar methods be applied to Minneapolis. Bankers noted that "rail shares touched a new low for the year" and that "while Wall Street felt relieved over the ending of the San Francisco strike, that had been expected and did not influence the market."

If the atmosphere of Minneapolis was normal on the day of the battle, twenty-four hours later it was not. It was as if a high voltage of electricity had been discharged into the social organism. Slowly as the news spread, was retold, embroidered, discussed, a new alignment of class forces appeared in the city. This process of invisible mobilization of emotions, prejudices, and opinions in the wake of an event is both the most interesting and, for our purposes, the real historical *meaning* of the event. Men and women react to happenings, and especially to violent ones, not only with the historic facts as data—they very seldom have them—but also with a whole complex of emotions and experiences. That is a commonplace of psychology. Bloody

Friday moved through the minds of Minneapolis citizens touching pity, fear, and hope, class fear and class pride and, above all, the instinct of "group preservation." It proved an invisible but infinitely potent mobilization of class forces. Above all it proved, even to the doubting, that a class alignment and a class battle did exist. In a word, coupled with the events that followed, it made Minneapolis people take sides either actively or in their hearts.

Some employers found their sense of decency and common humanity shocked by the "brutality of the police," but there is no record of a single business man offering public criticism of the events of the day. In place of this the most impassioned defense of the "bravery of the police" was found in the press. In effect the Employers' Committee took the event—as did the strikers—as a cue to widen their "mass base." They turned to the Kiwanis, the Rotary Club, the Lions, and the civic and commerce organizations, or those organizations turned to them, to "endorse" the police and the events of Friday, July 19. The Civic and Commerce Association in a letter to the mayor said, "Our citizens cannot help but admire the bravery of our police force." The Kiwanis in a letter to Joseph Cochran, chairman of the Employers' Committee of Minneapolis: "While we deplore the loss of life, we commend the Mayor and the Chief of Police of Minneapolis for their determination to maintain the law of the land and protect lives and property." Similar statements from Rotary and the Lions. The events of Bloody Friday, far from appalling them, strengthened their determination to continue and redouble the same tactics and won for the employers new allies in that determination. Two years later the secretary of the Citizens' Alliance indicated to me frankly and without embarrassment that that had been the Alliance's intention before the "unfortunate" interference of the National Guard. These were his words: "Nobody likes to see bloodshed, but I tell you after the police had used their guns on July 20 we felt that the strike was breaking. Mike Johannes—they call him 'Bloody Mike,' but I don't care—it was a religion with him to keep the streets open. And if the troops hadn't come in and interfered, the strike would have been soon over. There are very few men who will stand up in a strike when there is a question of they themselves getting killed. And I say there are very few of us, in view of what Minneapolis is today, who don't feel the strike would have been better ended that way." The secretary believed what he was saying, and there was emotion in his voice when he spoke these words. And from the viewpoint of the Alliance he was not only correct but possessed the courage of his convictions. If one believes passionately that unionism is a blight to an American city, it is romantic to count the cost of human life in annihilating it; and besides, the Citizens' Alliance correctly sensed that this was no ordinary strike and no ordinary trade union. Under the pother about a soviet in Minneapolis and Red Revolution there was a good grain of class sense. It was a strike and a union which promised actually to change the lives of tens of thousands of persons in Minneapolis, to the employers' detriment. And it did.

But to return to the high-voltage days of July, 1934, Bloody Friday, far from dismaying the Employers' Committee, heartened them to bigger and better battles toward what they called a "permanent settlement." Confidential letters from the archives of the Citizens' Alliance, subsequently published, revealed that they had no use for the Regional Labor Board or the government either; that they had defied them before, and were prepared to do so again. This view they only shared with other honest antiunion employers, and from their own premise they were quite correct. The Kiwanis said to the Employers' Committee: "We hope you will not make the mistake of conceding anything that will make for only temporary settlements of the present difficulty." The Rotary: "We urge you to agree to no concession, no compromise, that would make temporary rather than permanent industrial peace." The Lions: "We do not feel there should be any compromise with Communist propagandists or agitators." Note that none of the allies intimated that the employers might concede *too little* to insure "permanent industrial peace"!

I have said above that I thought the employers were entirely correct from their own point of view in their reactions to Bloody Friday. This requires qualification, or rather, explanation. Their class instincts were sound, their instincts as nonunion employers who had maintained the prerogatives of dictatorial control of their businesses in Minneapolis for thirty years, which were now being threatened, were sound. And who could blame any business man who had lived through the Battle of Deputies Run for having a few Red nightmares and wanting to shoot back? Arthur Lyman, Minneapolis business man, one of their own, had been killed by "those God damned truck drivers" in the May strike. One can appreciate their class instinct and sympathize with their emotions, but one cannot respect their intelligence. As a move for winning the strike, which after all was their objective, Bloody Friday was damn bad strategy. Subsequent events indicated, contrary to the hopes of the secretary of the Citizens' Alliance quoted above, that the storm of protest that Bloody Friday aroused not only in the entire working class of Minneapolis but in large sections of the middle class, was so great that the process of cumulative slaughter, even if the employers had tried it, simply would not have worked. The strike was not "beginning to break" after Bloody Friday, as the secretary had said. His class hopes were deceiving him. The strike was coming alive.

The Central Labor Union, containing all the most conservative and "respectable" labor leadership in Minneapolis, promptly filed a petition with the mayor that "Chief Johannes be ousted." The statement referred to him as a danger to the peace of the community. Farmer-Labor clubs, the Veterans of Foreign Wars, and local trade unions hitherto indifferent to the strikers, passed bitter resolutions condemning Bloody Friday. Unfortunately for the Citizens' Alliance, for each resolution of the Civic and Commerce Association or the Rotary, 574 acquired 100 new flesh-and-blood pickets for the front.

The *Organizer* summed up as follows, in words which while written at the moment in the fierce heat of class conviction were borne out objectively by the events of the next two weeks: "You thought you would shoot Local 574 into oblivion," says the *Organizer* editorial, which came off the press Saturday morning. "But you only succeeded in making 574 a battle cry on the lips of every self-respecting working man and woman in Minneapolis."

The invisible processes of mobilization in the thoughts of men and women culminated, so far as the workers of Minneapolis and their sympathizers were concerned, in the vast funeral cortege which accompanied Henry Ness, slain strike picket, to his grave. Ness, who had never left the picket car in which he arrived at the market place, had received thirty-seven slugs in his body from the shotguns of the police. Repeated efforts at blood transfusion failed to save his life. He died four days after the shooting. The workers of Minneapolis display a certain genius for public demonstrations. In the funeral of Henry Ness they outdid themselves both in drama and solemnity. Estimates of the crowd vary from fifty thousand to one hundred thousand persons. Some twenty thousand took part in the procession itself, which marched first from the funeral parlor, where a service had been held, to the strike headquarters on South Eighth Street, and thence to the cemetery several miles distant. Almost the entire labor movement of Minneapolis marched, together with several posts of the Veterans of Foreign Wars, of which Ness was a member. At the headquarters funeral orations were delivered over a loud speaker to a crowd estimated by the Minneapolis *Labor Review* at twenty-five thousand. The orations at South Eighth Street had a certain dramatic poignancy which did not escape the crowd, for the old garage in which strike headquarters was located, lay directly opposite the city's most select social gathering place—the Minneapolis Club, to which the most distinguished members of the Employers' Committee belonged. There were a few watchers at the club windows as Bill Brown and Albert Goldman delivered their funeral speeches over the loud speaker. Bill Brown broke down and couldn't finish his speech, but Goldman proceeded in detail to tell the crowd whom they should hold responsible for the death of Henry Ness. He looked up at the Minneapolis Club as he spoke. A black flag was raised over headquarters, which remained for the duration of the strike.

The funeral procession moving toward the cemetery passed through residential Minneapolis, and completely halted all movement of street cars, automobiles, and other traffic. There were no police and no disorder through the line of march. Strikers had appointed their own corps of traffic cops. Chief Johannes, fearing the worst, had actually sent a corps of armed police to the court house and fortified it with machine guns. Along the march bystanders removed their hats as the procession passed, till it reached Twelfth and Hawthorne Avenue, where few sympathizers with Henry Ness or the strikers lived. On this avenue pedestrians were disposed to keep their hats on. At the cost of several hot arguments and the loss of a couple of hats they did so. At the cemetery a firing squad of regular army soldiers from Fort Snelling, in accordance with military regulations, fired the last volley over Ness's grave. The dead striker was a member of the Veterans of Foreign Wars and had served in the regular army for fifteen years, two and a half of which were spent in active service during the World War.

In the war in Minneapolis, both armies could now claim their war dead, and incidentally both veterans of the World War. On the office walls of the Citizens' Alliance a framed parchment was hung: "In Memoriam to Arthur C. Lyman, who fought for his country abroad, and who knew how to fight and die for the same principles at home." The *Organizer,* reporting the funeral of Henry Ness, had said: "The last speaker was Chaplain Nelson, of the Post of the National Veterans Association to which Henry Ness belonged. His invocation was a touching tribute to the intrepid soldier who had so fearlessly fought for himself, for his family and for his brothers—for his union."

On July 23, a few days after Bloody Friday, the Federal conciliators published their plan of settlement and asked for prompt acceptance by both parties. The proposal in essence granted the union the right to represent the inside workers provided a post-strike election turned in the union favor. In addition, it asked a 2½-cent wage increase per hour, and subsequent arbitration of all wage scales.

The governor of the state promptly seconded the endorsement of the Federal conciliators and the United States Department of Labor and urged settlement of the strike in the "public interest," adding that if the plan was not accepted, clashes would follow, endangering the lives "not only of the contenders but of neutral persons." Unless the plan was accepted by noon of Thursday, July 26, by both parties, he threatened martial law.

At nine A.M. on Thursday both the union and the Employers' Committee went into session. By noon the union announced their acceptance, the employers their rejection. The employers, diplomatically, now found themselves in the tightest spot they had yet been called upon to occupy.

To the Federal conciliators the employers said: "We cannot

deal with this Communist leadership. . . . This whole strike is the result of misrepresentation, coercion and intimidation." They repeated through an elaborate series of counter-proposals their former stand on the inside workers. On wages: "To fix an increased wage scale by a vicious strike and then arbitrate from that point upwards only paves the way for a repetition of the same lawlessness." In other words, strikes should never result in wage increases.

To the governor the employers said: "Under threats of martial law you are attempting to force a settlement which will leave the issue and the methods of the present strike wide open for repetition in the future. . . . We as citizens of Minneapolis demand to know whether you will support local authorities with military aid in the discharge of their duty, or support the efforts of the few to lawlessly obstruct the flow of normal traffic in this city."

The governor replied in part:

"I do not agree with you that the plea for a living wage by a family man receiving only $12 a week is answered by calling that man a Communist.

"Neither am I willing to join in the approval of the shooting of unarmed citizens of Minneapolis, strikers and bystanders alike, in their backs, in order to carry out the wishes of the Citizens' Alliance of Minneapolis. . . .

"This organization is controlled and dominated by a small clique of men who hate all organized labor and are determined to crush it. This sinister group repeatedly prevented a settlement of this and the former strike. This group restrained the so-called fruit and produce employers from agreeing, on the eve of the present strike, to pay helpers, platform men and inside workers a wage scale of 42½ cents per hour. I know that many employers of Minneapolis are fair-minded and just but they are blocked from any group settlement of labor controversies by this clique. . . .

"You have repeatedly informed me that a contributing cause of strikes is the low wages paid by the so-called 'chiseler' employer. These 'chiselers' are members of the Citizens' Alliance. Have you ever attempted to hold them up to public scorn and contempt? Have you ever interceded in behalf of these low-paid employees? Your answer to these questions must be in the negative.

"You are constantly speaking in writing about the duty of the Government toward you. You must not forget that you also have a duty to the Government.

"You have already flouted the recommendation of the Minneapolis-St. Paul regional labor board, a governmental agency. If you had agreed to that recommendation there would have been no strike. You are undoubtedly preparing yourselves to flout the recommendation of the National Labor Relations Board, and the United States Department of Labor. These two agencies were created by law for the mediation of all labor disputes in the country. You can prevent disturbance in the city of Minneapolis by co-operating with your government instead of flouting it. The responsibility for what occurs in the city of Minneapolis, if this strike continues is entirely upon your shoulders.

"The agencies of government do not belong to you, as one would be led to believe from reading your communication. They belong to all the people and I propose to use the governmental agencies under my jurisdiction, including the national guard, for the protection of all the people of the city of Minneapolis and all people outside the city, including farmers, who desire to do business within the city.

"Respectfully yours,

"FLOYD B. OLSON,

"Governor."

Before twelve o'clock noon on Thursday, July 25, the union had voted to accept the Haas-Dunnigan peace pact by a vote of 1866 to 147. The governor, after he had given the employers another twenty-two minutes grace and then had received word from Father Haas of the employers' rejection, instantly proclaimed martial law.

What was it like? At first, not too bothersome. "No parking in the Loop" aggravated the average citizen most. No drinks after nine P.M.; night clubs and dance halls must shut down at midnight. *No picketing of trucks. No trucks to move without military permit.* Permits granted only for milk, fruit or other edibles. "Minneapolis put on Bread and Milk Diet," announced the *Journal* in a scare headline. Hottest discussion at the time waged over whether Minneapolis could continue community sings under martial law, a mass activity to which the city was particularly attached. The high command ruled in favor of the sings. A day and night "walkathon" was in progress outside the city limits and the walkers were for a time desperately afraid the midnight rule would stop them from walking. Military authorities ruled the walkers could keep going by themselves but fans and spectators must disperse at midnight.

During this period the employers addressed a letter to the governor as follows:

"Your communication of July 26 was delivered to our committee only a short time before your proclamation of martial law. Your proclamation suggests it would be dangerous to answer your letter in kind.

"May we have your official military permission to make and publish such reply as your letter calls for?

"Yours truly,

"EMPLOYERS' ADVISORY COMMITTEE.

"By J. R. Cochran, Chairman."

The governor answered:

"Dear Mr. Cochran: I have your communication of today in which you express some apprehension that the kind of letter you propose to write to me will infringe upon the laws of the state. Please be advised that you may write me in any terms you desire with complete immunity from any military regulation or the laws of the state with reference to libel. I solemnly warn you, however, to refrain from stating anything that will frighten the children of Minneapolis, for fear of the penalty that will fall thereon.

"Surely your group should have every opportunity to offer its defense, if any it has, for its failure to accept the strike terms proposal of Father Haas and Commissioner Dunnigan.

"May I suggest that in this communication your many collaborators discover some noun that you may use to describe those under-paid workers and perhaps describe me,—other than the terms 'Red' and 'Communist.'

"I shall look forward with pleasure to receiving your communication and to read the accompanying and supporting editorials of the Minneapolis *Journal*. I am sure that these two literary efforts will furnish an amusing interlude in the serious situation which confronts the citizens of Minneapolis.

> "Very truly yours,
> "FLOYD B. OLSON,
> "Governor,
> "State of Minnesota."

As may be surmised, in spite of the temporary gaiety which the above interchange, and which "uniforms everywhere" and the novelty of the new order lent the city, no one, and least of all the governor, the strikers, and the employers, failed to appreciate that a profound change in the order of events had overtaken them. Instantly, for the first time in the history of the nation, organized employers deplored and protested the introduction of the militia into a strike situation. They regarded martial law as an effort on the governor's part to force their acceptance of the Labor Board proposals, and not to break the strike. They were correct in their judgment of the governor's intentions. At the very start, Brigadier General Frank E. Reed resigned as camp commander with the statement: "I felt . . . that if I were not permitted to let trucks operate, I could not conscientiously act as troop commander. I therefore asked to be relieved." Promptly the governor appointed his own Adjutant General, E. A. Walsh, as commander. "Military veterans could recall no other instance in which the Governor of a state has designated his Adjutant-General to command troops in service. The legality of the procedure is not questioned . . . but it is an innovation in the military annals of the nation."

The employers' bitterness against the governor and martial law knew no bounds. They were soon to refer bitterly to the soldiers as "the governor's pickets" and to talk openly of impeachment.

On the other hand, it must have surprised members of the Citizens' Alliance over their breakfast coffee to read equally bitter denunciations of the governor and martial law on the part of the union. The union's problem with the governor's pickets was a far more intricate one than the employers'. Martial law, whatever the governor's intentions, promptly affected the strike in two ways. It reduced picketing to a shadow and under the pressure of business men at the permit office—fifteen hundred stood in line on the first day—put wider and wider categories of trucks on the streets in increasing volume. It increased chiseling. On the second day of martial law military authorities announced that "more than half the trucks in Hennepin County were operating with or without permits." A few days later General Walsh himself put the figure at six thousand. At that point it needed no Marxist arguments on the mistake of depending on soldiers as pickets to convince a piano mover that the governor of the state of Minnesota—*with the best of intentions*—was breaking his strike.

The leadership promptly went in person to the governor of the state of Minnesota with a specific proposal that he halt all movements of trucks for forty-eight hours and that union representation be allowed to advise National Guard officers in an overhaul of truck permits. They added an ultimatum that if the proposal was refused they would defy the governor's orders and military authorities by picketing all trucks with or without permits.

Class war in Minneapolis had reached a new high and was presenting unforeseen enigmas and contradictions to the first Farmer-Labor governor in America. Bewilderment replaced indignation in the news report of this encounter. "When Governor Olson walked out a half hour later he declined to comment. To observers there appeared to be an air of unreality about the whole meeting and the incongruity of strike leaders presenting flat demands to Governor Olson as the Commander-in-Chief of the National Guard which he summoned to the city to preserve law and order."

The governor was rapidly becoming the center of the strike and exchanging the position he had held in the May negotiations of "being all things to all men" for the most hated man in Minneapolis. The average citizen began to note with alarm that martial rule was costing $15,000 a day. Business men read angrily that bank clearings were down "a million dollars a day under pressure of strike and military rule." And the employers, far from yielding to military and moral pressure, continued to tell the Federal mediators that they would not deal with Communists "unless compelled to do so by the requirements of Section 7A of the National Recovery Act." Let Bolshevik Mr. Roosevelt put that in his pipe and smoke it! To balance the workers' ultimatum the employers prepared their

own for the governor of the state by initiating injunction proceedings against Olson and his use of the militia.

If the employers' ultimatum was to take a few more days
before it would be put to the testing, the strikers' was organized
into action the next day. Declaring Olson's reply to their
demands "absolutely unsatisfactory and unacceptable," they
called an open-air mass meeting of twenty-five thousand on
the Minneapolis parade grounds to "show them, militia or no
militia, no organization can break this strike." Bill Brown,
himself a Farmer-Laborite and *not* one of the handful of
"Marxist revolutionists" in the union, declared that "the Farmer-Labor administration is the best strikebreaking force our
union has ever gone up against." The truck drivers applauded
wildly. When they left the parade ground they prepared to
picket in the face of the bayonets of the National Guard and
against the orders of its commander-in-chief.

CHAPTER XI

THREE CITIZENS AND THE FATE OF A CITY

IT is a perennial task of the historian to mark, with what accuracy he can, the interacting role of individuals and the "impersonal forces of history." Three men in the crisis of the civil war in July held the fate of the city in their hands. And the history of events at this point is inseparable from their personalities. A. W. Strong,* guiding spirit of the Citizens' Alliance, proposed to smash the strike and the revolt of the rank and file it stood for by force. The ultimatum to the governor demanding freedom of interference in the "enforcement of law and order" had no other meaning. V. R. Dunne, strategist and organizer of the truck drivers' union, proposed to defend the strike by a forceful defiance of all its enemies— including the bayonets of the National Guard and its commander, the Farmer-Labor governor of Minnesota. The role of the governor himself, "on a picket fence" between left and right ultimatums, was still undetermined. With an obliging simplicity in this instance, history seems to have assigned lead-

---

* Since the writing of this book, the death of Mr. Strong has been reported. The decease of a living character suggests to the writer either a revision or an amplification of estimate. With this in mind I have carefully re-read the book in proof. I find nothing to change. Mr. Strong in his several interviews with me said: "I know you don't agree with me. All I ask is that you don't distort the statements that I make to you." If Mr. Strong could read this book, I believe he would respect the conscientiousness of my presentation, though he would differ of course from my conclusions.

ing roles to peculiarly typical protagonists in our story. The
lives of all three men exemplified the economic forces as well
as the philosophies for which each one stood. If, however, they
are symbolic protagonists, all three men were also highly individual, unique, and provocative personalities in their own
right. And within limitations, events gave all three of them an
opportunity to influence history decisively.

Two years after Deputies Run, I sat in the office of Strong,
Scott and Company, manufacturers of "uni-pulvo," a boiler-
stoking device, and of grain-elevator equipment. Mr. A. W.
Strong sat behind the president's desk and said to me, "All
of my industrial principles and practice I have put into the
Citizens' Alliance, of which I was a charter member and of
which I have several times been president, *and it embodies
them.*"

I looked at Bert Strong's face, as his friends call him. Firm,
regular features with deep lines around the eyes and mouth,
carved by responsibility, it was the face of a practical man and
an executive. I looked at it again, and it seemed to me not the
face of a business man at all. The head narrows at the eyes,
which are deep and smouldering, and the forehead is slightly
sloping and high. A. W. Strong has followed the steps of
empire builders, but as I talked with him, he seemed less a
disciple of the canny, ruthless, and imaginative Jim Hill than
the strict and kindly proponent of a moral sect. Bert Strong
is a man with an intense emotional adherence to both principles and persons. He showed me a letter from loyal employees with an emotion that shook him visibly. He spoke of
the labor leaders he had fought with a reserve of hatred which
only strict Christians employ against willful heretics.

As I sat there, he told me the story of his life with modesty
and dignity, and told me that I might quote him. "I came to
Minneapolis when I was fourteen years old and went to work

in a bag factory. I became factory superintendent. When I was still a young man—this was in the nineties—I decided I would like to be my own boss. I had no capital but I was young with plenty of blood and vinegar in me. I was ready to take a chance."

The desire to be his own boss, rising with youthful exuberance in Bert Strong's breast, has ripened with the passage of years into a moral passion as well as a fundamental principle of political economy.

"I had no capital," he repeated, "but during my years in Minneapolis I had made a good many friends. I went to one of them, for I had a plan to buy out this business of which I am now president." Here is, perhaps, the second basic trait in Mr. Strong's character. Independent and aggressive to the point of intolerance, he is also gregarious in his own way—in fact, a fanatical believer in mutual assistance and collective action among his own kind.

"I went to a wealthy man whom I knew and told him my proposition. He said how much money do you need? I told him and he wrote out a check." Mr. Strong indicated the writing of the check with his hands. "I said to my friend that he must understand there was absolutely no security I could offer beyond my signature. He told me he considered that sufficient."

It was impossible for me to doubt in Bert Strong's presence that he had been faithful to this trust and to all others who had reposed a similar faith in him in later years.

"One day in the middle nineteen-hundreds, a man whom I had never seen before came into my office and handed me a document which he asked me to read. I did so. It was an agreement which stipulated that no man could work in my plant unless he belonged to the union." Mr. Strong paused and looked at me steadily. "Now this may sound funny to you *but I had hardly heard of a labor union at that time.* He said, 'My name is Van Lear. I am president of the machinist union.' He told me that unless I signed the document my factory would be on strike the next morning. Well, I told him, then my plant will go on strike because under no circumstances will I ever sign that document." Mr. Strong then related to me how, on talking with his employees he had found no grievances over wages and hours among them, but that they were resolved to follow their leaders in a strike for recognition. "And so," he concluded, "they struck the plant for thirteen weeks and almost broke me. It was at that time that I founded the Employers of Machinists Association of Minneapolis." (Superseded in later years by the Citizens' Alliance.) "For the strike was all over the city of Minneapolis. *We won and established the principle of the open shop.* And Minneapolis has remained an open-shop town ever since, until the recent disturbances beginning in 1934."

Starting from the Employers of Machinists Association, Strong and his associates built the Citizens' Alliance. Many of the other charter members died or fell away, but the Alliance became A. W. Strong's life work. Strong, Scott and Company is not a rich or a powerful industrial concern. In 1934 A. W. Strong held the city's destiny in his hands, not through industrial or financial power as Jim Hill had, but through the weight of a single economic principle and the power of an organization which embodied it.

Strong "came to power" in the era of the city's decline. And he was destined to defend the city and "its principles," not with the exuberant spirit of the Golden Age, but with the narrower if more passionate fortitude of a man fighting for his economic life. Parallel Strong's life with that of the economy of the Northwest. When Bert Strong went to work as a boy in a bag factory, the empire was still at its height. But

A. W. STRONG

". . . kindly proponent of a moral sect . . . his life work was at stake"

V. R. DUNNE
". . . his whole life and character prepared him for the crisis of 1934"

when Strong was forty-five—Jim Hill at forty-five was beginning to reach out for imperial control—the economic basis of
the empire itself was being whittled away. And during the
post-War years, when Strong and the Citizens' Alliance exercised their greatest power, the empire was fully conscious of
its economic decline. The small and middle business men of
Minneapolis, struggling for success and survival, overwhelm-
ingly constituted the membership of the Alliance. Bert Strong
was their representative.

Nevertheless, Strong and his Alliance welded the big and
the little industrial interests of the empire into one fighting
organization, as far as he could. He met socially and prosely-
tized all the leading citizens of the empire although he was
not born one of them himself. His marriage to the daughter
of one of the empire builders perhaps helped. Bert Strong, who
had risen from a factory worker, became a member of the
Minneapolis Club. Sophisticated scions of the empire builders
have attacked Strong for years and with him the Citizens'
Alliance. Declaring themselves liberals and sensible men, they
condemned the "antilabor obsessions" of Bert Strong and
blasted the Alliance as an instrument of provocation. Presidents of national corporations have even scornfully named for
me small businesses who "were only able to exist in Minneapolis by taking it out of labor's hide." None of this criticism
has bothered Strong or his associates—an indifference which
events have seemed to justify. Given a strike or union to smash
in Minneapolis, the banks and empire builders have solidly
backed the Alliance with the munitions of war.

A. W. Strong would deny with all his force that the Citizens' Alliance was "antilabor." "When I was factory superintendent," he told me, "I treated all the men under me fairly
and they returned that treatment." On the walls of his office
is a poem wishing him "Merry Christmas" and signed with

the names of the oldest employees of Strong, Scott and Company. It accompanied the gift of a radio for Mr. Strong's Pontiac car. Formally, as we have seen in the history of the "peace parleys," even the Citizens' Alliance gives nominal allegiance to the principles of collective bargaining. But the core of Bert Strong's conviction and that of the Alliance is that the greatest "independence and freedom" for employers and employees alike will be established by keeping unions out of Minneapolis, or keeping them docile. After all, this is no more than the view common to the majority of American business men. But in Minneapolis it is a view heavily panoplied with organizational and theological equipment. The Alliance's fight to smash unions in Minneapolis Bert Strong regards as a fight to restore freedom to the workingman. I think he holds this view honestly. But the crucial point of this history is that *against the employer*—as well as the employee—who disagrees with its formula for independence and freedom, the Alliance is as ruthless and autocratic as a court of inquisition against heretics fallen from grace. There are many employers in Minneapolis with all of Bert Strong's rugged individualism who by the same token refuse to be bound by any employers' association that may limit it. Strong is not of that sort—he believes in the most disciplined collectivism in defense of the freedom "to be your own boss." Ruthlessly, before and after 1934, the Citizens' Alliance has cracked down on business men who differed from its version of industrial salvation. Bert Strong has built an industrial union, in so far as he could, of all Minneapolis business men, and no strikebreakers are tolerated.

I am ready to believe that in Strong's case, and in that of his emotional adherents among employers, the fact that a nonunion Minneapolis means higher profits for the Alliance membership doesn't consciously enter into their thinking. Ripening from the passion to be undisputed boss of one's own factory, the principle of "freedom" has acquired a theological character.

In 1936 I attended the annual dinner of the Citizens' Alliance. Dr. Neil Carothers, announcing he was speaking "not as a politician but an economist," described the economic system which he credited members of the Citizens' Alliance with supporting. "The reason I accepted your invitation [to speak] was because you do take your economics seriously," he said. "In the first place, it [the economic system] is somewhere between twenty and forty thousand years old . . . . this system cannot be hurried . . . . wages and income are determined by physical forces, by economic forces, and by biological forces governing the birth rate. . . . The wage rate is not determined by law. It's determined by the co-ordinated and co-operative activity of all these forces. It starts with the sun spots," etc., etc.

The net effect of this oratory was to convince the membership of the Citizens' Alliance that the strike of the underpaid truck drivers for a wage increase was a defiance of eternal law. The speech was received with stormy applause. I submit this is neither politics *nor economics*—it is theology.

I have no doubt that in July, 1934, Mr. Strong was prepared to ruin himself and the members of the Alliance in defense of eternal law and of a principle designed to give every man freedom. Indeed, equipped with both economic power and the spirit of evangelism, the Citizens' Alliance of Minneapolis is no ordinary employers' organization. In July, 1934, it possessed centralized committee control, a disciplined membership, a permanent staff of highly paid functionaries, the backing of the Minneapolis banks, the co-operation of the police, and one of the most thoroughgoing labor spy organizations in the country. It was a redoubtable antagonist for any rank-and-file rebellion. This was Bert Strong's creation, or at any rate he was its theologian and its organizer.

Mr. Strong himself says he was only "one of many" who

founded and who built up the Citizens' Alliance in Minneapolis. And other members of the Alliance have intimated to me that the real power has passed into other hands, that Strong today is simply the "grand old man of the Alliance." This may well be, but certain it is that in the historic crisis of the Alliance's life in 1934, A. W. Strong was the moral dynamo behind it, and to him the supreme task of negotiating the final strike settlement, which was to decide the Alliance's fate and the city's, was given.

In July, 1934, the challenge to all of the Alliance's principles and to the status of its control over the city's rank and file was dramatic and crucial. And I am willing to hazard that Strong knew it more accurately and more intimately than any of the truck owners or any other Alliance employers. Liberal employers were privately criticizing the Alliance's tactics, once more. Strong and his colleagues had outfaced them before and they would do it again. The truck-owner members of the Alliance had heartily endorsed the conduct of the police on Bloody Friday. They had pressed injunction proceedings against the governor. Citizens' Alliance stalwarts believed that "law and order could be restored" and the strike broken by the guns of the police if only the militia could be gotten rid of. If others wavered, there is little doubt in my mind that A. W. Strong was firm, willing to fight on to a bloody vindication of the Alliance's principles without counting the cost either in personal ruin or in the blood and treasure of his city. His life work as well as his economic faith were at stake, and the weapons at the disposal of the Alliance seemed ample. The Citizens' Alliance had made up its mind to use all of them in defense of the city's "freedom."

Vincent Raymond Dunne was born in Little Falls, Minnesota, forty-six years ago, a few miles from the Lindbergh home, many years before Charles Lindbergh, Jr., flew the Atlantic. V. R. Dunne, brought up a strict Irish Catholic, was taught to hate Lindbergh, Sr., as a Swede, a Protestant and a Red, and was told that Lindbergh's radicalism flowed naturally from his unfortunate race and religion. But by accident Dunne himself became a rebel at the age of eleven. Ray and his five brothers were studying for their first communion and one day, as an interlude to the catechism, Bill, the eldest, read aloud from Victor Hugo to the other kids. They were gathered around him on the lawn beside the parochial school. Unfortunately Father Dupont, the Little Falls priest, overheard the profane words of Hugo and, snatching the novel from Bill, tore it in two before their eyes. While the Dunne brothers stared at him in terror, he assembled the whole confirmation class and preached a sermon on the evils of worldliness. The Dunne boys were expelled from the class. The effect of this episode on the Dunne parents was to break their hearts. They felt the boys had brought disgrace upon the family forever. Ray, however, set to wondering what there was in the book which Father Dupont considered worthy of hell fire.

After the first shock was over, according to his own recollection, it roused the first dim sparks of intellectual curiosity. The fatal book itself had come from his grandmother's house, who alone among the Dunne relatives had a small library of English and European classics. Ray's father was too poor for books. With increased avidity Bill and his brothers devoured the rest of the little library. Today, although Dunne attended school for but part of one winter, he is well read and writes a clear and easy style. Perhaps Father Dupont is to be credited with his literary education.

Little Falls was at the edge of a forest in the early nineteen-hundreds and Ray Dunne's first job was driving a team for a lumber company. By fourteen he had "put on cork shoes," learned to handle a cant hook and earn a man's pay. When the call came for lumberjacks near the Black Feet Mountains in Montana, Ray applied for a job and got it. Most of the lumberjacks in the empire in those days were joining up with the I.W.W. and Ray became a Wobbly—it was the I.W.W. which gave Dunne his first political philosophy. "Although I wasn't interested in it at the time, I recall that I joined at about the time of the Russian Revolution of 1905 and the Wobblies were talking about it in Montana!" From the lumber camps of the Northwest he went to the Coast and, still a boy of sixteen or seventeen, was arrested in California for making an I.W.W. speech.

In 1908 he returned to Minneapolis, where he has lived ever since. All kinds of jobs in the Twin Cities followed, in factories and on the street, sandwich man for a lunch wagon, driver for the American Express Company. "There were horses in those days but I drove one of the first big motor trucks for a Minneapolis transfer company." Most of the jobs were in trucking, in the office or on the driver's seat. That is the Minneapolis industry V. R. Dunne knows best. Two of the jobs he lost through trying to organize a trade union. When the war came his boss fired him for refusing to buy war savings stamps.

As soon as the American Communist party was founded— at first as an underground party—V. R. Dunne became a member of it. Some revolutionists don't find time to marry. Dunne married in 1914 and has raised children ever since. "We have brought up three children of our own besides others we have adopted and raised from time to time." The family circle in Ray Dunne's mother's house in South Minneapolis is typical of educated workers' homes anywhere. The older kids are in high school now and conversation runs to baseball, high-school dances, news of the day, and the high cost of living.

From 1921 on V. R. Dunne earned his living in the coal

yards in Minneapolis. He had gone to work for the DeLaittre Dixon Coal Company and stuck with them for twelve years. He shoveled coal, drove a truck, became weighmaster, dispatcher, and for a time superintendent. All of these years he spoke publicly, wrote for his party's press, and gave a substantial part of his earnings to the revolutionary party to which he belonged. Why wasn't he fired from the DeLaittre Dixon Company for being a Communist?

The empire had dealt generously with the DeLaittres and they were millionaires several times over from lumber holdings. Ray Dunne they liked personally, and found him a highly intelligent weighmaster. Lecturing him repeatedly on his radical views, they nonetheless refused to fire him when he spoke at street meetings and attended plenums of the Communist party. When as a known Communist in Minnesota he ran for senator on the Farmer-Labor ticket, one of the DeLaittre brothers said, "Give me some of your literature, Ray, and I'll get you some votes." Dunne says that Tycoon DeLaittre swears that he voted for him. Not that the DeLaittre family were millionaire parlor Reds—their confessed ambition and life's work was to double the family fortune—but a streak of Tory radicalism made them despise the idea of firing a man for his political views. Besides they respected Dunne and found him a more than competent employee of the DeLaittre Coal Company. They even offered him stock in the business— though V. R. Dunne turned them down. Instead, he worked as hard as he could to organize a rank-and-file revolt against the empire builders and their inheritors. And in their own way the DeLaittres respected him for that too.

Finally, in 1933 the coal company entered into a business arrangement with Fuel Distributors, a Ford-owned corporation. V. R. Dunne was transferred to the new concern. For several weeks the Ford manager tried to make up his mind to fire his Communist weighmaster who had come to him with the O.K. of the DeLaittre Dixons. First he asked him to "resign." It was such a unique episode that I believe it deserves a place in this record.

"Is it because of my work?" Ray Dunne asked his boss.

"No, no. The work is all right; you know that, Dunne."

"Do I get along all right with the men?"

"Of course, relations with the men are fine."

"Well, what is it?"

Believe it or not, the Ford manager was embarrassed. He put off the firing until another day. But after all, it was too much for a Ford company to harbor a trade unionist who at that moment was organizing the coal heavers of Minneapolis under his nose, and was a Communist to boot. V. R. Dunne spoke publicly at an anti-Fascist rally. A week later the manager gave the weighmaster his last pay check.

There followed lean years of poverty and struggle. Ray Dunne had always shared his wages—which rose as high as $175 a month—with his political party, in addition to supporting his own family, and he had no reserves. Odd jobs, contributions from friends in the labor movement, relief groceries, and clothes donations by friends pulled the family through. Meantime he threw himself vigorously and full time into organizing the truck-driving industry of Minneapolis.

The truck drivers and the Strike Committee of One Hundred leaned heavily on V. R. Dunne in the crisis of civil war in 1934. It had been his foresight and his organizing ability which had been crucial in building the union. For that reason and that reason only, he held the fate of the city in his hands.

V. R. Dunne, forty-three years old, was still a little man, no taller, and weighed a pound or two less than he had when, age fourteen, he had gone to work in the Black Feet Mountains with a cant hook. But the truck drivers had come to trust in his "long head." The years from 1928 on, when the Communist Party had expelled him as a Trotskyite, had done things to him. He had studied the American and European political classics and got into the habit of independent thinking. This he combined with an unshakable faith in the rank and file of the empire and an intimate knowledge of the coal yards of Minneapolis.

The workers knew Ray Dunne as a good organizer, a man who smoked union-made cigarettes, was fond of the movies, lived in his mother's house in South Minneapolis, didn't get drunk, and was honest. They followed his leadership and many of them, if the occasion offered, would be quite willing to die for him. One reason was his physical courage. Life had made bodily fearlessness a matter of routine. In the past two years alone, Dunne has been beaten up several times by the police on picket lines, attacked in the street by armed thugs, thrown into jail, confined in a stockade under military guard by the governor. More important than physical fearlessness is his moral nerve. He tells workers what he thinks of a situation whether they like it or not. I have seen him argue down two thousand truck drivers who opposed his policies.

These were the bases of his power in July, 1934; he had no others. He was not an officer of the truck drivers' union, not even a paid organizer of Local 574. Along with the other strike leaders he was merely a member of the truck drivers' organizing committee. The organizing committee met to talk things over. Everyone said what they thought. The strike committee met with the organizing committee to talk things over. The strike committee asked Ray Dunne what he thought. "We must restore the picket line," he said. He told them his "analysis" without raising his voice.

V. R. Dunne's analysis of the strike situation in July, 1934, was diametrically opposed to Strong's, and it flowed as logically

from his class viewpoint, as well as the experience of a lifetime, as did Strong's. In distinction from much rank-and-file
opinion at the time, he saw as the main enemy not the Citizens' Alliance, not even the revolvers and machine guns of the
police, but at that moment, the Farmer-Labor governor of
Minnesota. "Restore the picket lines in the face of the governor's decrees and the bayonets of the militia," said Dunne.
"Follow Olson and you will win," urged a substantial majority
of the labor movement. "He's a Farmer-Labor governor—the
militia is on our side."

"Nonsense," answered Dunne. "Submit to the governor and
the strike is lost. *The militia is moving trucks.*"

Enemies and friends of V. R. Dunne, alike, would agree, I
think, that his whole life and character prepared him for the
position he took in the strike crisis of 1934. Son of a worker,
earning his own living from the age of eleven, a Wobbly at
fourteen, a revolutionary Marxist from the time he was twenty,
his life, as well as his philosophy, taught him that workers
"must rely only on their own organizations." Dunne had not
an atom of faith in anything else. When Governor Floyd
Olson called out the militia and the militia moved trucks for
the truck owners, Olson became an enemy of the strike. All
talk about a Farmer-Labor governor winning the strike was so
much nonsense. Dunne's Marxist theory told him so, but in
arguing with opponents he did not produce his theory to prove
it. He pointed to the six thousand trucks moving in Minneapolis and to the paralyzed picket lines. By the time of the
parade-ground demonstration that was argument enough for
the strikers he led.

What to do about it? He proposed, and the other strike
leaders with him: Tell the governor to his face he is breaking
the strike. Demand he stop moving trucks. Demand he permit

picketing. If he won't or can't because he's governor, picket anyway in the face of the tin hats.

The baldness of this tactic horrified most Farmer-Laborites, as well as average citizens, as a species of Communist lunacy.

Did it make *any* difference then that Olson was a *Farmer-Labor* governor and not a Republican? "Of course," Dunne answered, *"that's what the tactic means.* With the National Guard ordered to shoot us down, the situation would be all but hopeless. With a Farmer-Labor governor we can do something about it. Olson doesn't want to break the strike *if he can help it.* So force him to call off the Guard, but restore picketing at any cost."

After as cool an appraisal of forces as possible, revolutionists take chances. If they didn't they would not be revolutionists. V. R. Dunne and the leadership of 574 took a long chance in the summer of 1934. And knew they were doing it.

Floyd Bjorstjerne Olson was born in 1891 in a Jewish working class neighborhood in Minneapolis. Biographers have since pointed out that physically and racially he had the "perfect set-up" for a Minnesota political career. His mother was Swedish, his father Norwegian. Floyd Olson, a Norse amalgam, stood six feet one in his socks, weighed one hundred seventy-five pounds, and to his admirers looked every inch a "modern Viking." As if this were not enough, he married a Czechoslovakian wife and could speak Norwegian, Swedish, or Yiddish as the political occasion required.

Floyd Olson combined the qualities of a radical and of a self-made man, two elements equally vital to his role in Minnesota politics and to this history. Without question, he was the most brilliant and able, as well as colorful, "radical" of his generation. Mourned by millions of supporters and opponents, he died prematurely on the threshold of a career in the United

States Senate and with presidential aspirations, at the age of forty-four, on August 20, 1936. The qualities which distinguished Olson were courage, physical and moral, political sagacity (Republican opponents said he was the shrewdest politician in the northwest), ironic eloquence (he was a dangerous campaigner), and unlimited personal charm. Thousands of supporters who disagreed with Floyd Olson politically followed him with blind and dogged devotion.

Floyd Olson worked his way through school and one year at the University of Minnesota by selling newspapers and candy at night in the Opera House. He won a reputation on the debating team but otherwise found time only for his books and the business of making a living. After freshman year, he started to knock about the world—jobs as land salesman, traveling auditor for a tractor company, and for a time law student with an attorney in Saskatchewan. For some reason, the attorney's office didn't work out and Floyd went to work as a riverman on boats plying from Tete Jaune to St. George. Thence, mucker in a silver mine at Hazleton to installing telephone poles for the Grand Trunk Railroad. When news came of gold in Alaska, he joined the rush. On returning to Seattle without gold, he got a job as dock walloper and joined the I.W.W. He finally decided to try his luck once more in the home town, and with a wealth of experience and no cash the future governor of Minnesota rode blind baggage in freezing December weather back to Minneapolis.

From then on came a change of fortune. Law studies were resumed at Northwestern College, he was admitted to the bar in 1915, and at the age of twenty-eight was appointed county attorney—the youngest man ever to hold the office. He ran for governor as a Farmer-Laborite in 1924 on a radical platform but was defeated. Re-elected county attorney in 1928, it was in this job that he really got into his stride. "The ablest lawyer in the Northwest," his Republican enemies have assured me. His record as county attorney was sensational. He made large property owners responsible who rented buildings for gambling and prostitution; he convicted Henry C. Hanke, former county treasurer and Republican, for making off with $25,000 of public money; *he condemned Briggs, the president of the Citizens' Alliance, for attempting, through a private detective agency, to procure a labor official to plant dynamite for the purpose of discrediting organized labor.* Almost single handed he fought the railroads on price fixing and prevented the raising of rates on hard coal to the Northwest. Here was the basis in personal performance for the later career of the first Farmer-Labor governor which we have discussed in a previous chapter.

The contradictions of character, which friends and enemies alike discerned in their young and colorful governor, are important to this history. It came to be noticed that the Farmer-Labor governor picked most of his intimates from lawyers, bankers, and manufacturers. He entertained them with good food and good liquor and they entertained the governor in return. A. I. Harris, a close friend and devoted admirer of Olson, suggested to me in explanatory defense, "The governor took an almost sadistic pleasure in baiting these parasites of this capitalist system." His enemies among Farmer-Laborites said these intimacies proved the governor was selling out to their enemies. A far simpler explanation is, I believe, that the governor liked good food and good liquor and hadn't had much of either in his earlier career. They are the natural reward for an American self-made man. Though not without significance, this contradiction in our Farmer-Labor governor is not decisive to our history. More pertinent is the Olson trait of swift accommodation of political principles to election needs, the trait which enabled the party to say officially in 1930,

"Mr. Olson is not a radical . . . but . . . a progressive," and Olson himself to shout in 1934, "You bet your life I'm a radical" and advocate abolition of the capitalistic system. Still more crucial for an understanding of the governor's approach to the strike crisis of 1934 was the Olson characteristic of brilliant personal performance unfettered by party discipline.

Olson's whole life, sketched briefly above, had nurtured individual initiative in him with a vengeance. He had risen from newsboy to governor, his wits had pried him out of innumerable tough spots and invariably pushed him ahead. I have never met a man with a more imperious belief in his own destiny or a blither confidence that his own wits would give him his heart's desire. This man was head of the Farmer-Labor party of Minnesota. Yet he was not half the organizational man that Strong was with his reactionary Citizens' Alliance or V. R. Dunne with the truck drivers' union. We have already noted in a previous chapter that the Farmer-Labor party needed Olson more than Olson needed the Farmer-Labor party. That is important. The "high-handed actions of the Olson machine" were already causing a revolt among his more collective-minded rank and file. But the revolt was stillborn. Olson was too persuasive a leader and too valuable to rank-and-file Laborites.

Two other components in Olson's makeup are directly pertinent to an understanding of the *problem* presented to him by the ultimatums of Ray Dunne and Bert Strong in the civil war of 1934. However much he joked, baited, or drank the liquor of the capitalists—Harris is right—his heart and his emotions were with Wobblies, dock wallopers, factory workers, *and truck drivers.* He hated the reactionary stupidity of the Citizens' Alliance with genuine class emotions as well as an intellectual scorn. He wanted the strike to win. But the final factor, which to my mind must have been dominant in Olson's view of the crisis, was the political one. A far more stupid man than the Farmer-Labor governor would have realized that his political strength and that of the Farmer-Labor party was bound up with the issue of the civil war. And no one ever accused Olson of political stupidity. He was brilliantly and exceptionally aware of all the most subtle *political* factors of any situation that touched him or his party.

The problem which the ultimatum from the right and the ultimatum from the left presented to the governor of Minnesota was of arbitrating between the class forces he personally and politically represented and those he did not. As the United States has had only one Farmer-Labor governor, this problem was unique on American soil. In European politics there had been precedents aplenty.

In sum, and *politically,* the enigma handed the governor was this: at the historic conference with the strike leaders they had asked him in essence to turn over the National Guard permit authority to them. Had he yielded, he would in effect have abdicated sovereignty as governor and as the commander-in-chief of the National Guard. The strike leaders combined their demands with an ultimatum of forceful defiance. He could hardly have submitted to this rebellious defiance of the military and remained governor of Minnesota. On the other hand, if as governor and commander of the National Guard he broke the strike, he was politically dead. The Farmer-Labor party would lie peacefully in a grave beside him.

A variety of emotions must have jostled inside Olson's head as he left the Minneapolis Club on that hot July day and declined to comment. The hatred of all the business classes in Minnesota had risen to a new high against him. But he had counted on that and rather enjoyed it. Now, however, twenty-five thousand *workers* in Minneapolis—at the parade-ground demonstration—were hurling defiance not only at the National Guard but at *him* and at the Farmer-Labor party.

There is a personal factor to which, at this point, I believe, some weight should be given. Floyd Olson had a reputation, as well founded as Ray Dunne's, for never losing his grip on himself in an argument. In a long career as militant champion of the rank and file, no labor leader had ever defied him. Local 574 had now done so to his face. One of the participants in that crucial interview, who had known and also admired the governor for many years, said to me, "I have known Governor Olson for fifteen years; it was the only time I have ever seen him both angry and not quite sure of himself." Whatever transpired at the interview inside the governor's head and nerves, in the thirty-six hours that followed, Governor Olson devised a plan. Into it went all of his political acumen, his philosophy, and his ambition. It was this:

1. To raid and to occupy by military force the strike headquarters of Local 574. To arrest the leaders who had defied him and place them in a military stockade.

2. To call for the election of a "rank-and-file" committee "truly representative" of the truck drivers of Minneapolis.

3. Personally, as governor, to confer with that committee and so settle the strike.

The plan had a political inference of which the governor must have been aware—that the union, for its own good, must be beheaded. This was a reversal of the stand taken by the governor up until then. The plan offered advantages to its author: it gave an immediate answer to the defiance of martial rule by the strikers; it lessened the difficulties of settlement with the Employers' Committee by *forceful removal* of the "Communist leaders"; it would concentrate the kudos for a strike settlement in the hands of himself and the Farmer-Labor party which he represented. Such a plan would certainly re-

GOVERNOR FLOYD B. OLSON
His party's future hung in the balance—and his own

ENTER THE NATIONAL GUARD

"Pickets" or strikebreakers?—they pleased neither side

ceive support from the conservative labor leaders in Minneapolis, whose concealed hostility to the truck drivers' leadership was known. The attempt of the governor to carry out all
three steps of the plan is a matter of record. That the plan was
his own was admitted to Grant Dunne, strike leader. There is
no record to show that the political advantages listed above
were part of the governor's considerations; perhaps the governor regarded the plan as best in the public interests—and in
the interests of the workers. All the historian can record is:
(1) that the political advantages mentioned above would
accrue to the author, had the plan succeeded; (2) the price of
success was the destruction of the leadership, and—in the author's opinion—the demoralization of the union.

CHAPTER XII

TRUCE BETWEEN THE PAST AND THE PRESENT

T HE first step of Governor Olson's plan was executed by Colonel McDevitt, at four A.M. on August 1. With several hundred National Guardsmen, a battery of light artillery, and a detachment of machine gunners, he surrounded on all sides the old garage on South Eighth Street which served the strikers as headquarters. The leaders who met the colonel on his entrance into the strike headquarters recall that he was nervous and excessively polite. The colonel had left his troops outside awaiting the result of his parley with the leaders. He apologized and explained that it was a matter of carrying out military orders. He begged that the garage be evacuated without resistance. At the time he arrived it was still dark and as he conferred with the leaders the first rays of dawn came through the windows of the garage. Members of the Women's Auxiliary were pouring coffee and cutting bread while several hundred hungry pickets waited to eat their breakfast. The leaders requested that the men be permitted to finish their meal before the military occupation. The colonel consented.

V. R. Dunne, chief strategist of the strike, was immediately placed under arrest. Meantime Dobbs and Grant Dunne hastily left by a rear entrance. At the door they were halted by a guardsman. Dobbs remonstrated, "What the hell is this? The colonel ordered us to leave. If you don't believe me send up and ask him." The guardsman did so and returned with the colonel's permission. Of course, warrants were in the colonel's

pocket for Dobbs, Dunne, and all the other leaders. By this
ruse Grant Dunne and Farrell Dobbs escaped. They hastened
to set up temporary headquarters in friendly filling stations
and at other spots throughout the city. So that by four-thirty or
five, when the military settled into final occupation of strike
headquarters, picketing was resumed as usual in Minneapolis.
While the colonel was conferring he had removed his tin hat
and laid it on the table. An irreverent striker, placing it on his
own head, ran to the microphone and in view of the crowd
outside, strikers and Guardsmen alike, led the strikers in song
as they evacuated their headquarters. They went out singing
"The Daring Young Man on the Flying Trapeze" to the disgust of the colonel and the total demoralization of his military
escorts.

It is incorrect to say that picketing was resumed as usual.
It was resumed on an even wider scale than theretofore and
with redoubled fury as the strikers learned of the capture of
headquarters and the arrest of their leaders. All the other strike
leaders, except Skoglund who was out of town, were taken
into custody and incarcerated in the military stockade.

The governor's intention of cracking down on picketing by
capture of headquarters and the leadership failed dramatically.
"In place of the South Eighth Street headquarters," a union
man told me, "we established 'curb headquarters' all over the
city. We had twenty of them." And in place of the eight leaders walled up in the stockade fifty-odd picket captains took
charge of the strike on their own. They were fighting mad
and utterly fearless. In the next twenty-four hours, the vigor,
the scope, and the fury of the picket actions terrified the city
and gave pause to the governor himself. According to the
press,

"Marauding bands of pickets roamed the streets of Minneapolis today in automobiles and trucks, striking at commercial

truck movements in widespread sections of the city. . . . National Guardsmen in squad cars made frantic efforts to clamp down. The continued picketing was regarded as a protest over the military arrest of Brown and the Dunnes, strike leaders, together with sixty-eight others during and after Guardsmen raided strike headquarters and the Central Labor Union."

One might have anticipated that Step 1, the raid of strike headquarters and the arrest of the leaders, which was promptly followed by a raid on the offices of the Central Labor Union, would have raised the prestige of the military and at least tamed if not demoralized the strike. Its violently opposite effect, which must have become instantly apparent to the governor, did not deter him, however, from executing Step 2. With all the leaders but two in military stockade, he called for "election of a rank-and-file committee to settle the strike." A committee of two rank and filers was elected at his request—Ray Rainbolt and Kelly Postal. They were summoned to a conference with the governor to negotiate a settlement. Rainbolt's account of the conference follows:

"We met with the governor, Kelly and I. He said to us, 'Well, boys, we've got to settle this thing.' We said to him, 'First you let out our leaders; after that we'll talk.' Kelly called him a copper-hearted son-of-a- —— and I said to him, 'Governor, you're right in the middle, on a picket fence. Watch your step or you'll slip and hurt yourself bad.' He talked and talked. And I said to him, 'Why don't you start a school for strikebreaking governors?' He also asked us if we knew where Grant and Dobbs were. I said, 'Yes, I know, but you won't find out from me.' "

Ray Rainbolt is a Sioux Indian, and this was perhaps the first occasion since Little Crow's speech to the traders that a representative of his race had had to inform constituted authorities what he thought of them. Both Little Crow's and Rainbolt's words were singularly succinct.

The governor, having failed to negotiate (!) a settlement, decided for his own reasons that the finding of Dobbs and Dunne was the next step. From here on the narrative can be continued by Grant Dunne.

"After the raiding of headquarters and the arrest of Ray, Miles, and the others, there was of course a warrant out for Dobbs and myself. Well, the governor finally by a roundabout way got a message to me to call Bob Cramer, editor of the *Labor Review,* so I went way out to a filling station in the suburbs and called him up. Cramer said, 'Olson wants to see you.' I answered, 'To put me in the stockade, huh?' He said, 'No, he gives his word he'll forget the warrant.' I replied, 'I don't know whether to believe him. He has double-crossed us before.' He said, 'Will you believe him if he tells you so himself?' I answered, 'Well, let me talk to him, and right now, while I'm on this line, I don't want a patrol car picking me up out here.' So the governor got on the line—he was right there with Cramer. He said he'd withdraw the warrant. I asked, 'Does that go for Dobbs too?' He said it did. So I said, 'All right.'

"When I got there, I asked him if those arrests and the rank-and-file committee, etc., were his plan. He said he thought that was the proper way to proceed. I asked him if the tin hats around my house and the intimidation of my wife and children was also a part of his plan. He denied that and apologized, saying that he couldn't control all the actions of the militia. 'Don't you know by this time,' I said to him, 'that you're not fooling around with children? You can take me and Dobbs and throw us into the stockade with the others. There will be plenty of leaders left. The strike will go right on, picketing and all.' "

The governor has a reputation both as a judge of men and a realist. And fortunately for the strikers Dunne was not bluffing but stating a fact. A remarkable and important interview for the union under the circumstances, but the facts upon which Dunne rested his case were even more important. The strike's conduct had been such that a thousand lesser leaders had come out of the ranks and the pickets themselves by this time had learned their own jobs. The arrest of the leaders, instead of beheading the movement, infused it, at least temporarily, with a demoniac fury. The fierce ruthlessness of the picketing which had followed the leaders' arrest was not unknown to the governor.

· "So he turned up the palms of his hands like this and said, 'Well, Grant, what do you want me to do?' I said, 'Two things: first, release our leaders from the stockade; second, turn back the headquarters in exactly the condition in which you took it over.' 'All right,' he said, 'I'll do it.' He kept his word. The next day the leaders were let out of the stockade and the headquarters restored."

The next morning the public was to read in the newspapers: "Last night Grant Dunne and Farrell Dobbs went into conference with Brigadier-General Walsh. [What happened in the conference was not made public through the press.] At the close Grant Dunne confidently predicted that his three companions would be released [from the military stockade] and the military received orders to withdraw from strike headquarters."

One of the conversations at that conference which was not made public, but which refined into a few heated speeches all the class feelings of the situation, is significant for this record. When Adjutant-General Walsh transmitted the governor's orders to Colonel McDevitt, both Dunne and the governor were present. General Walsh said, "You are to withdraw your troops from the strike headquarters and turn back the building in the condition in which you found it."

The colonel's face flushed and, looking hard at Walsh, he said, "General, if I carry out this order, it will certainly lower the morale of my men."

Dunne spoke up. "If you carry out that order, colonel, it will greatly raise the morale of mine."

The general turned fiercely to Dunne: "See that you don't use any of those lead pipes on my men."

Dunne answered him, "What about the weapons your troops use on my people? They're hard and sharp enough."

The governor waved them both to silence.

Following this powerful blow of the chief executive at the truck drivers' union, which the rank and file had checkmated, Governor Olson turned about and struck out at the employers. On August 3 he ordered the National Guard to raid the Citizens' Alliance! The scions of the empire builders gasped as Lieutenant Kenneth Haycraft descended on the sanctum of the Alliance with a detachment of tin hats and retired with a sheaf of dictaphone records and confidential letters. The governor promptly announced: "The evidence seized corroborates my charge that the Citizens' Alliance dominates and controls the Employers' Advisory Committee, and that it maintains . . . stool pigeons . . . in . . . labor unions." Further, there was evidence that the Alliance "had coerced other employers" to do its bidding and opposed in principle, as it had in fact defied, the provisions of the NRA and the United States Department of Labor. The effect of this attack on the stronghold of big business was to soften the blow—for some if not all of the strikers—of the raid on their own headquarters and the arrest of their leaders.

One is sometimes struck with how curiously little originality there is in political life. A blow to the left, softened by a blow to the right—classic and time-honored formula for reformists "put in the middle" by class forces! As I write these lines today, two years later, Leon Blum, premier of France and chieftain of the Popular Front, has sent the Gardes Mobiles to evict strikers from a chocolate factory while he pacifies his electorate on the same day with a raid on the headquarters of the Croix de Feu.

To return to Minneapolis in August, 1934—several thousand trucks were now operating under military protection and the union threw itself into an organized picketing campaign, as ruthless as the spontaneous guerilla warfare which followed the leaders' arrest, but now better directed and more efficient. The union stuck by their dictum that *"Nobody,* militia or no militia, is going to move trucks and break the strike."* There is no question that without the picketing the militia would have promptly done so. Nine thousand trucks, according to General Walsh, were now operating under military permit in Minneapolis out of a possible thirteen thousand. To combat their new enemy—the Guard and the governor himself—the union appealed to the Central Labor Union for a general strike, which the Central body considered but did not execute.

Under the rank-and-file pressure and with the moral aid of his exposure of the Alliance, the governor issued an ultimatum that *unless a settlement was reached by midnight* of August 5 he would again halt all trucks. He excepted those carrying necessities, and added, *any employer signing the Haas-Dunnigan agreement would immediately be given a permit.* The press reported thirty-seven firms signing up and receiving permits by noon of the new dispensation.

The employers fairly exploded and denounced the decree as a "flagrant violation" of the rights of citizens. Shortly after, they brought their ultimatum against the governor to a test, by bringing injunction proceedings against the proclamation and against the governor's use of martial law. The governor was his own counsel and won. The judicial decision, however, contained a studied rebuke of the chief executive's wisdom. A prominent Minneapolis lawyer summed it up: "The court found it impossible to deny that the governor was well within his rights. Reluctantly the judges contented themselves with giving the distinguished defendant a legal slap on the wrist."

In the coming period of ten days—the "duration"—warfare settled into one of mutual attrition, moral and physical for both armies. For the employers it was a question of sustaining business losses. One large transfer company was dropping $25,000 a day and total business loss for both strikes was estimated at $20,000,000. Added to this, the National Guard was debiting the taxpayer's account with approximately $450,000. Middle and smaller firms faced actual bankruptcy which in some cases was turned to good account by the bigger ones. There is evidence that at one point the majority of the 166 were ready for surrender when a large contribution from a national fruit company "gave them courage." The firm in question had its strategic points of distribution *outside* the city and had increased its trade vastly during martial law.

As to the union, the strikers were asking, would there be food enough to keep alive? The picture at headquarters was not heartening—a crew of dirty, unshaven men, fatigued from weeks of picketing, were subsisting on a constantly diminishing diet of soup, bread, and coffee. Funds in the union treasury were all but exhausted. But the "moral factor" was even more disheartening. The workers who saw trucks moving with an increasing use of military escorts returned from the picket line with black looks. On August 14, in spite of the governor's latest decree, there were now 11,500 trucks moving under permit, only 4200 of which had signed the Haas-Dunningan agreement.

The embattled employers again conceived of the radio as their chief weapon for winning public opinion and discrediting and demoralizing the strikers. Each day employer after employer went on the air to pound with personal variations on two main ideas:

"Local 574, *and the wording of the mediator's proposal,* make it appear that the wage question is the real issue. The real issue is Communism." [italics mine]

"The Communists hope that this strike is the beginning of a revolution that will overthrow all existing government."

The *Organizer* countered by satire. Bill Brown was quoted "authoritatively" as saying that he was "practically convinced that the rumor that Father Haas is a paid Communist agent is grossly exaggerated!"

But the most imaginative and effective job in political satire was performed by the *Organizer* of August 8, when it purported to give the confession of the editor on the "real issues of the strike" to a Kangaroo Court.

Asked to tell who Father Haas really was, and his true connection with the strike, the editor replies:

"His real name is Haasky. He's a Russian Bolshevik brought over here by the Brain Trust to put across a modified form of Communism through the NRA. . . . His proposal of 42½ cents an hour is practically the same thing as Communism."

Officer: Spill the rest of it. What about Dunnigan, Olson, Brown, and the Dunne brothers—how many of these here Dunne brothers are there all told?

Editor: Their real name is Dunnskovitsky. They are Irish Jews from County Cork, smuggled into the country about six months ago disguised as sacks of Irish potatoes. There are seventeen of them in Minneapolis, all the same age, and they all holler for 42½ cents an hour. They say that's the beginning of Communism and they are all strong for it. They have a brother in New York who is a famous acrobat.

Officer: How about Governor Olson? He's wit youse guys in the Communist racket, ain't he?

Editor: Sure! That's the slickest part of the whole game. That guy's a card. His right name is not Olson, and he's not a Swede either—that's just a gag to get the Scandinavian vote. He's a Russian importation—direct from Moscow—and his real name is Olsonovich. He's been a big help to the strike. *That raid he pulled off at the union headquarters, and the throwing of the pickets into the stockade, was all a trick to get sympathy for the strikers.*

Officer: Who cooked up this scheme anyway?

Editor: . . . . Some of the boys worked a week driving trucks and saved up enough money to take a trip to Europe. They went over to Constantinople to see Trotsky and get instructions for their next move. Trotsky said: "Boys, I want a revolution in Minneapolis before snow flies." They said "O.K." and started to leave.

Just as they were about to take the boat, Vincent Dunne stepped up to old man Trotsky and said: "What's your last word of advice before we go?"

Officer: What did Trotsky say?

Editor: He said, "Boys, keep your eye on Olsonovich. He is liable to double-cross you any minute."

On a less imaginative level one of the best answers—from a conservative point of view—to the millions of words by the employers on the "issue of Communism" was made by George W. Lawson, president of the State Federation of Labor. Going on the air on August 13, Lawson said, "I cannot subscribe to the belief that if the members involved in this dispute accept the recommendation and agreement of Father Haas and Mr. Dunnigan that we should turn over the destiny of Minneapolis to the control of the Communist Party. . . . When there is a strike to force recognition, the clever thing to do . . . is to hunt around for a Communist and call the strike a Communist plot."

Though it failed to break the strikers' morale, the Employers' Advisory Committee propaganda and pressure did succeed in breaking the "weakest link" in the stalemate. The Federal mediators had originally proposed a settlement reasonably favorable to the strikers, the acceptance of which had put the union in a superior moral position. Now Father Haas and Mr. Dunnigan, under pressure from the employers, broke and came back to the strike committee with a new proposal which eliminated most of the favorable provisions.

To the discomfiture of the ace mediators, the coal heavers and piano movers tore into the heart of the new plan: "If you had been a picket and were now asked to sign an agreement which might bar you forever from a job, would you do it?"

No answer.

"Then why did you bring it up?"

Father Haas grew pale under the inquisition.

"Why do you go over the heads of our negotiating committee? . . . Are you trying to insult our committee or question their sincerity?" (The mediators, suspecting exhaustion on the part of the rank and file, and hoping to force settlement "over the heads of the leaders," had insisted on presenting the new plan to the Strike Committee of One Hundred.) Pursuing his question logically, the worker added, "Why don't you force the 166 bosses to get together and take a secret ballot on the *original* Haas-Dunnigan plan?"

Answer: "We can't."

"Why didn't you make the bosses accept the original plan?"

Answer: "We did not have the power to make them do anything."

"Then how do we know you will have the power to make them live up to the government decisions on the basis of this settlement?"

No answer.

Toward the conclusion of the discussion a worker, a Roman Catholic, rose with a flushed face and said: "All my life I have been a follower of the Church and I say it's a crying shame when a man wearing the cloth of the Church as you do stands up before his brother workers and attempts to swindle them into acceptance of such a sell-out as you are giving us."

After full discussion the Strike Committee voted to reject the plan. A new mediator, a Mr. Donoghue, was sent in from Washington. At the conclusion of the strike Father Haas was taken to a sanitarium.

In the final week before the settlement, however, despite the bravest efforts, the strike's morale began to ebb; thousands still held out, but a small, significant trickle of men back to work had begun. Behind the scenes on the employers' side revolt against the Citizens' Alliance was threatened. Four employers of the sacred 166 had broken and signed up with the Haas-Dunnigan agreement. Still the strikers held out. In the last few days before the settlement came mysterious pressure from Washington against the intransigeance of the "little clique" of dominant figures in the Alliance. With relative suddeness, on August 21, the new Washington mediator secured acceptance from Mr. A. W. Strong, "grand old man of the Citizens' Alliance," of a strike settlement which gave the strikers, in the words of V. R. Dunne, "substantially what we have fought and bled for since the beginning of the strike."

Scarcely had the terms of the settlement been endorsed by the union when the rank and file of Minneapolis joined the coal heavers, market drivers, and piano movers in a "victory celebration" that lasted for twelve hours. The civil war was over.

What had thirty-six days' warfare, martial rule, the loss of a half million dollars in wages and the extinction of two lives decided for the future of our American city? A few commonplaces of labor relations. Look at them! The settlement provided that seniority should prevail in the employment of truck drivers, that the workers in warehouses were to be allowed to belong the union—*if they voted to do so;* that the wages of Minneapolis truck drivers might now be submitted to arbitration! Finally, that henceforth the union could bargain collectively with the employers!

This was the victory! But inwardly the civil war had raged over far deeper issues, the first of which was the historic dictatorship over Minneapolis and the lives of its workers by the tightly organized camarilla of the Citizens' Alliance. The strike had challenged and broken that dictatorship. All the best energies, brains, and resources of both combatants had been expended and each side knew acutely what they had won and lost. The amazing machinery of the conflict and its recruitment of the persons and passions of so large a part of the city's population is only significant—and indeed only intelligible—in the light of the empire's past, *and its present.* The dispute itself, between truck drivers and owners, has doubtless seemed to the reader as petty and perhaps unworthy of the elaboration I have given it. But the truck drivers' revolt had not only struck at a *crucial* link in the city's economy, but struck at a moment when the world crisis acutely revealed decline in the whole fabric of the empire. In the minds of both combatants the petty dispute had been endowed with the fate of a city.

Two years later, an officer and the chief strategist of the Alliance said to me, "If we had only held out for a few days, we would have won"—which is probably true—"and the history of Minneapolis since 1934 would have been a different one." Whatever the White Papers said in depreciation of the union's victory—White Papers which were promptly used as Republican campaign documents—the Citizens' Alliance never for a moment had any doubt of their crucial defeat.

On the other hand, attacking the settlement "from the left," the Communist party, like the official White Papers of the employers, belittled its importance. In fact they denounced the union's leaders as "strikebreakers" and the settlement itself as "betrayal—not victory."

In the course of the next two years they were to acknowledge this as a mistake, for the truck drivers of Minneapolis, out of the bloody lessons of civil war, forged the strongest labor union in the Northwest; and their tiny but vital foothold of victory in two years time they were to extend into a plateau. Not one of the 166 employers had actually signed a union contract—though the Labor Board stipulation was a *de facto* recognition of the union. Two years later, not 166 but 500 employers in Minneapolis *had signed contracts* with Local 574. The engine of rank-and-file struggle forged by the strike was promptly turned into a peace-time dynamo which speedily changed the economic fortune of five thousand truck drivers, and as part of a wider movement has served to energize a whole series of successful strikes and of trade union organizations, not only in Minneapolis but also throughout the Northwest. The dynamo and its allies have continued to function

A LESSON IN CLASS POLITICS
The troops of the Farmer-Labor Governor raid the Central Labor Union

"The Daring Old Gent On the Flying Trapeze"

Minneapolis Communism---42½ Cents an Hour

THE STRIKERS' NEWSPAPER ANSWERS THE RED SCARE

up to the present time, and to alter the balance of power between the empire builders and the rank and file.

During that twelve-hour victory celebration, a final episode of the civil war occurred which was deeply characteristic of the whole battle and the truck drivers who had fought it. On the night of the settlement, a small committee of workers visited the governor and demanded the release of all the 167 pickets still incarcerated in the military stockade. After discussion he gave his word that the men would be released. The truck drivers were not satisfied but asked the governor to put it in writing. He hastily dictated a memorandum: "I intend to release the prisoners confined in the stockade—Floyd B. Olson." One of the truck drivers skeptically scrutinized the note. "What is meant by this word 'intend,' governor?" There was further discussion. The governor scrawled in three additional words. The memo which the skeptical victors carried away from the commander-in-chief of the National Guard read: "I intend to—*and I will*—release the prisoners confined in the stockade."

Chapter XIII

EVERYDAY LIFE

TWO turbulent years of partial civic peace have followed
the summer of civil war in our American city. Many dramatic and reverberating events in the main current of our
rank-and-file history occurred in this era, which all parties
agree is a transitional one, and in concluding chapters we shall
touch on the most important of them as well as face the
question which everyone in the city is asking—transition to
what? But meantime—throughout the civil war and today—
what have the combatants and noncombatants alike been
doing with their everyday lives? Whole reaches in the city's
life and in the lives of men and women in it have been
neglected in our narrative of civic crisis, just as history itself
for a time neglected them. Even our interlude of "Personal
Lives" has hinted at only some of the omissions.

The city of Minneapolis has, to be sure, its own destiny,
but that destiny is primarily an American one. And the American common denominator is as important as any of its differences. The way you earn your living and *how much you
earn* is an invaluable key to what you do in time of crisis as
well as in everyday life. But the key can be misused. The very
mechanism of industrialism which tends to make for economic
class differences among Americans also tends to blot them out.

So far as I can discover everyone in our American city
goes to the movies—the empire builders and the rank and file

—and by and large they go to the same movies. The current feature, and the lives and current loves of its stars, are discussed with different shadings but a common human curiosity in the Woodhill Country Club, at a Methodist church social, and at a 574 picnic. The prosperity of the movies is *relatively* independent of social crises. Minneapolis has sixty of them and many reported increased attendance during the depression. Thousands, if they could afford the dime or the quarter, went "to forget." During Minneapolis' summer of civil war there was no falling off in movie crowds and two strike leaders sought everywhere by the police were finally arrested in a downtown movie "palace." There has been no study attempted in Minneapolis—as there has in some cities—to gauge the mental impact of this vast instrument of mass culture, but unquestionably it is a prime cultural common denominator in our American city. During a Red purge in Minneapolis initiated by the President of the American Federation of Labor in 1935 and ably seconded by Minneapolis bankers and business men, "The Informer," starring Victor McLaglen, was shown. Purgers and purged sat in the same theater and applauded. A member of the Civic and Commerce Association and V. R. Dunne (both movie fans) each told me it was the best picture they had ever seen!

Second only to the movies, the radio is an amalgamator of culture. Of course with the radio there is perhaps a greater element of selectivity. But only within limits. You can select swing music or Bach, but if you're getting the news of the day, you take what the announcer gives and as he gives it, and the children of all classes ask for the tooth paste or cereal for which their favorite program is the advertising medium. Nearly everyone of those six- or eight-room homes, like the one I lived in, has a radio. The houses on Lowry Hill and the estates around Lake Minnetonka have them too, but where

I lived you turned on the radio for news, for dance music, for a sermon, or for Major Bowes' Amateur hour. However, when Minneapolis' own KTSP broadcast strike news in 1934 everyone listened, and also during the political campaigns. Taking politics very seriously and with a star radio performer for six years in the person of its Farmer-Labor governor, all Minneapolis has become radio conscious. During the funeral of Floyd B. Olson, when a Lutheran minister, a Catholic priest, and a Jewish rabbi were severally preaching their funeral sermon over the dead governor, I drove through Minneapolis in a car. It was a hot August afternoon with the thermometer registering ninety-six. All windows were open. The words of the sermons could literally be heard all over Minneapolis, soft or loud, pouring into the streets from the windows of homes and apartments.

But the long arm of mass production has other ways of providing a common cultural background for Minneapolis—clothes. Prices and fabric are aristocratic or proletarian, but American shops and manufacturers have democratized *style*. You buy a lady's gown for $150 at Harold's. You will see the same model at the Leader for $15. Last summer during the heat wave all the girls took to split-skirt culottes. They were selling them in Power's basement for a dollar. On display, beautifully tailored, further up the avenue, $45.00. In late August Paris sent word to America—"*black* for sport." Minneapolis responded. Elegant ladies turned up in yachts on Lake Minnetonka in small chic black linen dresses. On the same day office girls hurrying from their typewriters to meet a boating date on Lake Harriet, were in black linen—the same model.

Within limits every Minneapolis home, whether it costs $3,000 or $300,000, enjoys a certain cultural common denominator in gadgets. In all the income levels, from $1500 to

$150,000 a year, the electric ice box and the washing machine are found, though they are less frequent of course in the lower brackets and usually bought on installment. As for the simple gadgets for the kitchen, no one in Minneapolis is too snooty or too poor to buy most of them at Woolworth's. In routine equipment American kitchens reveal amazing uniformity.

But the most typical and important gadget of all is, of course, the American automobile. The flying squadrons of strike pickets which have distinguished most of the recent Minneapolis strikes would have been out of the question on European soil. Most of the picket cars were either trucks or pleasure cars owned by the strikers. Social distinctions are of course easy to discover in automobiles or in anything else. The parking lot at the Minneapolis club will show a scattering of Cadillacs and Lincolns, where none can be found at the employees' entrance of the Strutwear Manufacturing Company. But since the depression the real key to your income is not the make of the car but the year. Workers and shopkeepers and leading business men in Minneapolis all buy Fords and Chevrolets and Buicks and so forth. But it is a question of a 1929 as against a 1936 Ford. There is a great deal of propaganda in Minneapolis, as everywhere else, about the universal ownership of automobiles by American workingmen. This is false. In Minneapolis the majority of workingmen and of the so-called lower middle classes ride in street cars and walk. Nevertheless, the automobile is a basic common denominator in the city's cultural life. The mobile-minded worker, even if his wages are in the lower brackets, can buy a second-hand car for "thirty-five bucks" and often does. And everyone I ever met has a "friend with a car." This is all-important. Especially in Minneapolis is the automobile a key to a large sector of everyday life. With the enormous park acreage within the city, and a hinterland of lake country, the automobile becomes strategic to what two-thirds of the population does with its Saturday afternoons—if they have them—and Sundays. Perhaps of all the elements in the vaunted "American standard of living" automobiles are the most important in cultural life, for they mean escape from daily drudgery, drab houses, and a measure of the freedom of movement which is among the most valued possessions of modern man. Social workers and members of the upper classes are in the habit of recounting with indignation tales of workers selling bread from a relief order to buy gasoline—a sacrifice which in terms of the human spirit is open, perhaps, to a different interpretation.

As I hinted in the first chapter of this book, Minneapolis provides a cultural common denominator in sport. Any Sunday afternoon reveals the parking lot at the Nicollet Ball Park crowded to the gates with Cadillacs and Lincolns as well as early American Chevrolets and Fords. Baseball is universally patronized by all classes and impecunious or busy fans follow the games by radio or in the sport sections of the newspapers. Besides a bewildering number of amateur club teams, all the leading trade unions in Minneapolis have their own nines. Golf and tennis have become increasingly democratic in the last decade. The midsummer Woodhill tournament draws all tennis-minded society, but apart from the private clubs, the city provides free municipal links and tennis courts, as well as those which can be rented for a small sum by the hour. Eighteen-year-old Patty Berg, described by the Civic and Commerce Association as "Minneapolis' nationally known golfing sensation," has become a recognized civic asset.

The only exclusive sports, as in most cities, are horses and yachting—though boating, canoeing, and ice-boating are enjoyed by thousands. There are eleven lakes within the city limits! The football exploits of the "Golden Gophers" of the University of Minnesota are the pride of the whole city. The *Organizer,* 574's belligerent newspaper, reports gridiron news with interest and civic pride. As an instance of quick transmission of sport fashions, from the exclusive to the universal, two years ago, bicycling was the last word for fortunate vacationists in Bermuda. Last summer, every lake boulevard in Minneapolis had a batch of cyclists, and bicyles could be rented in the parks for twenty-five cents an hour. Frederick J. Allen, the author of "Only Yesterday," after an exhaustive study of American sport reports that the most popular and universal of all in America, even topping baseball, is bowling. This is certainly true in Minneapolis. The bowling clubs are legion and in our American city the sport has a number of features that recommend it. In a land of long winters it can be played the year around; and in a city fond of its beer the bowling alley is an easy adjunct to the ubiquitous beer garden—not that Minneapolis fails to take advantage of its cold and snowy winters to put half the population on skates and skis.

Minneapolis, like nearly every American city, claims the life of the middle classes as its norm. The movies as well as the church express the mores of these classes, the auto manufacturers sell their new cars to them, the empire builders praise them, and many empire builders and rank and file, even when they do not live according to middle-class mores, insist they share their ideals in spirit. And of course the Citizens' Alliance claims to champion middle-class economic interests. What is the character and the everyday life of the "great American middle class" in our city?

First of all, it is the class that touches in its income brackets and its way of looking at life the working class on one side, and on the other the "leaders of business and society." It is a class in flux. In good times it draws a few recruits from the working class and graduates others into the ranks of the empire builders and their colleagues. In bad times it drops a substantial number into the class below it. Numerically it is perhaps a third as large as the working class, but ten times as large as the group above it.

John Carman is a respected member of the middle class. He owns an independent hardware store, and lives in a house slightly larger but much like mine at the heart of the brown residence district. The hardware store opens at eight and John is there every morning at ten minutes to. He lunches downtown on Hennepin Avenue at twelve and returns home in time to smoke a cigar and dine at six, except when he works over his books in the store at night. Unlike many American cities, especially larger ones, a definite neighborhood life has held over into the fourth decade of the twentieth century in Minneapolis; and a goodly segment of John's everyday life outside of business hours, and still more of his wife's and his children's, are bound up with that life. Within limits the neighborhood is like a village, with the grocery, the drug store, and the filling station as its social centers. One of Mrs. Carman's best friends is the wife of the proprietor of the grocery store and between them they exert a definite social pressure, which is felt for several blocks around, to trade at the neighborhood grocery and not cheat the neighborhood by going to the big chain stores over at Lake and Hennepin.

Both the drug-store proprietor and the grocer work a sixteen-hour day and the grocer's wife spends part of the day in the store. They always keep open a part of Sundays in order to outdo their monopoly competitors. Mr. Carman, himself, claims what with Saturday night at the store, and the work he does Sundays and sometimes nights on inventory and bookkeeping, he puts in more hours a year than the average working man in Minneapolis. But he takes a trip to Chicago occasionally and accords himself two weeks vacation in the summer. This independence he cherishes as much as anything in life, and he has no intention of retiring, though the nest egg he has in the savings bank makes him play with the idea. A neighbor of his, a furniture-store proprietor, has already done so, however, at fifty-five.

Only one family in the block has a full-time maid, but most wives like Mrs. Carman call in a cleaning woman once a week. (The top wage for cleaning women in the city is twenty-five cents an hour these days. The average full-time maid receives $3 to $8 a week.) There are two high-school girls in the neighborhood who hire out for twenty-five cents an evening as "baby sitters" when the family wants to go to the movies.

Porch life in the summer is a distinctive feature of Minneapolis life. The Carman porch, like most others in the block, is glassed in and really adds another room to the house. It is furnished with a couch, chairs, table, reading lamp and radio. A lot of evenings are spent out there. About once a month, however, the Carmans have a party. They serve grape juice for those who don't drink and beer for those who do. About 9:30 Mrs. Carman announces "lunch," which consists of substantial sandwiches, cookies, and always coffee.

The neighborhood penetrates everyday life both socially and practically. There is a lot of interyard exchange of news, and borrowing of eggs and butter, stepladders and kindling wood. Sundays Mr. Carman washes his 1933 Plymouth and mows the lawn.

Minneapolis is distinguished culturally for the attention it pays to music. Apart from the community sings which even martial law did not interrupt, there is the Apollo Club, the Cecilian Singers, and the Odin Club Singers. Then a lot of musical life centers in the choirs of the churches, in one of which Carman's eldest daughter sings. All the Carman family go to the Parade Ground Sings, but only the daughter as a rule attends the Symphony Orchestra. The younger Carman kids join heartily in the gang life of the neighborhood when they're not at public school. And John's eldest boy is a sophomore at the University of Minnesota. He has horrified Mr. Carman by joining the American Youth League, which demonstrated against "war and Fascism" on the campus last summer. The University, third largest in the United States, has been infected somewhat by the turbulent rank-and-file movements of the state and the city. A conservative emissary of William Green who addressed the student forum there in 1935 found to his chagrin that his audience were violent partisans of the "radical truck drivers' union." But the president, Lotus Delta Coffman, has to date kept his faculty ideologically innocuous to the empire builders, and a careful card index is kept of student defections both sexual and radical. We have remarked before that for the most part the sons of the empire builders go east to Harvard, Yale, and Princeton, rather than round the corner to the University of Minnesota.

Apart from the neighborhood life there are other collective social activities that claim a measurable segment of John's everyday life and that of his neighbors. Added to the Kiwanis, the Lions, and the Rotary, the whole middle class is crisscrossed with a complex web of fraternal, commercial, and social units. Among those that meet regularly in Minneapolis are the Optimists Club, the Automobile Club, the Boosters Club, the Nature Study Circle, the Women's League for Peace and Freedom, the Readers' Club, the Architects Club, the Association of Hardware Merchants, etc. But unquestionably more embrasive and decisive in the cultural life of the city than any of them are the churches. Unlike St. Paul, where the Roman Catholic church dominates the religious life of the city, the great majority of churchgoers in Minneapolis are Protestant. There are 290 Protestant churches in the city, 27 Roman Catholic ones, and 10 Jewish synagogues. The overwhelming majority of the Scandinavian population are, of course, Lutherans. Oddly enough, in the Golden Age and for a time afterward it was possible to distinguish the empire builders professionally by religion. The millers by and large were Congregationalists; lumbermen, landed proprietors, and real-estate men tended to be Methodists; and the bankers and manufacturers, Episcopalians. These religioprofessional demarcations have come to be obscured, however, in recent years. John Carman and his wife attend the Wesley Methodist church because they enjoy the crusading sermons of Dr. George Mecklenberg against vice, and sympathize with what his church did for the unemployed during the early years of the depression.

John Carman's attitude and that of his neighbors toward the empire builders on the one hand and toward the series of rank-and-file revolts during the past turbulent years has varied. To begin with, all the government agencies for relief of the unemployed and the unemployed themselves are far closer to the neighborhood's life than they are to the residents of Lowry Hill or the estate owners at Lake Minnetonka. Several of John's neighbors have relatives who are on WPA and during the hard times of 1933 his own nephew spent six months in one of the CCC camps. On the other hand, John has a cousin who is a prosperous Minneapolis real-estate proprietor and a member of the Citizens' Alliance. John's admiration for his cousin is unbounded, and once or twice a year they have lunch together. At the last luncheon a couple of months before the election John agreed with every word his cousin

said about high taxes, the bad effect of the dole on the workingman, extravagance, and all the rest of it, but somehow when
the election came around he voted for Roosevelt and not for
Landon. He didn't like Landon's radio voice and he felt in the
end that Mr. Roosevelt would do more for his hardware
store than Alf. Being intensely anti-Farmer-Labor, he voted
a Republican ticket in Minnesota. His neighbor and friend the
grocer, on the other hand, remembering the tax on chain stores
passed under Farmer-Labor auspices and Olson's veto of the
sales tax, voted a straight Farmer-Labor ticket.

The neighborhood has been distinctly divided in its opinions
of the various events of recent rank-and-file history in Minneapolis. It condemned universally the violence of the strikes,
not only the ones in 1934 but all the others that have followed,
and held the radical leadership responsible. On the other
hand, in most cases, it felt the workers were underpaid. Mr.
Carman has little use for unions, however, as such; thinks
they cause trouble and are unnecessary in America. On the
other hand, the proprietor of the neighborhood grocery store
and to some extent his friends favored the workers in the
recent strike led by General Drivers 574 against the Wholesale Grocers. He found that the strike was mainly felt by the
chain stores and he actually increased his own business while
the fight was on.

In a far more dramatic way the veering and unstable attitude
of lower-bracket representatives of the middle class toward
strikes and trade unions was illustrated by the petroleum
workers' walkout in the summer of 1936. A large number of
filling-station attendants were suddenly faced with making up
their minds whether they were "little capitalists" whose interests were with the Standard Oil Company from whom they
leased their stations or "petroleum workers" who should fight
for higher wages. Large numbers couldn't make up their

minds, and the strike was a flop. Here was the anomalous situation in which the filling-station proprietor in John Carman's neighborhood found himself. The Standard Oil Company leased him his station and he bought his oil and gas from Standard. He was free to hire an assistant and pay him what he pleased or not hire him at all. His hours were his own. By putting in about twenty more a week than when he had worked for wages the year before, he could make about $25 more a month. So he was against the union which wanted to abolish leases. But to make that $25 he had to pay his gas station assistant under the going wage; and besides the man in the next block was making *less* under his lease than he had working for wages, and called him a fink and a strikebreaker. He found himself in an economic no man's land between two classes, and the whole thing worried him like the devil. But after a week the strike collapsed.

Although there were other borderline cases in these years, large sections of the middle class never faltered in their economic loyalties and many of them found their economic life far more directly affected by the turbulent events of this history than Mr. Carman or his neighborhood.

One of these was Joe Conway, who told me that his everyday life in Minneapolis for three years had been hell. Mr. Conway is the owner of a small breakfast-food manufacturing company and he is fighting for his economic life. When I talked to him we sat in the little shipping room of the Conway factory right back of the office. "My father was a workingman," said Mr. Conway. "He was quicker and cleverer than most of the men, and they elected him their union delegate. But father could see no reason why he shouldn't cash in on his abilities for himself, and not the union, and he started a factory of his own. The business grew and we made money. Our peak year was 1929. Then came the depression." By

1931 Mr. Conway found that the big cereal mills were still making money, but he was not. To begin with, they had all the chain-store business. "I held a special meeting with the boys in the factory and asked them if they would stick with me through the depression. They agreed." Sticking with Mr. Conway meant working for forty per cent under the going rate for cereal workers. "We got along fine till a union delegate walked into the picture. And then——"

From then on, according to Mr. Conway, twenty-four hours of his everyday life has gone into worrying about the union—for he kept dreaming about it at night. He fought a strike which gripped his factory with all there was in him and lost. He has had to raise wages all along the line. Mr. Conway is still wrestling with the union and says it has taken three years out of his life, but it has also given him a painful education in the economics of his American city.

When I saw Joe Conway last, he was saying, "Sometimes I think I'm wrong on the labor factor," and he mentioned what has been worrying all the small manufacturers; long distance from the centers of dense population, freight rates, and the "squeeze" of chain stores, factors which University of Minnesota economists, more statistically and less emotionally, had been worrying about for years. At the same time, part of the routine of everyday life for Mr. Conway when I saw him was nurturing a little cereal factory a few miles outside Minneapolis where there were workers who weren't "bothering about the union." He was paying them fifty per cent under his Minneapolis rate.

Mr. Conway's life and that of his father illustrate the effort to secure a position of relative economic independence and power and to hold on to it—come hell or high water or workers demanding a living wage—a struggle which characterizes the middle class everywhere, but which shows itself with peculiar fierceness and militancy in our American city.

Let us examine in contrast the life of one of the latter-day empire builders, taking as an example the president of one of the largest Minneapolis corporations whose factories are situated not only in this American city but scattered through other parts of the United States. The man I have selected is himself a conscious defender as well as an admirable product of long-headed, broad-gauge, big business activity. In the past few years in Minneapolis while Mr. Conway has been meeting in his own way the impact of a declining economy on independent cereal millers, this corporation executive, in collaboration with his economic equals, has met the squeeze in another way—consolidation. His corporation is the product of one of the many successful mergers of the last decade. The executive's everyday life has concerned itself with working out in practice the more efficient as well as more profitable effects of that merger. In contrast to Mr. Conway, the president entertained me in one of the private rooms of the Minneapolis Club, and his general outlook was both more tolerant and more optimistic. He said he had heard I had "radical views" but didn't care as long as I was honest. When instances comparable to Mr. Conway's were mentioned, of small business men fighting trade unions, he said frankly that there were certain companies who could only keep alive in Minneapolis by "taking it out of the hide of labor." He indicated they would have to go under or go elsewhere. He said he believed in the principle of collective bargaining, if some way could be found to make labor leaders "responsible." As to his own corporation, they dealt with unions in some plants, and in some did not. One felt that not only a temperament of personal tolerance, but an economic position of great power and security—the destiny of his corporation was far from dependent on the fortunes of the Northwest alone—gave him the foundation for

BASEBALL
". . . a cultural common denominator in sport"

SWEDISH "MIDSOMMARDAGEN"
Customs emigrate too

107° ABOVE
Luckily there are eleven lakes within the city limits!

40° BELOW
"A land of long hard winters"

a philosophic outlook denied to Mr. Conway. As to his everyday life in these turbulent years in Minneapolis, he admitted
with disarming frankness that he had made a lot of money
and maintained an expensive scale of life, because he "liked
to live that way." (He has one of the largest domestic establish-
ments in Minneapolis.) He had started as a poor boy in a
small town, and felt he had earned his own way up. But the
scale of imperial living troubled him for his sons. Feeling that
they'd get wrong ideas about life and that at the same time
he was responsible for their luxurious tastes, he had solved the
problem in this way—granted them a "subsistence allowance"
and agreed to pay their doctor's bills the rest of their lives.
"This may be socialistic of me," he said, "I don't know."
I asked him what the subsistence was. He said $6000 a year;
"every penny over that they have to earn for themselves." To
any member of the rank and file of Minneapolis or even to
Mr. Conway, this "subsistence" may sound like a grim joke.
But it was no joke to the corporation president, and the very
fact that it was a sincere and incidentally an unusual exercise
of honest conscience makes it significant for this record.

The way Mr. Conway or the corporation president earn
their living and how much they earn has clearly made a
profound difference in the way they spent their everyday lives
in the past three years in Minneapolis. It has also provided
them with differences in political and economic philosophy.
As the secretary of the Citizens' Alliance put it, "men like
the corporation president in question can afford to be tolerant
and philosophical about labor unions." Mr. Conway cannot.
The former can afford the luxury of worrying about his chil-
drens' overluxurious upbringing; Mr. Conway doesn't need
to. On the other hand, Mr. Conway at heart not only admires
the executives of big business, but he will submit in the end
to the way they are organizing America. On the whole he

accepted branch banking in Minneapolis as against the old small independent banks. A great many Mr. Conways are giving up the management of small independent factories and becoming the manager-employees of big business. Some of the middle and particularly the lower middle class in Minnesota, as we have seen, have thrown in their lot with the Farmer-Labor party to fight the chain stores, branch banking, etc., but the bulk of the middle class, like Mr. Conway, despite their differences are bound to remain on the side of big business. In the big truck drivers' strikes and in all the many strikes which, as we shall see, followed in three turbulent years, it was the local middle-class business man who was most directly involved. But it was the empire builder and the top few—the bankers and big industrialists—who provided financial support and moral backing. Whether the local middle-class business man is against big business or for it, the national corporations which control the aggregate of individual and financial power will only tolerate the "independence of the great American middle class" if it plays ball. A good many of the middle class want to, but more don't or can't.

Why don't these dissidents who are for the "little fellow" organize against the giant corporations on the one hand and against the trade unions on the other? Modern history records no successful organization of the middle class against their economic and financial superiors. In Germany and Italy the middle class successfully consolidated itself against the working class. But it was then taken over by big capital for its own purposes. The truth is there is no essential difference in class division between Mr. Conway and the corporation head, except in degree of financial and economic power. Possession of this sovereignty has given the economic leaders in our society power as arbiters in most social and cultural matters as well.

They endow the art schools, symphony orchestras, and universities. They organize the horse shows and give fashionable parties which the rest of society reads about in the newspapers. Mr. Conway and Mr. Carman no more dispute these standards of taste, fashion, sport, liquor, or whatnot than they dispute the fundamental economic opinions of their financial superiors, *in fact far less*. They imitate, approximate, and exemplify them sometimes fanatically "keeping up with the Joneses" and sometimes quietly conforming with decent self-respect, according to temperament. But the middle class as such invents little that is new. It hasn't the time or the inclination. Nor is it properly speaking a class in itself, in distinction from the smaller group of financial and industrial leaders above it. The top and the middle in a true *class* sense are *one* in our society; the middle is on the move and the top has stopped long enough to set up the standards.

The working class in Minneapolis, as elsewhere, is in a different category. In everyday life it tends with slenderer means to approximate the social fashions and cultural content handed to it. But members of the working class, as the history of the Northwest and our city amply shows, are united by a common insecurity and despite variations a common way of making a living—by wages and not profits. They are united as well by the union against them—in time of crisis—of all other forces of society. At such times, the working class for brief periods develops ideas of its *own* interest apart from the middle class, and the faint beginnings of an original culture. It produces leaders, thinks up fresh forms of organization and strategy, and above all scans skeptically its own relation to the rest of society. This is what the dirt farmers of the Northwest under the impact of the empire builders' aggression did. This is what the workers in our American city have increasingly done in the past few years. I have talked with Minneapolis iron workers who discussed with great acuteness—in reference to their own lives—the election of Roosevelt, the events in Spain, the latest campaign by the *Journal* for restoring the declining economy of Minneapolis. "In reference to their own lives" is the key.

Trotsky's remark that the culture of the working class is *politics* is clearly enough illustrated in Minneapolis. The political and economic ideas, the organizational forms, the speeches, songs, and heroes which proceed from its struggles are its only original class contributions to cultural content. And Roy Bauman and his fellow workers have taken over a part of this content in fainter form into their everyday life. A May Day demonstration, the annual union picnics, the Ness Memorial Day demonstration held once a year in the Minneapolis market where Ness was shot—these are its outward signs. Mr. Strong and Mr. Conway are of necessity either indifferent or hostile to these signs, but more important, the signs themselves suggest a world of different assumptions and values to which they lack the key—as decisively as though they were observing the customs of men from Mars. Make no mistake—the tens of thousands of workers in Minneapolis who share these memories and ideas also share the great common denominator of American life, and most of their everyday life they absorb the standards, cultural and otherwise, that Mr. Strong and Mr. Conway accept. Occasionally, however, both in time of crisis and in everyday life, they do not. To the many average citizens who accept either with fatality or enthusiasm the *status quo* of American society, such elements of institutionalized class culture as I have mentioned are an aberration from the healthy norm of American life. They are clinical exhibits of an unfortunate sickness in our economic organism. But to those who find them normal processes, and who believe that the working class as such—like other classes in the past

—has its own historic contribution to make to a civilized culture, they are signs of progress. However that may be, it is as impossible to omit them from a survey of our American city as it is to omit the neighborhood life in Mr. Carman's block.

The part played by the so-called underworld in the everyday life of Minneapolis is neither as profound nor as famous as that of her sister city of St. Paul, whose kidnaping ring attracted national attention in 1934. It is more modest in its operations and less obtrusive than in many American cities, but it is there. In 1904, when Lincoln Steffens included Minneapolis in his famous series, "The Shame of the Cities," its organizational nucleus was called "The Syndicate." In 1936, with new leaders and new methods, it is still The Syndicate, which controls the illegal enterprises of gambling, prostitution, slot machines, and racing bets. In the days of Coolidge prosperity the annual "take" exceeded a million a year, and pay-offs to police and city officials are alleged to have run to $15,000 a month. In the present relatively hard times and under pressure of complaints, reform investigations, etc., the take has been decimated, although a veteran police reporter in Minneapolis estimates profits for The Syndicate in the week of the Fourth of July, 1936, as $12,000.

Before repeal in 1934, the story of the Minneapolis Liquor Syndicate—not to be confused with The Syndicate proper which controls slot machines, etc.—is a typical success story. From small gallon-lot dealings and liquor running in small quantities, the stronger, the tougher, the luckier pushed their way to the top. Minneapolis operators made connections with Chicago, Cleveland, New Orleans. Liquors arrived by the carload, and rectifying plants were installed. The perfume business became an excellent source for alcohol. There was an occasional shooting to facilitate business mergers, and competition amongst bootleggers was occasionally, in Minneapolis as elsewhere, liquidated with firearms. With repeal in 1934, this phase of underworld activity, which along with bootlegging elsewhere had attained a kind of semirespectable status, ceased. Some of the operators went into slot machines and gambling, some into the legitimate liquor business, a few to jail.

Periodically, since the muckraking days of Lincoln Steffens, Minneapolis, like other American cities, has declared a holy war on its underworld. The most recent vice crusade to interrupt the routine of everyday life ran its course in the spring and summer of 1936. The Reverend George Mecklenberg of the Wesley Methodist church gave it his moral support by fiery denunciations of vice fron the pulpit. The Law and Order League of Minneapolis made investigations, and as has been common in late years, an effort was made to discredit the recent labor revolts in the city by connecting their leaders and their unions, as well as the Farmer-Labor party, with the underworld. This political by-product of the investigations failed, but certain results can be credited to the crusade. A panderer was sent to the penitentiary and two men were indicted under the Mann Act. The best information obtainable two months after the close of the crusade reveals The Syndicate showing a certain circumspection, but in business as usual.

Everyday life in recent years has been enlivened for many by the presence in society—or rather outside of it—of a unique salon attended by the most diverse characters. Judges, prize fighters, governors, utility magnates, radicals, artists, racketeers, all have attended the informal social gatherings in Minneapolis, sponsored and inspired by Mrs. Annette Fawcett. An immemorial cause of dullness in most American cities is the difficulty of "meeting interesting people," or meeting them under interesting conditions. Mrs. Fawcett aimed at abolishing this difficulty in Minneapolis. Annette Fawcett is the divorced wife of Captain Billy Fawcett, the publisher of *Whiz Bang, True Confessions,* and *Hooey.* Her gatherings were usually held in the Hotel Radisson, in a high-ceiled double room, with robin's-egg blue walls, plenty of chairs, sofas, drinks, and conversation. Representatives of at least half a dozen socially insulated groups found it possible to meet at Mrs. Fawcett's and nowhere else. A district attorney would discuss Hollywood with a visiting movie star, a radical reformer argue government ownership with a utility magnate. But whether the guest was a bootlegger or a Federal judge or an artist, Mrs. Fawcett skillfully arranged that nobody should be a bore to the other guests. Inside information on all phases of the city's life was the current coin of conversation, which included gossip on the lives of its leading citizens. Both conversation and liquor were free, but Mrs. Fawcett was careful to see that her guests, whatever they *said,* behaved with decorous courtesy to each other. Frowned on by conventional society, Mrs. Fawcett's rooms at the Radisson in their own way were a salon of the city's "interesting people," and so far as I know the only one the city has ever had.

Despite preoccupation with their personal lives, the citizens of Minneapolis since the summer of civil war have been continuously aware that a change has come over the city—for better or (as many think), for worse. I have heard the dramatic events of this history discussed with bitterness or enthusiasm not only at the bar in the union hall of 574, but at the Minneapolis Club and in the homes of the empire builders. Last summer two ladies over their tea at the Woodhill Country Club were discussing the truck drivers' union. "The leaders of 574 are Communists, aren't they?" "Well," replied her friend, "they're Trotskyite Communists, not Stalinites." It is difficult to find another American city where the distinctions of revolutionary politics are current in social circles. The reason is simple. Few have escaped the impact of the rank-and-file revolt in any walk of life in the city. The distinguished board of governors of the Minneapolis Club were appalled last year to find that the veteran waiters of the club who had served them so faithfully for a generation were abruptly *all* members of the cooks and waiters' union! The governors at a board meeting promptly voted them a bonus.

Indeed, the whole city in one way or another is conscious of the impact of organizational change in its economic life. The source, apart from basic economic forces, is visible and tangible enough. Labor has created in the midst of the city a dynamo which for three years has made change a fact of everyday life. To some however, the force has seemed not a dynamo of change but a demon which is malignantly pushing the city further and further from its cherished Golden Age of prosperity and peace.

CHAPTER XIV

THE DYNAMO OF CHANGE

WHEN the tired pickets returned to their jobs as drivers of trucks and the tin hats of the National Guard became civilians again after the civil war of 1934, few on either side gauged the long-term effects of the rank-and-file victory. But wider and wider circles of men and women in Minneapolis who had no connection with the craft of driving a truck were to feel the impulse of the drivers' strikes and to act on it. In one sense, the class instincts of the Citizens' Alliance were vindicated. They had militantly refused to grant a 2½-cent wage increase, arguing that even this modest gain would increase the prestige of the "Red union" and all Minnesota labor in the end would be Communized. All Minnesota labor was not Communized, but the union's prestige grew prodigiously and workers all over the Twin Cities joined in a wave of organization that grew rather than diminished with the passing years.

But for the immediate rank-and-file combatants, the first stage after the civil war became one of disorganization, discouragement, and retreat. Paradoxically the union membership, which had reached several thousands at the peak of the strike, two months after victory had fallen to 900. *None of the militant strike leaders had been officers of the union, with one exception.* With the dissolution of the Committee of One Hundred, the machinery of power reverted to the same officers who before the July revolt had succeeded in "stabilizing" the union in weakness and impotency for twenty years. By October, 1934, the progressives in the union were saying, "Either we take over the union's leadership, or the leadership will break the union." Bill Brown—the only officer favoring this internal revolution—called for a resignation of all officers and a progressive slate was elected by the rank and file. The veteran officials consented to resign in full confidence that the rank and file would promptly restore them to office. Their surprise was as great as their disappointment. At the time few in Minneapolis realized the importance of this peaceful revolution.

But scarcely was the union well on its way to becoming a functioning peace-time dynamo than it received another blow which greatly heartened the Citizens' Alliance, the Republican party and the empire builders. It was expelled from its American Federation of Labor International by President Daniel Tobin. After all, he had denounced it as consistently through the civil war as the empire builders themselves. Mr. Tobin's reputation in the American labor movement as a czar and reliable bulwark of reaction was already a national one. But he now outdid himself, to the delight of all the dynamo's enemies. From Daniel Tobin's point of view 574, harboring Reds and progressives, had committed the *craft unionists'* sin against the Holy Ghost. They had combined into one powerful union crafts which the Law and the Prophets said should be split into eight. Mr. Tobin offered to receive back the stormy petrel into the fold of the International on condition of atomic dismemberment into its craft parts. He added: *expulsion of all strike leaders* and the admission of no new members without his consent. Moderate delegates to the Central Labor Union of Minneapolis remarked that even the Citizens'

Alliance hadn't demanded of the truck drivers terms as devastating as those of the president of their union.

In the fall election of 1934, the rank-and-file farmers and workers of Minnesota returned Olson, Farmer-Labor governor, to office. The platform, as we remarked in an earlier chapter, was the most radical in the party's history, and reflected both the effects of the depression and the temper of the electorate. Many workers who voted for Olson still resented the blows which the governor's militia had dealt the drivers' union in the summer of civil war—but the opponent was a Republican! They voted for Olson. And besides, many of the party were convinced by his admirers that the governor's tactics had *won* the strike for the workers of Minneapolis. A working-class electorate still further evinced its strength by ousting the Republican mayor of Minneapolis and electing a Farmer-Labor mayor, Thomas E. Latimer.

Meantime, more and more workers—at first those closest to the driving trades—were pouring into unions, asking recognition, striking and getting it.

The skilled auto mechanics whose level of pay was far below that of their fellows in other Midwestern cities, struck two thousand strong in both St. Paul and Minneapolis. They set up a commissary, a cruising picket line, a strike newspaper, and won all their major demands. In Minneapolis, following an unextinguished tradition, the employers fought hardest. Special company police and armed guards were thrown against pickets, but after all, the workers of Minneapolis had now been through Bloody Friday and out the other side. On January 11, three union organizers who attempted to enter the Tri-Motor Garage to meet and talk with the employer were shot and wounded. The organizers, however, persisted, *disarmed the thugs* who had been sent against them and *talked with the employer*. A new morale pervaded the rank and file of the city and the *Labor Review* recorded the thanks of the strike leadership "to the leaders and members of Local 574" for "tireless and valuable assistance."

By the summer of 1935, however, the rank-and-file trickle into "trade unions of their own choosing" had become a torrent, and spread far beyond the driving crafts or any industry related to them. Two bitter strikes occurred, rivaling in militancy and counter-violence the truck strikes of 1934, one among the iron workers of Minneapolis and one in a large hosiery manufactory which had successfully maintained sweatshop conditions throughout the depression. The tactics of combatants in both struggles and on both sides were replicas of the civil war, but the issue was now a wider one of translating the moral gains of 1934 into practical ones for *the whole rank and file of* the empire's capital. This was clearly recognized and not least by the strategists of the Citizens' Alliance.

Labor conditions at the Strutwear Knitting mills were characterized by low wages—even for skilled operatives $4 to $6 a week below other textile plants in the Middle West—the "stretch-out," child labor, and the use of labor spies in the plant. The strike itself was characterized by new and unusual features, some amusing, others ironically tragic. The plant was owned by a Mrs. Struthers, widow of the company's founder, who leaned heavily for strategic guidance on the Citizens' Alliance; but though they stood together in sentiment and principle, her own ideas of the class struggle were far more naïve than those of her generals. She prejudiced the company's case severely in the public's mind by (1) admitting she received advice from the Alliance and (2) declaring *she could not recognize the union as the American Federation of Labor was an illegal organization in the United States!*

For a time the company attempted to operate the plant with a scab crew under heavy police protection and in the face of a militant picket line, but late in November they added a new and original chapter to employer strike tactics. Attempting to move finished goods out of their struck factory, they could find no truck drivers in Minneapolis or St. Paul to move them. Local 574, in solidarity with the strikers, was at the root of this difficulty. So they set up a dummy corporation in another state and called upon the Federal marshal to move the goods under heavy guard—which he did. Mrs. Struthers again failed her more sophisticated colleagues by admitting on the witness stand that the company to whom the marshal was delivering the goods was nonexistent and had been fictitiously organized for the purpose.

For a time Governor Olson closed the plant with National Guard troops, but later withdrew them in the face of a Federal injunction. After eight months, the strikers won with "wages adjusted to conform with those in other hosiery mills." Again the issues and the modesty of the victory underscored the intransigeant philosophy of the employers.

If the Strutwear strike had been a violent one, the revolt of the iron workers—which paralleled a part of it—repeated even more nearly episodes of the civil war. The grimmest of these were the shootings at the Flour City plant, which in workers' minds were made the more terrible because of their open sanction by the Farmer-Labor mayor of Minneapolis. On July 26, the mayor in person, at the head of sixty-eight police, escorted thirty scabs *through the picket lines* into the plant. The workers of Minneapolis have never ceased marveling at this naked exhibition of open treason on the part of their "class leader." Latimer had won his election on a pledge "to keep the police from breaking strikes." But the mayor topped his performance by an attempt, on September 10, to wipe out the picket line itself with gas and bullets. His chief of police began the battle by discharging gas from an armored car against

strikers meeting in a vacant lot, seconded by a gas attack on
the picket line, clubbings with night sticks, and repeated vol-
leys from the revolvers of the police. Two bystanders were
killed.

We have attempted before to seek an explanation of such
violence, psychological or otherwise, in terms of self-interest
or class strategy. Is there any explanation of this savage
massacre at Flour City—under the orders of a Farmer-Labor
mayor? Yes. On the heels of the civil war, it seemed that to
the average citizen had come not peace, but an ever widening
circle of industrial strife. Conservative labor leaders, instinctively timid before militancy, and employers fearful for "law
and order," had for months "brought pressure on the mayor."
Tom Latimer, unlike Floyd Olson, was no skilled manipulator
between hostile classes, and having been told that the strikes
were incited by the "Red leaders" of 574, he struck out boldly
in the "interests of law and order." In the end the rank-and-
file revolt swept over him; but it was in a confused effort to
preserve himself, the labor movement (as he thought it ought
to be), and "law and order" as the employers conceived it,
that he murdered two people—and betrayed all three of his
objectives.

The wounded pickets were replaced at Flour City by new
recruits, and on September 24, after a seventy-four-day strike,
the iron workers of Minneapolis won. They got the wage scale,
within a penny or two, that they had fought for.

While both the Strutwear and iron workers were on strike,
Mayor Latimer, with a rather more masterly fumble, had set
up a Board of Mediation composed of "liberal employers" and
conservative labor leaders and called upon all workers on strike
to *return to their jobs without a settlement*. Thereupon he announced the Board "would adjust their differences." Employers hailed the Board as the city's salvation, but the leaders of

both strikes promptly termed it a strikebreaking agency. The Board, although it continued in existence for two years, never settled a *major* strike in Minneapolis.

Meantime the rank and file of the city were exercising their growing power in other activities than those of the picket line. They had won a partial political control over the destiny of the city's unemployed, in part through the Farmer-Labor party which for a time controlled the Board of Public Welfare for the city of Minneapolis, and in part by direct pressure from organizations of the unemployed. They measurably stepped up the amount of relief and altered its manner of dispensation. The largest of the unemployed "pressure groups" was the tightly organized Federal Workers Section of 574 with a membership of eight thousand.

As was to be expected the truck drivers' union, whose strikes had detonated a far wider revolt than their own, continued to play a co-operating role in the whole movement. They contributed pickets to the iron workers' strike as those workers had contributed soldiers to the Battle of Deputies Run. More especially they loaned organizers, leaders, negotiators, and "staff" advice. But they never attempted to "capture a union," nor, as was charged, set up a rival labor movement in the city of Minneapolis. As one of fifty examples, on May 29, in a strike of building workers, they tied up the job in forty minutes, winning *for the building trades* an all-union job. To the employers such tactics constituted a "serious blow at responsible trade unionism." To 574 it was in the tradition of labor solidarity. V. R. Dunne, truck driver, *not a hosiery worker,* went on the picket line at the Strutwear Knitting plant and received for his pains three broken ribs, but through his assistance and that of other union men—also not knitting workers—the knitting workers got a wage raise. Nor did this practical assistance of 574 to the rank and file confine itself

to Minneapolis. Organizers were "loaned" throughout Minnesota and North Dakota, and Miles Dunne on request in the
winter of 1935 directed a successful strike of gas-house workers
in St. Louis. In each instance, where the workers organized
were not under truck-driving jurisdiction, 574 turned them
over to their respective unions. In two years while still an
"outlaw union" in Minneapolis, the truck drivers organized
and turned back to A. F. of L. unions five thousand workers.
Was this extracurricular activity the fruit of altruism? Of
course not. With enlightened class instincts the leadership
knew that the survival of the drivers' union depended on the
whole labor movement. "A victory for one is a victory for all."

Inevitably workers in trouble were magnetized by the labor
dynamo the drivers had built, especially as its electrical energy
was at their disposal. Last summer, besides jewelry workers,
breakfast-food makers, and sash-and-door workers, even the
workers from a Minneapolis cemetery asked the drivers' help
for their strike on Memorial Day! No wonder conservative
labor leaders, watching the dynamo from their Eighth Street
headquarters, and the Citizens' Alliance watching it from the
Northwest Bank building, laid the charge of a "labor dictatorship" on the drivers' union. Legends grew up. For workers,
the numerals themselves became slightly magical, and their
mention a force potent enough to snatch victory from defeat.

Most employers who have had actual peace-time experience
report their contractual relations with the drivers' union as
reasonably tolerable. Joseph Cochran, the chairman of the
Employers' Committee during the civil war of 1934, told me
he "had had no trouble with the union, except on seniority
rights," and that he respected the honesty and ability of its
leaders. But outside the truck owners, and especially amongst
employers subscribing to the "confidential bulletin" of the
Citizens' Alliance, there is a well-articulated legend of "con-

STRIKE AT FLOUR CITY ORNAMENTAL IRON CO.
"The mayor attempted to wipe out the picket line with gas and bullets"

FLOUR CITY
An innocent bystander

LEGENDARY BOLSHEVIKS—THE DUNNE BROTHERS
What irritated the employers most was the Dynamo's efficiency

STEWARD'S MEETING, 544
"When we have a strike or a picnic we do it right!"

spiracy." Its objects are no longer said to be "the setting up of a Russian soviet in Minneapolis," but turning the labor movement into a "racket." A former member of a mediation board in Minneapolis told me that 574 was simply a money-making scheme so that the Dunnes and Bill Brown could spend the union's funds in riotous living. He informed me that the Citizens' Alliance needed strikes in order to keep its staff busy, and that there was a "definite understanding" between the Alliance and the Dunnes. After a strike all money collected by either party was split three ways, to the 574 leaders, to the officers of the Citizens' Alliance and to Governor Olson! There are other "versions," but this illustrates sufficiently the more imaginative and legendary by-products of 574's history.

As to the actual post-war exploits of the drivers' union, the documents in the record are open to all. And the internal functioning of the dynamo itself is neither mysterious or legendary. On examination it shows itself as practical and functional as a Ford tractor plant. American qualities of organizational ingenuity and audacity have penetrated not only business but also the American labor movement. The May strike machine at 1900 Chicago Avenue, which we examined in some detail, is one example of it. But the same principles of economic engineering the leaders of 574 translated with equal precision into a peace-time dynamo of change. That translation was to have more concrete significance for our American city and the Northwest than the strikes themselves. Many militant strikes have been fought and won in America, but few have transferred their militant strike energy into a permanent trade-union dynamo.

"What is the organizational secret of 574's success?" Several Minneapolis employers have told me they would like to know. I can answer that there are several elements in that "secret"— which is no secret at all. First, harmony of aim in the leadership—which even the enemies of the dynamo have never denied. No member of the executive board ever attacks another outside of board meeting. A union rule. "Inside we fight like hell!" says Bill Brown. More personally, in the turbulent post-strike years V. R. Dunne, a remarkable character, has been to the union, besides a strategist, a personal amalgamator. "That guy can bawl hell out of you, and you'll take it; you know he has a way of doing it, and besides he's right." But more basic than this accident of personality is that none of the leaders are or can afford to be indispensable. "One of us may get bumped off or go to jail." In search of new leaders the officers are constantly dumping responsibility on the shop stewards, the organizers, and the membership. "At the last membership meeting did you see how the boys fought us on that tactic before they took it? Now they know what it's all about." During the strikes and after, 574 educated fresh strata of leaders they didn't have when they started.

Examining the dynamo itself, the union combines centralized control plus "home rule for the sections." It is semi-industrial, which made Daniel Tobin so angry. Ice-wagon drivers or taxi drivers meet separately on craft problems, but have behind them the drive and support of their united strength. "One big union like the Wobblies," charged the employers in 1934. "That will mean a general drivers' strike every five minutes." Actually the opposite has been the case. Sectional strikes there have been in the past three years, a handful of men, backed morally and financially by the five thousand men still on the job. But there have been no general strikes of drivers in Minneapolis since the civil war. They haven't been necessary. "574 gives the lie," says Farrell Dobbs, "to the craft union philosophy."

Through its stewards, one or more in every trucking company, and a crew of cruising organizers, most of them former members of the Strike Committee of One Hundred, 574 keeps in close touch with its far-flung economic organism. And it spends most of its time enforcing old contracts, according to its lights, and making new ones. On June 5, 1935, union drivers charged Kabish Contracting Company with chiseling their pay. The union tied up the Kabish jobs. At three P.M. *the same day* the men got their chiseled pay, amounting to $723.24, and "work was resumed." The Skellet Transfer Company refused after the strike to re-employ a union driver. The Regional Labor Board ordered reinstatement. Still Skellet refused. Orders came from 574, "All Skellet drivers out." The man was reinstated. But as far as the record shows there has been no striking for striking's sake. In the winter of 1935, the *Organizer* answered its critics with partisan and characteristic irony. Referring to certain sectional strikes, it editorializes:

"These strikes took place because the employer was not abiding by the terms of the strike settlement of August, 1934. It seems that some employers are not in possession of a memory capable of functioning over a twelve-month period. It is therefore necessary from time to time to refresh their power of retention."

Such an "approach" has consistently delighted the unions' friends and irritated its enemies.

Whatever one's appraisal of 574's philosophy, the union has impressed all observers with its salty flavor of realism, partisanship, and gusto. Nor is it only the employers who are aware of it. For the humanitarian concerned over the "wrongs of the under dog" or the radical who takes the revolution with a touch of piety, Local 574 is indeed a shocking experience. It is difficult to find a Board member who won't stop, while you tell him your funny story, and then tell you one back before he goes into "conference with the market bosses." Perhaps it is because most of them have been truck drivers and a truck driver refuses to take anything too seriously or be in a hurry about it. The favorite species of truck-driver humor is a form of extravagant badgering, physical and vocal. You can find three or four executives, some officers, and a couple of stewards, any evening between meetings accusing each other with affectionate violence of being finks, fakers, wife beaters, or whatnot, from sheer animal spirits. But there is another aspect to this practice, the instinct to debunk the next man's ego. When thugs were sent onto the street in the spring of 1936 to smash the union by terror, George Frosig came to a union board meeting badly beaten by black jacks about the head and ears. The newly wound bandages about his head were still bloody. Half humorously but half seriously his fellow board members told him he deserved it. If he had handled himself right he'd have kept his head out of the way. Another sympathizer remarked that George's brains were in his feet, adding the suggestion he be hung up by his toes for a few hours to shake his brains into his head—if possible.

As indicated, 574 for its leaders and organizers has other aspects than those of a dynamo. For the rank and file too, besides being an economic weapon, it is a club, a recreation center, and a school. Except when a hostile police administration decided for a time last summer that truck drivers were better off without beer, the recreation hall at union headquarters contained an overworked bar; and three or four hundred coal heavers, ice drivers, etc., could be seen of an evening playing checkers, drinking beer, and telling extravagant stories in truck-driver lingo. At intervals the union's own band of eight pieces has provided music for 574 dances held in the large hall on the top floor. But the climax of social activities is the 574 picnic: "When we have a strike or a picnic we do it right!" summarized Moe Hork, chairman of the 1936 picnic committee. Last summer ten thousand men, women, and children attended, according to news reports. Baseball, a merry-go-round, automatic autos for the kids, beer, loud speaker for union and Farmer-Labor speeches, listened to by nobody. With the usual attention to organizational details the union mobilized all the Yellow Cabs in Minneapolis to provide free transportation. The picnic was boisterous and hearty "but no fights." Showing foresight, the Union had its own strong-arm squad to remove drunks and belligerents.

On the serious cultural side, the union holds classes three or four times a week in economics and labor history. But 574's most powerful educational instrument is *The Northwest Organizer,* a labor newspaper with a circulation topping that of the Central Labor Union's official organ. The reader has some idea of the militant partisanship of this sheet from war-time quotations. In the turbulent years of peace its character hasn't changed.

"The leadership of 574 is biased and partisan," one business man in Minneapolis said to me, "in favor of their own particular brand of radical trade union. They see everything from that point of view." Local 574 would doubtless cheerfully agree with this criticism.

There is, as we have seen, humor in the dynamo's newspaper, with a pro-working-class bite to it. Take this one: "Famous Lines in History—'Officials of the closed plants blamed agitators for the trouble and said there were no serious differences between the employer and the workers.' " Or in a lighter vein: "Society notes: Attendance at union meetings will soon drop off as the time is rapidly approaching when the drivers will be off to Florida to spend the winter at golf and deep-sea fishing." "The coal heavers are setting the vogue for ebony tinted eyelashes this winter. The Scotch cap will also be popular— worn at a rakish angle over the ear. Out at the Fuel Distributors the boys are setting the fall mode with chic blue or red bandannas pinned on the upper bosom. Gloves with red cuffs will be quite common." Or: "There's wan sure way to keep them immygrunts out—teach thim all about our insti-choochins before they come."

Against such an animated and cocky dynamo it was inevitable that innumerable monkey wrenches should have been thrown into its working parts. Indeed, the story of the effort to smash 574 since 1934 is almost as dramatic and violent a one as the narrative of the civil war itself. A few of the monkey wrenches included revised versions of the Red scare, provocateurs inside the union, wholesale and retail firings, several efforts to bribe the leaders, and physical attacks upon them by imported thugs under police protection. But the stockiest monkey wrench of all was fabricated and dropped into its gears by a hostile alliance between conservative elements in the labor movement and certain employers. The monkey wrench nearly smashed the dynamo. But its failure opened a new chapter and new prospects not only for our American city but in certain spheres, economic and political, for the Northwest.

This alliance from its inception reflected in the life of our American city a basic and nationwide struggle which gave it more than local significance. After expelling the stormy petrel of the truck drivers' union from the fold of the American Federation of Labor in the spring of 1935, Mr. Tobin created by decree a rival truck drivers' union in Minneapolis. It was called Local 500. The "legitimacy" of this new child of Mr. Tobin's was widely proclaimed in Minneapolis. It was said to have the blue blood of respectability in its veins as contrasted with the bastard Red of General Drivers' Local 574. Instantly bankers, lawyers, business men who had been indifferent for a generation, took a friendly interest in the "legitimate labor movement."

The new union, which started life with a membership of twenty-six as against the then three thousand truck drivers in 574, promptly received the approval of most of industrial Minneapolis, including the Citizens' Alliance.

Local 574's expulsion and the creation of Local 500 preceded by several months the wholesale excommunication of the C.I.O. unions by the Executive Council of the American Federation of Labor, but in the smaller microcosm of Minneapolis its effects on the labor movement were similar. It threw everyone into confusion. This was not altered by the fact that 574 is technically *not* an industrial union. The local had been guilty of industrial practices, it was militantly progressive, its sympathies were pro-Lewis and anti-Green. The creation of Mr. Tobin's "legitimate" A. F. of L. baby precipitated one of the fiercest interlabor wars in the history of the Northwest, a war in which (as we have seen) the employers promptly took sides, and one with the immediate object of smashing the drivers' union. Delegates to the Central Labor Union of Minneapolis were in a tight spot. A number of the honest conservatives among them believed sincerely that 574, useful as it had been to the labor movement, must be "curbed" and that draining its "responsible" members into Local 500 was the way to do it. Others openly stuck by the stormy petrel. The rank and file throughout Minneapolis remained militantly loyal to the victors of the civil war, and the truck drivers themselves, shouting "treason," treated the unhappy twenty-six who had been beguiled into Mr. Tobin's local, as "finks, traitors to the true cause of labor, scabs, and strikebreakers."

The truck owners themselves also found they were in as tight a spot as the labor leaders. Mr. Tobin's agents, visiting them one by one, offered peace and a "safe and responsible union." "But what about our contracts with Local 574?" "We'll take care of that," said the legitimizers. The employers thought it over. They stuck to 574. "After all," said a veteran Minneapolis truck owner, "574 isn't so bad; we're still doing business. Why ask for trouble?" And another, "It's all very well for Tobin's Teamsters Council and for the secretary of the Citizens' Alliance to talk about "saving the city" by recognizing this other union. Let the Citizens' Alliance stick out its neck if it wants to. I'm damned if I'm going to be put in the middle!" For their own reasons, the truck drivers and the truck owners of Minneapolis remained faithful to the drivers' union.

The recalcitrance of "Red 574" finally won Minneapolis a share of the national spotlight. Mr. Meyer Lewis was dispatched from the executive office of the American Federation of Labor in Washington to Minneapolis as Mr. William Green's personal emissary. It was announced that the Federation was starting a national campaign to purge the American labor movement of Communism, and that the crusade would start in Minneapolis! This proclamation made first-page headlines throughout the United States. The Citizens' Alliance rejoiced and many of its members went into conference with Mr. Meyer Lewis—at the latter's request. But Mr. Lewis, though he won a few adherents to his cause—and was, I believe an honest crusader—made little real progress toward smashing the dynamo. At all events, the *Organizer* was able to sum up his first month's effort to lay low the union in these terms: "Meyer Lewis' record shows thirteen times at bat, no hits, no runs and thirteen errors." During the month, they continue, "We took in 117 new members—a fairly lively corpse."

But the truck drivers were over confident of their independent strength. The forces behind Mr. Lewis and Mr. Green were powerful and when defied entirely ruthless. Mr. Green's emissary regretfully concluded that he couldn't break the truck drivers' union through the aid of the employers and by propaganda, and expressing horror at the rough treatment the truck drivers visited on the luckless members of Local 500, decided, to quote his own words, "to fight fire with fire." Suddenly armed thugs appeared in considerable numbers from Chicago, and for three turbulent weeks openly attacked officers and members of the truck drivers' union on the streets of Minneapolis. *The Organizer* openly accused Mr. Lewis and the Teamsters Joint Council of unleashing the terror. Among others, V. R. Dunne and Vice President George Frosig were viciously beaten with blackjacks near the Omaha loading platform. As several arrests of victims were made and none of the gangsters, 574 concluded that the plan of open terror involved an "understanding" with the Minneapolis police force. During this period of illegal violence, I discussed these methods with two leading liberal members of the mayor's mediation board. While disclaiming official sanction, they expressed the hope and the belief that the union would be destroyed by the Chicago importees. This was a logical if lurid reflection of class emotions in Minneapolis at the time.

On the other hand, the rank-and-file workers in Minneapolis' trade unions became roused to a pitch of fury at the open terror they had not felt since the great strikes of 1934. The truck drivers themselves, especially after the attacks on Dunne and Frosig, and the declaration of open war against them, mobilized to fight for their lives. On May 24 they called a special membership meeting to consolidate their forces and build their defense. In many ways this was the turning point in the internal labor warfare in Minneapolis and developed into one of the most extraordinary exhibitions of union patriotism in the history of the city. Repeated suggestions of how to "kill off" the gangsters and "return them to Chicago in coffins" were made at the meeting but dismissed by the cooler heads of the leadership. Instead a campaign of mobilization of rank-and-file support throughout the city was adopted as a counter to the Lewis terror.

Just before the close of the meeting Miles Dunne asked for the floor.

"There is no doubt in my mind," he said, "that within this hall and listening to my words are stool pigeons and agents of the Citizens' Alliance. And I have a message for them. I want to say to these people who to my mind are the lowest and vilest of living creatures: Go back to your bosses, go back to your paymasters, and tell them every word that you have heard here. Tell them that nobody here is afraid of you or of the group which pays you. Tell them that the finks and the gangsters will be cleaned out of this town in thirty days and there'll be no job left for you in Minneapolis."

The meeting closed with the two thousand men present standing and repeating aloud after the chairman the oath of loyalty to the union.

The day after the meeting, 574 appealed to the protective arm of the Farmer-Labor party, asking all candidates and office holders to declare for or against the terror. The Farmer-Labor candidates declared for General Drivers' Local 574. Meticulously every fact of the conspiracy against the union was dug up and publicized by 574 throughout the city of Minneapolis, including such telling details as the license numbers of the gangsters' cars and who they belonged to, the salaries of the thugs, and the names of their paymasters. The union publicized as well the "hopes" of the Citizens' Alliance in the matter, and the threat of destruction to the whole labor movement if 574 were crushed.

Whether the "heat" became too intense or those responsible concluded they had chosen the wrong way to purge and legitimize Minneapolis labor, the attacks of the gangsters suddenly ceased and a historic phone call was made by the Teamsters Council to V. R. Dunne to come and "talk it over." A series of conferences followed, the dénouement of which opened an entirely fresh perspective for the rank-and-file history of our American city. The stormy petrel was reinstated in the American Federation of Labor and into the Central Labor Union of Minneapolis. Local 500 was liquidated—the official word was "merged"—into its former enemy. Tobin's terms of two years before were thrown into the waste basket. The dynamo was readmitted with no dismemberment of its parts, all militant organizers retained, *no change in its policy*. The gangsters were, of course, withdrawn. Mr. Meyer Lewis told me afterwards that he regarded this dénouement as a victory for his policy and himself. I did not argue the point. In this sense it was a victory for himself and his colleagues: unity in the trade union movement of the Northwest is a victory for all its members—a strategic victory. The abrupt shift from friendship to hostility toward the new though "legitimate" drivers' union by the Citizens' Alliance was to confirm this.

The International officers at the historic conference proposed a fifty-fifty division of former 574 officers with new officers of the International. The union accepted. So far as I know the re-entry of a militant trade union under such circumstances into the American Federation of Labor with no expulsions, and no change in basic organization or policy, is unique in the history of American labor.

In recounting the history of these years of "change" I have followed the lead given me by the majority of Minneapolis citizens in stressing the role of the belligerent truck drivers' union. But I have tried to emphasize as the history of events has emphasized that the movement of revolt was city-wide. The most diverse currents and economic forces went into it, till in the end it actually did what the most class-conscious of the empire builders feared on the eve of the civil war: measurably alter the balance of economic power in the city of Minneapolis between the workers and themselves. A concrete description of this altered balance is difficult in each of its corollaries. For example, in the "sense of greater freedom on the job," and in the crucial matter of what the rank and file cherishes far more than high wages, "job protection," the change is difficult to evaluate. Thousands of workers dropped for their political views and for belonging to a union were reinstated, and the whole rank and file felt that a bulwark had been built up in the city around themselves and their jobs. But if this generalization is a vague one, it is possible to be more concrete on the actual change in standard of living of specific sections of the Minneapolis working class. According to the Industrial Commission of Minnesota (a state agency) the average wage in "motor transportation" (buses and trucks included) was $14.50 per week in May, 1934. In June—after the first strike—$19.09. Two years later, in May, 1936, the average was $32.16, a rise of one hundred and twenty per cent in two years. Auto agencies, garages, and filling stations, affected by strikes in both 1935 and 1936, show a two-year rise from $15.89 to $31.47. In the iron-working industry, which had its strike in the fall of 1935, for the same period there is a wage rise from $22.44 to $25.73. Increases also occurred in nonunionized industries and where there was no rank-and-file struggle. In most cases, however, the increases were relatively so slight as not to compensate for the rise in living costs between 1934 and 1936. In firms where no union contracts existed but which belonged to partially unionized industries, there were notable "protective" wage rises. Dayton's Department Store, a famous antiunion firm, topped each increase of drivers' wages as they came along. And as the retiring president of the Citizens' Alliance put it, "We are now paying high wages in Minneapolis—either because of unions or as in my case in order not to be bothered by union agitators." Thirty-eight new unions were chartered in Minneapolis in two years. These changes, while substantial, must not be exaggerated. While thousands of rank-and-file citizens in our American city have substantially more to spend on houses, food, clothes, medicine, and the movies, many thousands more—doubtless a majority—have been unaffected in a direct economic sense by the shift in class forces within the city. Among employers directly affected, the majority have reconciled themselves—at least for the present—to dealing with labor unions. A minority like Mr. Conway feel desperately that the unions are ruining their business and their lives. And the Citizens' Alliance has told its members that unless a "solution" is found, the city is doomed.

The real significance of the shift in class forces is not, however, in the wage changes of one city, important as they are to individuals and to the city, but that the whole dynamics of the change is part of a wider movement. Not only are the basic factors which precipitated the rank-and-file revolt present in other cities, but the form and expression of the movement is national and not local. The meaning of rank-and-file experience in our American city for these wider movements—both political and economic—we shall return to in a final appraisal of the city's destiny.

The last recorded struggle between the Citizens' Alliance and the newly unified labor movement of Minneapolis occurred in the fall of 1936. Encouraged by the Alliance to make a "firm stand against racketeering 574"—the truck drivers called it a "last stand"—the wholesale grocers of Minneapolis refused recognition of the drivers' union. After a two-month strike the drivers won. At the same time a bitter and violent strike broke out in Minneapolis' historic flour-milling industry—the first since 1919. The cereal workers' union won partial but significant gains.

Two months before the state elections of 1936, I discussed the Republican campaign with two well-known sons of the empire builders, both active in the politics of the state. One of them said: Unions will be with us *for some time now,* I believe. We must have a moderate and progressive Republican candidate for governor. And we have one in Mr. Nelson." The other said: "Our only hope in Minneapolis is to jail the Communists and the union racketeers. I believe Nelson will do it if he gets elected."

Whatever the true qualifications of the Republican candidate, the farmers and workers of Minnesota took no chances in the fall elections. In spite of the death of Floyd Olson, the party's leader, they elected a Farmer-Laborite governor by a two-to-one majority and for the first time in the history of the party won all state offices except one.

The rank and file have consolidated their forces in our American city on both fronts, the economic and the political. What is the next phase? Will it mean the collapse of Minneapolis business as the Citizens' Alliance predicts, or the introduction of the co-operative commonwealth? Neither.

CHAPTER XV

CROSSROADS

WE have briefly told the story of one American city, which in less than three generations sprang from the frontier, flowered in a Golden Age of economic power, and entered its decline. The events of its history, as they occurred, gave a practical education to the workers and farmers of the Northwest in the principles of Capitalism, and we have dwelt more on the activities and lives of these anonymous pupils than on those of their schoolmasters.

In 1936, the workers in the city of Minneapolis and the farmers of Minnesota consolidated a remarkable measure of power in their own hands—both political and economic—more than at any period in their history. But it would be a mistake to exaggerate their conquest. Nothing basic in the American order of things has changed. Add up the farmers' revolts from Ignatius Donnelly to Olson and throw in the summer of civil war and its effects—the "American system" is intact, though with a somewhat battered sovereignty. But it is also easy to understate the meaning and impact of the rank-and-file victories. To the truck drivers, iron workers, dirt farmers, etc., of Minnesota their meaning is personal and concrete. More important, they are part of the dynamics of a shift in class forces that is country-wide.

What is to be the next phase in the life of our city? The decline, the turbulent years, the militant victories of workers and farmers, the challenge to the *status quo,* are certainly a transition—but to what? The citizens of our American city are asking the question, and they have different answers for it.

There are, first of all, the invincible optimists; second, there are those who are properly economic traditionalists; and third, the tolerators and mild ameliorists—"sensible men"; in another category, on the extreme left politically and economically, the Marxist revolutionists and the handful of citizens who have more or less absorbed their philosophy.

Many intelligent and able leaders of Minneapolis industry find it possible to recognize all the prime factors of their city's decline but to dismiss them by an appeal to the progressive role and the infinite productivity of Capitalism itself. One of the founders of the Northwest Institute of Scientific Research said to me, "Here in Minnesota there are vast areas of peat and lignite. We are on the verge of perfecting their commercial conversion into coal. That is only one possibility. If labor will co-operate, technology, enterprise and ingenuity will solve our regional problems." Most business men, especially since the national upturn in business, have a measure of this optimism. They are less specific as to a "way out," but from a belief that the whole country is "sound" insist Minneapolis must share in the national prosperity. Their viewpoint basically was admirably expressed by Dr. Neil Carothers at last year's annual dinner of the Citizens' Alliance. "The system we live under is the most productive the world has ever seen." It has another characteristic, he added: "It unceasingly and automatically improves itself."

In contrast to the relatively pure optimists are those who face the fact that the city's economy is sick, diagnose the disease, and propose what I call a traditionalist cure. There is of course some intermixture between these categories, but the purest statement of the latter's position I received from a joint

ANNOUNCING THE FIRST STRIKE SETTLEMENT

".... few on either side gauged the long-term effects of the rank-and-file victory"

WHAT NEXT?
"We're going to town . . ."

conversation with the president and the executive secretary of the Citizens' Alliance. Labor racketeers and political radicals have established a dictatorship over the city and the state. They are ruining business. Prosperity can be restored by a *strong government*—meaning in Minnesota a traditional Republican one. The radicals—"who have no more respect for law and order than a jackrabbit"—will be jailed or run out of town, and "constitutional rights" restored to business men. *"All those laws* can then be repealed," said the president of the Alliance, "and we can conduct our businesses as we used to do." Economic restoration of a traditionally unfettered industrialism and a political restoration of the Republican party as a broom to sweep the radicals out. From conversation in certain other circles I find a strong nostalgia for the days and the dictatorship of the Committee of Safety. Given a restoration of power "to the right people," it is felt that the prime factors of decline—sabotage of business—can be liquidated.

The third category of tolerators and "sensible men" takes a less aggressive but more reasoned view of the city's plight. Chief among these in Minneapolis is, I believe, Dr. Prosser of Dunwoody Industrial Institute, who has published a kind of balance sheet of civic assets and liabilities. He has listed very honestly all the prime factors of decline which economists stress, and balanced them with such assets as educational equipment, home ownership, etc., most of which I have mentioned in this book. On the prime factor of the class war, or as he terms it "industrial strife," his solution is a carefully veiled blow to the right and the left. Prosser says that the heart of the problem is "lack of responsible leadership on *both* sides."

In contrast to all of these analysts of the city's destiny, the extreme left, Marxist revolutionaries and their followers have almost nothing to say about the city's destiny at all. They insist that the fate of Minneapolis is bound up at bottom with the destiny of the whole country and with the economic system of modern society. They do not believe, however, in any basic economic change in Minneapolis or the Northwest before such a change overtakes American capitalism as a whole. They deny that the gain in economic well-being of the working class won by trade unions is "ruining" the city of Minneapolis.

To the objection that union wages forced upon the struggling manufacturer under a *declining* economy will force an exodus of business and infinite distress to the workingman they have a double answer. First an appeal to the facts. No firm in the city's strategic industry, trucking, "has either failed or emigrated since it paid a living wage and recognized the union." And one manufacturer who *did* move from the city in search of a "low wage area" found the union waiting for him in his new location! It is not labor's business, by lowering living standards to prop up the marginal producer. *But* if business *as a whole* either regionally or nationally cannot pay decent wages, the logical answer is not victimization of the worker, but a wholly different organization of productive forces. Such an admission of defeat by business is a decisive indictment of Capitalism.

No one can confidently predict the future for Minneapolis or any other American city. To quote the words of the Unemployment Stabilization Research Institute, manned by economists from the University of Minnesota, some "unforeseen fortuitous circumstance" may occur to restore economic health to the region. But what? Perhaps a "technological change," and I suggest the not improbable circumstance of a world war which, reviving agriculture, would for a time restore economic vitality to the Twin Cities. But barring "fortuitous circumstances," the Institute soberly predicts continued decline.

What connection is there between the remarkable rank-and-

file movement of Minnesota and the larger ones of which it is
a part? The surge of workers into progressive and industrial
unions is conspicuous throughout the United States. And significantly, John L. Lewis's phalanx of industrial unions in the
Committee for Industrial Organization is a challenge not to
the Citizens' Alliance of a single city but to the United States
Steel Corporation, the automobile manufacturers, and indeed
to the traditional open-shop policy wherever found. It is of
more than passing significance that the annual convention of
the Minnesota State Federation of Labor endorsed the C.I.O.
Closely akin to the qualities of originality and daring which
have distinguished the Minneapolis labor movement is the
nationwide epidemic of sit-down strikes, originating in the
mass production industries of Akron, Toledo, and Detroit.
Minneapolis workers were quick to adopt the technique and
a series of successful strikes occurred.

Seconding this widespread economic ferment of the rank
and file throughout America, and tied to it, is a political trend
which Minnesota because of peculiar factors in her history
was able to anticipate. Workers and farmers in Minnesota for
a generation and more have tied their ballots to their economic
interests, but now serious political observers are forecasting a
national Farmer-Labor party by 1940. Whether or not that
prediction is sound, it is certain that for the first time in American history the workers of America, as far as they knew how,
took their economic and class interests with them into the
presidential election of 1936. The importance of Minnesota's
rank-and-file experience, both in its successes and its failures,
cannot be overestimated as a laboratory of social experiment
for a future America.

The most striking characteristics of the economic revolts in
the Northwest recounted in this biography are their freshness,
their efficiency, and their Americanism. The leadership ad-

hered to what might be termed the "principles" of militant class struggle everywhere. But they gave to those principles imaginative adaptation to the American scene. Analyzing the weight of class forces in a particular state and city, they invented a strategy as flexible as it was bold to achieve practical success. The durable nature of their aims and methods, long after the initial militancy of revolt, is a matter of public record.

These phenomena contain, I believe, more than a temporary significance for the American labor movement. The present nationwide drive to organize the basic industries of America requires for success similar militancy, a foresighted leadership, and class understanding. The slogan for industrial unionism is not enough. "Sell-outs," deals with employers which whittle away victory, fatal compromise with new and more ingenious Haases and Dunnigans, will also be possible under industrial unionism, as they were under the conservative craft philosophy. If the rank and file of American workers are to achieve substantial gains from the expected wave of organization they must display an acute class vigilance, and find somewhere the imaginative and ruthless ingenuity that is so striking in Minneapolis. Already they have the will and the morale for the struggle.

In the political sphere of rank-and-file organization one can discover to date no comparable burst of originality in theory or action in our American city or in America as a whole. For the Farmer-Labor party, while presenting definite possibilities of usefulness to the rank and file, is, for reasons I have indicated elsewhere, in no way the final answer for the emancipation of the rank and file; and the best of those parties calling themselves Marxist and revolutionary have, without exception, been lacking in precisely these qualities of imaginative realism and courageous and principled adaptability which some of their adherents have been able to bring to the trade-union field.

Throughout this book I have tried to stress the cultural—the intimate and the personal connection of these phenomena with the lives of men and women—as well as the broader outlines; to try and strip the class struggle either of the clinical gauze that sociologists have put on it, or the trappings of the economic theologians who teach that it is a little malodorous, unrespectable and un-American. It is, on the contrary, real, universal, human and important. Reaction to the phenomena of this history as well as particular hopes and fears for the city's destiny—and the country's—depends of course on the outlook of the observer. To those who believe the rank and file as such has no destiny, other than absorption into the American economic system which is the best of all possible ones, the phenomena of this book must appear as clinical symptoms of a passing sickness. Like hundreds of business men in Minneapolis, they envision Capitalism both in Minneapolis and throughout the world as at the threshold of new triumphs, new and undreamed contributions to culture, progress and well-being. If this be true, the class-conscious activities of the Minneapolis working class and the ideas and exploits of its leaders are at best political nightmares, at worst the fruit of a conspiracy which society must for her own protection destroy. To those, however, who believe that the working class *as such* has a historic and progressive role to play in the modern world, the development of its independent culture and power—even in such limited ways as exhibited in this history—is a heartening demonstration of human morale, of fighting strength and of real progress. The achievement of a civilized world is brought the nearer by them.

SELECTED BIBLIOGRAPHY

BEARD, CHARLES AND MARY R., *The Rise of American Civilization*. New York: The Macmillan Company, 1927.

Bill Haywood's Book, An Autobiography. New York: International Publishers, 1929.

BRUCE, ANDREW ALEXANDER, *Non-Partisan League*. New York: The Macmillan Company, 1921.

BUCK, SOLON J., *The Agrarian Crusade*. New Haven: Yale University Press, 1921.

Bulletins of the Minnesota Employment Stabilization Research Institute. Russell A. Stevenson, director. Minneapolis: University of Minnesota Press, 1932 and 1933.

DE KRUIF, PAUL, *Seven Iron Men*. New York: Blue Ribbon Books, 1934.

EDGAR, WILLIAM C., *The Medal of Gold*. Minneapolis: The Bellman Company, 1925.

Employers' Advisory Committee, Joseph R. Cochran, chairman, *The Truth about the Truck Drivers' Strikes*. Minneapolis, 1934.

Farm-Holiday News, The, 1933-1936.

Farmer-Labor Leader, The (after 1934 The Minnesota *Leader*), 1930-1936.

FINE, NATHAN, *Labor and Farmer Parties in the United States,* 1828-1928. New York: Rand School of Social Science, 1928.

FOLWELL, WILLIAM WATTS, *History of Minnesota*. 4 vols. St. Paul: Minnesota Historical Society, 1921.

GASTON, HERBERT E., *The Non-Partisan League*. New York: Harcourt, Brace, and Howe, 1920.

GATES, REVEREND FREDERICK T., *The Truth about Mr. Rockefeller and the Merritts*. New York: G. P. Putnam's Sons, 1911.

HAINES, LYNN AND DORA B., *The Lindberghs*. New York: The Vanguard Press, 1931.

JESNESS, OSCAR B., AND ASSOCIATES, *A Program for Land Use in Northern Minnesota*. Minneapolis: The University of Minnesota Press, 1935.

JOSEPHSON, MATHEW, *The Robber Barons*. New York: Harcourt, Brace & Co., 1934.

Land Utilization in Minnesota. A State Program for the Cut-Over Lands, by the Committee on Land Utilization. (Editorial Committee: William Anderson, Oscar B. Jesness, Raphael Zon). Minneapolis: The University of Minnesota Press, 1934.

LANDIS, PAUL, "Cultural Changes in the Mining Town. A sociological study of three Mesabi Iron Range towns: Eveleth, Hibbing and Virginia." *American Journal of Sociology,* vol. 41, no. 2, July, 1935.

LINDBERGH, CHARLES A., *Banking and Currency and the Money Trust.* Washington, D. C.: National Capital Press, 1913.

LINDBERGH, CHARLES A., *The Economic Pinch*. Philadelphia: Dorrance Publishing Co., 1923.

LINDBERGH, CHARLES A., *Why Is Your Country at War, What Happens to You After the War, and Related Subjects*. Washington, D. C.: National Capital Press, 1917.

LUNDEEN, ERNEST, "The Minnesota Farmer-Labor Party—History, Platforms, Programs." Washington, D. C.: *Congressional Record,* vol. 80, no. 128, part 2, pp. 11232-11263, July 9, 1936.

Minneapolis *Journal,* 1934-1936.

Minneapolis *Labor Review* (official organ of the Minneapolis Central Labor Union), 1934-1936.

Minneapolis *Star,* 1934-1936.

Minneapolis *Tribune,* 1890, 1934-1936.

Minnesota Commission of Safety, Report of, St. Paul, 1919.

Minnesota History, a Quarterly. St. Paul: Minnesota Historical Society. Articles too numerous for separate mention.

Monthly Bulletins, Department of Labor and Industry, Industrial Commission of Minnesota. St. Paul, 1934-1936.

MYERS, GUSTAVUS, *History of the Great American Fortunes.* 3 vols. Chicago: Charles H. Kerr & Co., 1910.

Northwest Organizer (originally the strike newspaper of General Drivers' Union, Local 574, continued as union's official organ, today organ of Teamsters' Joint Council of Minneapolis). Minneapolis, 1934-1936.

PYLE, JOSEPH GILPIN, "James J. Hill." St. Paul: *Minnesota Historical Bulletin,* vol. 2, pp. 295-323, 1918.

PYLE, JOSEPH GILPIN, *Life of James J. Hill,* authorized. 2 vols. Garden City, N. Y.: Doubleday, Page & Co., 1917.

RUSSELL, CHARLES EDWARD, *Railroad Melons, Rates and Wages; a Handbook of Railroad Information.* Chicago: Charles H. Kerr & Co., 1922.

RUSSELL, CHARLES EDWARD, *The Story of the Non-Partisan League: A Chapter in American Evolution.* New York: Harper & Bros., 1920.

St. Paul *Pioneer Press,* 1890, 1934, 1936.

St. Paul *Union Advocate* (official organ of the St. Paul Trades and Labor Assembly), articles and editorials, 1930-1936.

Stanley Committee on the Investigation of the U. S. Steel Corporation, (vol. 3), Washington, D. C.: Government Printing Office, 1911.

TEIGAN, HENRY G., series of articles on the history of Non-Partisan League and the Farmer-Labor Party, St. Paul *Union Advocate,* 1927.

VORSE, MARY HEATON, *Footnote to Folly.* New York: Farrar & Rinehart Inc., 1936.

WHIPPLE, BISHOP, "The Sioux Massacre." St. Paul *Press,* 1862.

Specific quotations in "The Golden Age of Economic Empire" and "Fate of the Rank-and-File Empire Builders" are from the following:

BLEGEN, THEODORE C., articles in *Minnesota History,* a Quarterly, 1933.

HALSTEAD, AUSTIN L., "Minneapolis, The Greatest Milling, Lumbering, and Agricultural Implement Center in the World." *Northwest Magazine,* September, 1899.

JOSEPHSON, MATHEW, *The Robber Barons.* New York: Harcourt, Brace & Co., 1934.

KING, CAPTAIN CHARLES, U. S. Army, "Twin Cities of the Northwest." *The Cosmopolitan Magazine,* October, 1890.

LARSON, AGNES, "On the Trail of the Woodsman in Minnesota." *Minnesota History,* a Quarterly, December, 1932.

PYLE, JOSEPH GILPIN, *The Life of James J. Hill.* Garden City, N. Y.: Doubleday, Page & Co., 1917.

RALPH, JULIAN, "The Capitals of the Northwest." *Harper's New Monthly,* March, 1892.

For the political differences between the Communist Party and the "Trotskyists" upon the events in this history, see:

DUNNE, WILLIAM F., AND CHILDS, MORRIS, *Permanent Counter-Revolution, the role of the Trotskyists in the Minneapolis strikes.* New York: Worker's Library Publishers, 1934.

New Militant, The, New York: 1934-1935.

SOLOW, HERBERT, "War in Minneapolis." *The Nation,* September 5, 1934, pp. 274-275.

STRANG, HARRY, "A Labor Lieutenant and Top Sergeant." *The New International,* vol. 2, pp. 163-166, August, 1935.

United Action (official organ of the ninth district of the Communist Party), 1936.

CHARLES RUMFORD WALKER (1893–1974) was a journalist, editor, and labor activist. He was author of several books, including *Steel: The Diary of a Furnace Worker.*

MARY LETHERT WINGERD is assistant professor of history at St. Cloud State University. She is author of *Claiming the City: Politics, Faith, and the Power of Place in St. Paul.*